History of the People of Israel

© Ross & Perry, Inc. 2001 All rights reserved.

Protected under the Berne Convention. Published 2001

Printed in The United States of America

Ross & Perry, Inc. Publishers
717 Second St., N.E., Suite 200
Washington, D.C. 20002
Telephone (202) 675-8300
Facsimile (801) 459-7535
info@RossPerry.com

SAN 253-8555

Library of Congress Control Number: 2001096571
http://www.rossperry.com

ISBN 1-931839-15-8

Image on cover provided by Rev. John DeLancey, Tour Leader,
www.biblicalisraeltours.com

⊗ The paper used in this publication meets the requirements for permanence
established by the American National Standard for Information Sciences
"Permanence of Paper for Printed Library Materials" (ANSI Z39.48-1984).

All rights reserved. No copyrighted part of this publication may be reproduced,
stored in a retrieval system, or transmitted, in any form or by any means,
electronic, photocopying, recording, or otherwise, without the prior written
permission of the publisher.

Volume 3

History
of the
People of Israel

**From the time of Hezekiah
till the
Return from Babylon**

By
Ernest Renan

Ross & Perry, Inc.
Washington, D.C.

CONTENTS.

	PAGE
PREFACE	xi

Book V.

THE KINGDOM OF JUDAH ALONE.

CHAPTER I.
Hezekiah 1

CHAPTER II.
Policy and Administration 8

CHAPTER III.
Definite Constitution of Iahveism 17

CHAPTER IV.
The Anavim 31

CHAPTER V.
Fusion of the Two Narratives of Sacred History . . 41

CHAPTER VI.
Literature in the Reign of Hezekiah 57

CHAPTER VII.
Invasion of Sennacherib 79

CHAPTER VIII.
The Last Years of Hezekiah.—Triumph of the Theocratic Democracy 94

CHAPTER IX.
Reaction against the Anavim.—Manasseh and Amon . . 103

CHAPTER X.
The Revolutions in Asia during the Seventh Century b.c.—Nahum 114

CHAPTER XI.
Recrudescence of Anavite Prophetism.—Sophonius, Jeremiah 120

CHAPTER XII.
Jeremiah and the Civil Power 137

CHAPTER XIII.
The Reforms of Josiah 142

CHAPTER XIV.
Centralisation of Judaism at Jerusalem 154

CHAPTER XV.
The New Thora 168

CONTENTS.

CHAPTER XVI.
First Appearance of Socialism 185

CHAPTER XVII.
Literary Work about the Time of Josiah 196

CHAPTER XVIII.
Revolutions in the East.—Death of Josiah 210

CHAPTER XIX.
Jehoiakim.—The Pietists in Disgrace 221

CHAPTER XX.
Nebuchadnezzar and Jeremiah.—The Scourges of God . 232

CHAPTER XXI.
The First Captivity 243

CHAPTER XXII.
The Reign of Zedekiah 256

CHAPTER XXIII.
Pious Dreams 274

CHAPTER XXIV.
Destruction of Jerusalem.—The Second Transportation . 282

CHAPTER XXV.
The Last Convulsions of Judah 299

Book VI.
THE BABYLONIAN CAPTIVITY.

CHAPTER I.
THE FIRST YEARS OF EXILE 309

CHAPTER II.
CONSOLATIONS OF THE PEOPLE 321

CHAPTER III.
PLANS OF RESTORATION.—EZEKIEL 333

CHAPTER IV.
SACERDOTAL AND LEVITICAL THORA 341

CHAPTER V.
LITERARY WORK DURING THE CAPTIVITY 361

CHAPTER VI.
APPROACH OF THE SIEGE OF BABYLON 368

CHAPTER VII.
CAPTURE OF BABYLON 373

CHAPTER VIII.
CYRUS AND THE ACHÆMENIDÆ 379

CHAPTER IX.
THE GREAT ANONYMOUS PROPHET 390

CHAPTER X.
THE NEW JERUSALEM 398

CHAPTER XI.
IAHVEH, THE UNIVERSAL GOD. 406

CHAPTER XII.
DOUBTS AND HESITATIONS 414

CHAPTER XIII.
THE RETURN 423

PREFACE.

This volume will show how the work of the monotheistic prophets acquired such solidity that the terrible blow which Nebuchadnezzar dealt to Jerusalem failed to destroy it. By a miracle of faith and hope unparalleled in history, the Iahveists of the prophetic reformation disseminated along the banks of the Euphrates will bring about the return to Judea, the re-establishment of holy worship, the rebuilding of Jerusalem. I hope that I may be given the strength to delineate, in a fourth volume, the train of Jewish ideas up to the appearance of Christianity, and thus to complete the cycle of religious history which I have taken as my task. It is a hope which I scarcely ventured to nourish a few years ago. I now think that I may without presumption look forward to the completing of the work which has been the principal aim of my life.

I have been blamed for having, in the previous

volume, drawn too many comparisons between the ancient events which I am relating and movements of the present day. It is not my fault if, in the present volume, I have again been led to offend, in this respect, the susceptibility of rhetoricians. The history of ancient Judaism is the most striking instance of the opposition of political and social questions. The thinkers of Israel were the first to revolt against the injustice of the world, to refuse their submission to the inequalities, the abuses, and the privileges without which there can neither be an army nor a strong society. They compromised the existence of their petty nationality, but they founded the religious edifice which, under the name of Judaism, Christianity, or Islamism, has served as a refuge for humanity down to the present day. Here we have a lesson upon which modern nations cannot reflect too much. The nations which abandon themselves to social questions will perish, but, if the future belongs to such questions, it will be a grand thing to have died for the cause which is destined to triumph. All the plain, sensible people of Jerusalem, about the year 500 B.C., were furious with the prophets, who rendered all military or diplomatic action impossible. What a pity, nevertheless, it would have been if these sublime madmen had been arrested! Jerusalem, perhaps, would have remained for a little longer the capital of an insignificant kingdom; but she would not be the religious capital of humanity.

As regards the current dates at the head of these pages, the reader must be referred to the remarks at the close of the Preface to Vol. II. I am keeping for the fourth volume a map of Palestine and a plan of Jerusalem, brought down to the most recent data of science; and as regards the oriental typography of this and of the two preceding volumes, I have to thank the Director of the National Printing Press for the loan of the type required for a satisfactory execution of the work.

HISTORY OF
THE PEOPLE OF ISRAEL.

BOOK V.
THE ONE KINGDOM OF JUDAH.

CHAPTER I.

HEZEKIAH.

THE destruction of Samaria led, in accordance with an ordinary law of history, to the exaltation of Jerusalem, its rival. The religious and literary work which had been wrought by the two divided halves of Jacob will in future be accomplished by Judah alone. Now Judah was Jerusalem. The religion of Israel had not, up to that date, any distinct name, but in the form which the genius of Jerusalem is about to give it, it will be known as Judaism. Thus concentrated, the force of the religious movement kindled by the prophets acquired a fresh degree of intensity. The small city of David became a focus of creation, such as there has never before been of the religious kind. Moral and social problems were started with an originality beyond compare. The earliest organised religion is in process of formation; Christianity, Islamism, Protestantism, and, *mutatis mutandis*, modern Socialism will spring from it.

Iahveism, Elohism, and the worships connected with them, even the disciplines which for centuries constituted Prophetism, were not, as yet, religions having a principle of identity which would ensure their duration. They were vigorous germs from which was to spring the stem of the religious tree of humanity; but they were only germs of the reforms of Hezekiah and Josiah. The books which were the outcome of these reforms, the terrible fanaticism of Jeremiah, the captivity, the return, were the knot which bound all that into a bundle which it would henceforth be impossible to break. The kingdom of Israel having once disappeared, its religion disappeared with it; the kingdom of Judah will disappear, but its religion will survive it. Judaism, from being a local religion, will become a religion not tied down to any particular country, susceptible of being practised in all countries and embraced by the most divergent races.

Two great men, Hezekiah and Isaiah, are at the bottom of this extraordinary movement, which decided the fate of humanity, though circumstances aided very much. The eleven years over which the siege of Samaria lasted and those which followed were a time of ardent fever for Jerusalem. Every moment, men were expecting that the scourge which was crushing Ephraim would be diverted upon Judæa. A sort of patriotism prevented Isaiah and Micah from uttering too loud shouts of triumph at the capture of Samaria; but, in reality, the victory of Iahveism was complete, the predictions of the prophets of Jerusalem were realised, the kingdom of Ephraim had fallen a victim to its infidelity towards Iahveh. Alone of the cities in Syria, Jerusalem had been spared. What could be clearer? If it were admitted that the Assyrians were the scourge with which Iahveh chastised the peoples, this immunity of Jerusalem could only be the effect of a divine protection. A beautiful surate in Isaiah,* which appears to relate to this period, contains the complete theory of Providence as understood by the prophets, a theory which has remained the universal philosophy of history down to Bossuet's day.

God governs the world by punishment. In order to punish, He has need of instruments; but these instruments do not know the hand which makes use of them; they imagine that they are themselves doing that which God causes them to do. "It is by my own strength," says Asshur, "that I have done all this; it is by my wisdom and my intelligence that I have altered the frontiers of nations, sacked the treasures, overthrown the kings, and

---

* Isaiah, from ch. x. v. 5, to end of ch. xii.

crushed the peoples." What folly! the pride of Asshur will be punished. His policy is to exterminate the peoples one after the other. Calno and Karkemis, Hamat and Arpad,* Damascus and Samaria, have succumbed.† Jerusalem, upon whom the example of Samaria has been lost, will have the same fate. The prophet hears, so to speak, the tramp of the enemy marching from the north and crushing everything upon his passage.‡

It is just when Asshur thinks himself sure of taking Jerusalem that Iahveh seizes His axe and lays it at the root. Asshur was like a Lebanon covered with tall forests; Iahveh hews them down and humbles him.§ The defeats of Israel are in this respect peculiar, that they are never complete. A remnant of Israel is always preserved by Iahveh to form the nucleus of a renaissance which will be the era of happiness.‖ The just have been the cause of victory; the just shall reign beneath the sceptre of a perfect king, who, in the mind of the prophet, is at once Hezekiah and the ideal king of the future theocracy.

The two families of Israel reunited¶ will defeat the Philistines, the Edomites, the Moabites, and the Ammonites. Iahveh, renewing the miracles of the

* Tell-Erfad, to the north of Aleppo.
† It is remarkable that there should be no allusion to Tyr.
‡ See Isaiah, ch. x. v. 28 and following.
§ Isaiah, ch. x. v. 33, 34.
  See vol. ii. p. 427.
¶ See Isaiah, ch. xi.

Exodus, will make Euphrates passable for the remnant of his people dispersed in Assyria, so that they may return dryshod. The just of the ideal kingdom then burst forth in triumphant song. Victory will be the fruit of moral improvement; for, in order to have the countenance of Iahveh, a man must be pure. True policy is that based on moral order. The nation which maintains order may be sorely tried, but not overcome.

At no moment is the conception of the pietists of Israel more clearly seen than now. The State is a function of religion; the enemies and the lukewarm servants of Iahveh wreck the public weal; the guardians of the public weal are, therefore, in duty bound to see that Iahveh is served as he deserves to be. The true worship of Iahveh is purely of heart and deed, a loathing for material symbols, whether in wood or in metal. The servants of Iahveh are the poor and the humble. The rich are, as a rule, hard, impious, and violent. The first duty of the pious sovereign is to be just towards the poor of God, and to repress with rigour the oppression of the poor by the rich; the poor will in their turn reign.

Such was, without any sensible difference, the doctrine of all the Iahveist prophets. Now, during the years which followed the ruin of the kingdom of Israel, the prophets' party was all-powerful in Judæa. The king surrendered himself to it unreservedly. His temperament was naturally inclined towards piety and justice. The body of Hebraic writings was already a very considerable one, and sufficed to serve as a basis for a moral education, Hezekiah deriving from them many of his good qualities and the serious bent of his mind. He appears to have been much younger than Isaiah, and to have possessed even more profoundly the literary culture which distinguished that prophet and Micah. He was almost a man of letters,* and he was above all a pietist; but the excesses of zeal into which pietism lapses were in this instance avoided.

One is sometimes tempted to believe that the ardour with which Hezekiah devoted himself to true religion was the result of a conversion, of a powerful moral revulsion which brought about an irrevocable attachment to the ideal which he held to be absolutely true.† The official proclamation of Judaism would thus have been very similar to that of Buddhism, brought about by the conversion of King Asolkva. The Jewish psychology does not seem to call for any step of the sort. The language of Isaiah and of Micah, in the first years of Hezekiah, does not differ materially from what was said under Ahaz.‡ Iahveism implied a theocratical leaven which could not fail to develop itself. The Iahveism of the prophets of Judah is essentially a social

* Proverbs, ch. xxv. v. i.
† 2 Chronicles, ch. xxx. and xxxi.
‡ See vol. ii. pp. 435, 436.

religion; its aim is the reformation of society in accordance with justice. The king is the keystone of the Iahveist edifice. The king is chosen, consecrated by God.* He is the *mesih* (anointed) of God. His duty is to cause God to reign, and to be guided by the advice of the men of God, that is to say by his prophets. Hezekiah, therefore, merely followed the indication of events which, in his eyes, were the clear manifestation of the will of Iahveh, the taking of Samaria, the captivity of Hosea. There were not two men in Hezekiah: he had become convinced by more or less striking signs. If Shalmanezer had not undertaken his campaign in Syria, it is probable that Jerusalem would have continued, in spite of Isaiah and Micah, to have gone on vegetating in the sort of religious mediocrity from which she was unable to extricate herself. I may go further and say that, but for the great events which seemed to be the justification of the Iahveist oracles, Isaiah and Micah would not have been what they were. Iahveh is the living God of history, the God who governs the world. He triumphs in history; the great revolutions of the world are His manifestations.

* Analogous ideas prevailed with Iehaumelek, king of Byblos. *Corpus inscr. semit.* 1st part, No. 1.

CHAPTER II.

POLICY AND ADMINISTRATION.

FROM about 721 to 711 the condition of Judæa appears to have been fairly prosperous. In the first years following the capture of Samaria the situation of Hezekiah with respect to the empire of Assyria was that of a vassal. One circumstance, however, occurred which made his position less untenable than might be imagined. Shalmanezer died before the war with Samaria was over, and was succeeded by one of his officers, named Saryouhin, or Sargon. The commencement of a new dynasty is always a favourable moment for those whom the preceding dynasty has left in subjection.

Sargon was too powerful a sovereign for the prudent Hezekiah to think of rebelling against him. The proposals, real or imaginary, of Egypt were, nevertheless, a standing temptation, just as at the present time the Russian alliance is for uneasy spirits in France. The political advisers of the king were in favour of it, among them a certain

POLICY AND ADMINISTRATION. 9

Shebna, or Sebent,* who was perhaps a Sebennyte, and certainly a foreigner, a man without any family, who attained the rank of *soken*, or privy adviser of the king, and was invested with the functions of prefect of the palace. Isaiah and the prophets were opposed to the Egyptian alliance, in harmony with their general principle that human means are an insult to Iahveh, and also because of the correct view they had formed as to the military situation of the time.

In 711 the temptation was stronger than ever,† when the tartan, or general, of the armies of Assyria traversed the land of Judah to conduct an expedition to Egypt and to Ethiopia. The first act in the campaign was the siege of Asdod. A general league of Egypt and the Palestine countries seemed to be clearly indicated, but Isaiah offered the most strenuous opposition to this policy, and resorted, in order to combat it, to the ocular demonstrations which were customary with him. On a certain day he was seen walking through the streets of Jerusalem barefooted, in a state of shameful nudity. He declared that Iahveh had ordered him to show himself in this state in order that men

---

* The two forms שבנא and שבנה come from the form שבנת, by the confusion of א and ת, which frequently occurs in ancient writing, and from the confusion of ה and ת, which is frequent in modern writing. See vol. ii. p. 47, note 4.

† Isaiah, ch. xx., borrowed from a book in which Isaiah is alluded to. Compare Dillmann, *Del Proph. Jessura*, pp. 182-183.

might see in what an ignominious * state the king of Assyria would bring back the prisoners from Egypt and Ethiopia.

The hatred of Isaiah against the man whom he calls the "shame of the house of his master," is expressed in a less eccentric form, in a fragment where the internal dissensions of the court of Hezekiah are rendered very palpable.† Shebna, whose father is never mentioned, and who must have been of low extraction, lived in great state, and hewed for himself, like the parvenu that he was, a court in the rock of the royal hill. This infuriated the pietist coterie. "Iahveh," they said, "will hurl him down from the summit of his honours; his chariots will avail him nought." The intrigue for the displacement of Shebna was evidently matured. The candidate of the theocratic party was Eliakim, the son of Hilkiah,‡ who was, in accordance with eastern usage, to raise all his family to places of honour with him. Iahveh apostrophises Shebna and extols the merits of the sainted man, who will make good his misdeeds.§ Eliakim, as a matter of fact, succeeded Shebna ‖ as master of the household, but the latter none the less retained great authority at court.¶ In reality, Isaiah was

* See vol ii. pp. 26 and 419.
† Isaiah, ch. xxii. v. 15-25.
‡ Compare Isaiah, ch. xxxvi. v. 3.
§ Isaiah, ch. xxii. v. 20-25.
‖ Isaiah, ch. xxxvi. v. 3 ; 2 Kings, ch. xviii. v. 18.
¶ See below, pp. 93, 106.

right, despite the strange character of his arguments. Egypt did not furnish anything solid to lean upon; it was Assyria who was the true organ of Iahveh, for Assyria was strong. The prophets, who saw the action of Iahveh in whatever triumphed, were in duty bound to be for Assyria. It is not with impunity that one executes the decrees of Iahveh, that one is his minister, the executor of his plans.* Pagan force charged with such a mission must have appeared something sacred. It is thus that the prophetic party was led to greet Assyria and then Persia as divine institutions. The court of Rome, always on the side of the strongest, is the true heir of this policy. The strong man does the will of God, and to disobey him is to disobey the will of God. Let me add that, being almost indifferent in matters of religion, the Assyrians were regarded by the pious populations of Syria very much as the Moguls were by the crusaders. They did not exercise any restraint upon religious liberty, which was clearly one these races always cared for. Subject in political matters to an empire which respects its religion, such, from the earliest antiquity, has been the position logically sought by Israel. This state of vassality towards Assyria had for Hezekiah substantial advantages. Assyria does not appear to have attempted to define very strictly her frontiers. Several towns of the kingdom of Israel were

* In Isaiah, ch. x. v. 10-11, Asshur reasons as a Iahvist.

attached to Judah. Upon the Philistine side,* the armies of Hezekiah were completely victorious. The country, no doubt exhausted by its struggles against Assyria,† fell into the hands of the king of Judah up to its southernmost borders, that is to say as far as Gaza.

The organisation of royalty appears to have again become, during the good years of Hezekiah's reign, what it was at the best epoch of the dynasty of David. The king is surrounded by *soferim*, constituting a sort of administrative class, and by *sokenim*, who were ministers or councillors. The prefect of the palace, or majordomo, is the chief *soken*, a sort of vizier. This place, as we have seen, in connection with Shebna and Eliakim, conferred great power and was the object of keen competition. The priests appear to have been subordinate, and to have been reduced to the service of the temple. The prophets were everything; they had gained in proportion as the civil order had lost by the victories of Assyria.

The public works at Jerusalem, which seem to have been carried on with great activity under Ahaz, were still more active in the reign of Hezekiah. The city was completely transformed, the population was largely increased, and it is probable that many Israelites, with no home since the break up of the kingdom of the north, came to settle there.

* 2 Kings, ch. xviii. v. 8. † Isaiah, ch. xx. v. 1.

POLICY AND ADMINISTRATION. 13

The water supply was always the great difficulty in Jerusalem, the city being situated close to the watershed between the Mediterranean and the Dead Sea, and with only a few very distant summits above it. The population of Jerusalem has always depended upon its cisterns, which are very numerous and well executed. The small spring of Gihon, upon the slope of Sion, sends forth only a tiny stream. The waters collected at the commencement of the western valley are of little use, and are derived entirely from the surrounding land. Hezekiah endeavoured to make the most of this scanty supply,* and at the same time to take the necessary precautions so that, in the event of a siege, the city could not have its water supply cut off. He had built within the city a vast basin,† and had dug a conduit underground to bring in, during the rainy season, the waters of the upper pool (*Birket Mamillah*), itself fed by the waters of the tableland.

---

* The basins of Etham were certainly made for supplying the city with water. They are never alluded to in the Bible. This able piece of work, the only defect of which is that it presupposes a very precise administration in the country, appears to have been due to Pilate (*Jos.* B. J. iii. 14, 4).

† 2 Kings, ch. xx. v. 20. It is probably *Amygdala*, or *Birket Hammam el-Batrak*. If the pool of 2 Kings, ch. xx. v. 20 is the same as the old pool of Isaiah, ch. xxii. v. 11, it is to be assumed that Hezekiah merely repaired an ancient work. The description between the two walls given by Isaiah would just answer to this site, which Hezekiah would merely have covered with a second wall.

The works of the *Siloh* appear to have been executed in the time of Ahaz,* though they were perhaps completed in Hezekiah's reign, and were, at all events, attributed to him.† This *Siloh*, or "emissary," was an underground canal destined to bring to the royal gardens and to the south-eastern gate the waters of the Gihon fountain, perhaps to safeguard them from the action of the enemy. A recently discovered inscription ‡ tells us that the work of piercing the soil was undertaken at the two extremities, and shows the trouble which the two squads of workmen had to meet under the hill. An examination of the underground works testifies at once to a good deal of boldness and to no little hesitation in a work which must, in the absence of perfected calculations, have presented enormous difficulties.

Hebrew art appears to have attained its highest degree under Hezekiah. The carrying away of the objects of art which occurred in the time of Ahaz § was soon made good. The palace recovered all its ornaments, and we shall find Hezekiah, at the end of his reign, proud of the richly-chased treasures he had succeeded in amassing.‖ The Assyrian style was already competing successfully against the Egyptian imitation which the Phœnicians had

* See vol. ii. pp. 509, 511.
† 2 Chronicles, ch. xxxii; Sirach, xlviii. 17.
‡ See vol. ii. p. 427, note 1.
§ See vol ii. p. 429.
‖ See below, pp. 117-118.

brought into fashion; another symbolism was beginning to prevail.* The temple was re-established in its splendour, although the simplicity of the worship was not affected. We know nothing of the priestly dress of that time.† The troops of Levites and singers, which are supposed to be as a vast choir around the temple, are merely the imagination of the author of the Chronicles, borrowed from the second temple. At Easter, canticles were sung, and the pilgrimages were accompanied in their march by the sound of the flute; ‡ religious sentiments were expressed by the sound of the *neginoth*, but there is nothing to prove that the music of the temple was already organised.§ The prophets, who had so depreciated the *cohanim*, were not in favour of the application of art to religion. Their worship was entirely abstract. What was the good of all this pomp and external show ? God only demands of man justice and a pure heart.

Socialist utopisms need, in order to develop freely, a fairly prosperous epoch. People do not declaim with full effect except when they are not so very badly off. Whatever Isaiah may say when he is in a very bad humour, the government did realise as full a measure of order and justice as the

* Isaiah, ch. vi.

† The lengthy details given in Leviticus refer to the second temple.

‡ Isaiah, ch. 30, v. 29.

§ The thanksgiving of Hezekiah (Isaiah, ch. xxxviii. v. 20) does not give the idea of a regular liturgical music.

country and the time were capable of. But great races of men are insatiable. They always exclaim against the insufficiency of the dose of liberty and equality which is assigned to them. It is not well to be too resigned. The state of holy disquiet in which the prophets lived was the great religious propeller of the genius of this people, the guarantee of its future. The impossible character of the dreams which prevented these marvellous agitators from taking their sleep could not as yet be discovered. They wanted justice, and time was needed to make it clear that the abuses which they called injustices were inherent in the natural conditions of existence, and that to suppress them it would have been necessary to suppress human life.

CHAPTER III.

DEFINITE CONSTITUTION OF IAHVEISM.

It is just within this period of relative peace and prosperity which marked the reign of Hezekiah that we may approximately place the definite fixture of the Iahveist religion such as the prophets of Ahab's time had conceived it, such as Isaiah and Micah had worked it out. Iahveh no longer has any connection with nature. His character as a national God is for the moment effaced; the victory of Monotheism appears to be complete. Iahveh is the God who has made heaven and earth. He wishes to do that which is good. Man does Him homage by acting with justice. This is a worship which all the world can pay Him, and in this sense all humanity is called to the worship of Iahveh.*

Iahveh exercises justice in the ordinary human way, governing the world in the smallest detail as an absolute master.† The reality here often sug-

---

* See vol. ii. p. 405 and following.
† See vol. ii. pp. 241, 242.

gested to the thinker who was the easiest to satisfy strange objections, the good man being often unhappy and the perverse man seemingly rewarded. Iahveism floundered in this morass. Iahveh, questioned with regard to His providence, only replies to man by thunderclaps. The government of the world is perfectly just, though man is not to know how. There is never any appeal made by the wise men of that day to rewards or punishments beyond the tomb. The justice of Iahveh, moreover, is summary; He punishes corporate offences at the risk of involving more than one innocent person. This justice is above all things intermittent; Iahveh varies from day to day; He lets human perversity reach its height, and then He appears upon the scene and punishes it.

The whole history of the world is the development of a plan conceived and desired by Iahveh. The race of Israel is the pivot of this history. Iahveh has chosen it from among the Aramean family as a privileged tribe; His eyes have been following it for over two thousand years. The great mark of affection which He showed it was to take it out of Egypt by the hand of his servant Moses, to whom, in the desert of Sinai, he gave several manifestations of His desires, without the source of these miracles being exhausted. Iahveh constantly speaks through his *nabis*, who are a permanent source of revelation. In the eighth century B.C. divination by means of the ephod had nearly

DEFINITE CONSTITUTION OF IAHVEISM.

disappeared, but necromancy was in greater vogue than ever; the *qosem* was almost as much consulted as the *nabi*. But, according to the pure Iahveist, Iahveh alone ought to be consulted. Any other oracle than His was an insult to His majesty, and implied the supposition that there existed some prophetic and divine power inherent in nature.

Assyria is the force which Iahveh sets in motion for the execution of his secret plans, which are neither more nor less than the realisation of a just world by means of Israel. The kingdom of Samaria, which was so far removed from this perfection, was already destroyed; that of Judah probably will be as well. But the destinies of Sion are eternal, Sion will be the centre of a regenerated humanity. The true king of Bethlehemite dynasty, the ideal David, who has not yet been seen, will appear and reunite in his hand the whole of Israel. At once king and prophet, he will lead the people into the way of pure Iahveism. The world will then recognise the superiority of Sion; the universe will become Iahveist; the sacrifices will be abolished; the true worship of Iahveh will be justice and happiness.

Such is the splendid dream in which was concentrated all the power of loving and believing possessed by the pious Judaists about 720—710 B.C. The reign of Hezekiah was the period in which the chief characteristics of this golden age were definitely delineated. Messiahnism is a creation of

Jerusalem, not of the Northern tribes. David, Sion, a legitimate dynasty, these were all a *sine quâ non*. The king was a necessary feature in the new ideal conceived by Judah. Hezekiah answered to some of these characteristics of the perfect Davidic king. At times, it might be thought that the great destiny of Israel would be revealed through him,* notably when surrounded by pious persons like Eliakim and his family. The coming signs, however, were not sufficiently in view; the times were too severe. The theocratic king was relegated to the future; he became as it were a sun which would appear at the end of all things. But this evening of the world would be so grand that people resigned themselves to not see it; it was enough that they should have laboured to bring it about.

This singular religious system, the least mythological and metaphysical ever conceived by a civilised brain, was not, in reality, anything other than the old patriarchal Elohism brought to life, become humanitarian and imported into history. Deism was so deep-rooted in these incorrigible nomads that it succeeded in expelling, by a long process of elimination, the strong dose of paganism which had pervaded Israel with the false God Iahveh, a deity essentially local and national. The nabis, stubborn representatives of the old Monotheistic spirit, had succeeded. Iahveh was no more

DEFINITE CONSTITUTION OF IAHVEISM.

than a symbol of Elohism.* What was said of God was said of Iahveh, and as God had created heaven and earth, so had Iahveh, who, in short, purely and simply signified " God," † without any distinction.

The two words came to be used indistinctively. The word Iahveh was given an etymology which made it mean the only God. The very dominant idea was that the name of *Iahveh* was part of the Sinaiatic revelation, that God himself had explained it to Moses, deriving it from the root *haïa*, or *hawa* (Aramean), which means *being*.‡ This idea, a very taking one assuredly, did not, however, exclude two older systems, which had their partisans. Upon the one hand it was held that Abraham offered sacrifices in the name of Iahveh§; upon the other, that the use of that solemn name dates from the earliest ages of humanity, from the patriarch Seth, son of Adam.|| From the period, already possessing a certain dose of philosophy, at which we have arrived, many minds no doubt said to themselves that there was a good deal of false reasoning in all this; that this Iahveh, with his personal policy and providence, was, after all, a special God, very dis-

---

* See vol. i. p. 71 and following, 218 and following; vol. ii. p. 221 and following.

† It is thus that in the middle ages Christ was assigned all the functions of God, and that in our day the removal of the crucifix from schools has been regarded as tantamount to excluding God from them.

‡ Exodus, ch. iii. v. 14. § Genesis, ch. xv.
|| Psalm xiv. v. i.; liii. v. 2.

tinct from the absolute El of the sages of old, whose school was continued in the Themanites and the Beni-Qédem.* The great contradiction which resided in the inner conscience of Israel—on the one hand the abstract and universal God of the universe, upon the other the special God of Israel—was masked by a rough sort of palliative, which served the purpose. We see no sign that the pure Elohists, like those who wrote Job and the Proverbs, ever protested against what was pagan and in a measure Polytheistic in a proper name given to God; nor do we see that the Iahveists ever stood up against a party of pure Deists, denying that Israel had, like the other tribes, a special protecting God. Both had for a common adversary the group of fools who said "there is no God."† These alone were the perverse and the dangerous men.‡ As they were careful not to commit their ideas to writing, we do not know how numerous they were. History sees only the surfaces, but in reality there are only surfaces in humanity; they are the appearances, and, outside the pure scientific order, human things are but mere appearances. The battle won is that which one believes that one has won. The triumphant opinion is that which succeeds in proving, at a certain hour, that it was entitled to triumph.

* The book of J **b** sh ws a trace of this duality.

† Psalm xiv. v. i.; liii. v. 2.

‡ The symbolic name איתיאל (Proverbs, ch. xxx. v. 1, seems an affirmation (El existe) made to refute these foolish people.

It is because the Iahveist movement of the prophets was a retrogression, an effort to revert to a more ancient and a purer religion, that the great prophetic movement of the eighth century so resembles Protestantism. The work of the prophets who surrounded Hezekiah, without being entirely his masters, consisted in refining, in eliminating the dross. The essential character of Judaism is henceforth clearly marked; it is a Puritan reformation, a negation, a religion of preventive measures and of precautions. Ancient Iahveism had never succeeded in setting absolutely upon one side superstitions, whether they were derived from the ancient nomads or were the imitations of Cananean and Aramean forms of worship. The wise were content to smile at these frivolities, and did not much care if their wives carried grotesque little gods in their pockets and their baggage. About the middle of the seventh century there was more notice taken of these matters. Two duties were, as the Puritans thought, incumbent upon them; first of all, to expel all that was not Iahveism, and then to disencumber Iahveism itself of the tolerances which, according to the prophets, tarnished its purity.

The destruction of the kingdom and of the sanctuaries of the North gave considerable importance to the temple of Jerusalem. Up to that time, as I have said, this petty *naos* had been little more than the private chapel of the King of Jerusalem. Now, each day saw its destinies grow, and it gradually grew to be the national sanctuary of all Israel; while it became the focus of an ardent piety, a host of zealous worshippers regarding its absolute purity as an article of faith. Isaiah, no doubt, gave too little thought to this small house of stone to have offered the king any advice on this subject. Nor do we find that it was his habit to select the porticos near the temple for his preachings, as did other prophetic schools. The temple under Hezekiah was purified and sanctified, not embellished or developed.* It was with it as with a church of the middle ages, St. Peter's at Geneva, coming under the influence of Calvin. It is possible that several of the ornamentations made in the time of Solomon, not remarkable for their good taste, may have been carefully overhauled at this period; and perhaps the absence of figured work in the description of the decoration of the temple,† which seemed rather strange, was due, not to the taste of the founder, but to acts of vandalism committed by the zealots of a later age. But this is no more than mere hypothesis. If these aftertouches had been upon any considerable scale, it seems probable that there would be some written allusion to it, for we know, by means of a formal text,‡ the boldest step which

---

* The amplifications of the Chronicles (Book 2, ch. xxix. and following) have no historical value.

† See vol. ii. pp. 128-129.

‡ 2 Kings, ch. xviii. v. 4.

DEFINITE CONSTITUTION OF IAHVEISM. 25

the spirit of iconoclasm impelled the new reformers to take.

Of all the utensils of the temple, that which most displeased the prophets was what was called the *Nehushtan* (abbreviation, with a play upon the words, of *nehas nehost*, serpent of brass), an ancient talisman which Moses was said to have had made against the stinging of serpents. The Israelites had hitherto offered incense to it as to a god, and it may very possibly have been an ancient image of Iahveh, derived from a time in which this god was represented under forms borrowed from Egypt.* Hezekiah had it broken to pieces.† To effect so bold an innovation as this a religious party need be very strong, for the Nehushtan was a national relic of the first order, and a national religion is always superstitious. The day upon which Hezekiah ordered the brazen serpent of Moses to be broken he did what the Protestants, emulating him in a measure, did in the sixteenth century, when they mutilated the Gothic saints and broke down the most venerable altars. The horror of priestly imposture and of religious materialism overrode respect of tradition. Devoted to abstraction and to the absolute truth, the Jewish prophet is more than a patriot. The falsehoods with which the patriot is so easily satisfied cause his gorge to rise. The fabulous attribution of some virtue

---

* See vol. i. pp. 125, 152.
† 2 Kings, ch. xviii. v. 4.

to a natural object seems to him an encroachment upon the power of Iahveh. More and more the religion of the prophets of Jerusalem becomes a humanitarian religion, and ceases to be a worship in keeping with a race or a country.

Neither Solomon, nor any of his successors up to the date we have reached, thought of making the temple of Jerusalem the exclusive place for sacrifices. The high places of ancient times continued to be places of worship. Iahveh was worshipped there, and in many cases local divinities as well. The country was covered with *masséboth* or sacred pillars, and with *aséroth* or phallic stelæ, bearing the sign of Astarte ⚥. These objects shocked the Puritans, who obtained the permission of Hezekiah to suppress them.* Did they also demand the unification of the place of worship—a demand which, as it appears, would have been calculated to please royalty, which is always inclined towards centralisation? The Judaic prophets of the eighth century are constantly expressing their desire for this. Their ideal is Iahveh adored in Sion, and in Sion only.† It is probable that Isaiah more than once entreated Hezekiah to suppress the extra-urban sacrifices.‡

---

* 2 Kings, ch. xviii. v. 4. † Isaiah, ch. xxx. v. 29.

‡ The passages, Isaiah, ch. xxxvi. v. 7, and 2 Kings, ch. xviii. v. 22, would lead to the supposition that this reform was, as a matter of fact, effected. But there is a misapprehension here, the Assyrian message confusing the idolatrous worships upon the high places which Hezekiah did away with (2 Kings, ch. xviii. v. 4) and the sacrifices of Iahveh which were offered on these same high places and only abolished in the time of Josiah.

But although the king was in perfect accord with the pious party, he never allowed himself to be entirely led by it. His attitude reminds one of that of St. Louis—so deeply religious and yet maintaining a certain independence with regard to the clergy. The suppression of the local sacrifices would certainly have entailed unpleasantness and disturbances, as it did in the reign of Josiah. Whereas the characteristic of the movement set on foot by Hezekiah and Isaiah, in opposition to that for which Josiah and Jeremiah were responsible, is that it was not, at all events in its first phase, accompanied by any crisis or by any rigorous measure.

Here we have a very remarkable fact, and it would be difficult to find its parallel in religious history. More than once, no doubt, the king was advised to strike hard at the impenitent,* but there is no proof that he ever gave way. He did not do more than give the places in his household and all the important charges in his gift to pious men who were recommended by Isaiah, such as Eliakim, the son of Hilkiah. So far as we know, he did not persecute any one. Even the city of Jerusalem was not given over to a state of absolute purification. Representations which were regarded as idolatrous, or at all events as scandalous, by austere Iahveists were still to be seen there.† The

* See below, p. 39, and following, p. 97.

† Isaiah, ch. x. v. 11; ch. xxvii. v. 9; ch. xxix. v. 11 and

king did not think he had the right to suppress these representations, which were repugnant to his personal feelings, but which the customs of the time tolerated.

Circumcision grew from being a simple preparation for marriage, which it was at first, to be more and more a religious rule at Jerusalem. It was one of the oldest usages of the nation, but its religious signification was not at first very clear.* The prophets never allude to this practice, evidently regarding it as very secondary.† Neither the book of the Alliance nor the Decalogue contained anything in this respect, doubtless because the thing was treated as a matter of course, and was not yet regarded as a precept The religious character, nevertheless, grew more and more decided. The law of the circumcision was soon to become a fundamental law.‡ Important fragments of the Elohist narrative seek to demonstrate that this operation is compulsory upon the descendants of Abraham.§ All clearsighted persons, well-ordered heads of a

---

following; ch. xxx. v. 9 and following, 22. Compare Micah, ch. v. v. 11-13. See vol. ii. pp. 435, 436. Micah only saw the first years of Hezekiah, anterior, perhaps, to the reforms.

* See vol. i. p. 104 and following.

† In the same way we should find no allusion to vaccination in all the sermons and catechisings of our day.

‡ Exodus, ch. xii. v. 48 ; Leviticus, ch. xii. v. 3; ch. xix. v. 23; ch. xxvi. v. 41; Joshua, ch. v.

§ Genesis, ch. xvii. Compare ch. xxi. v. 4; ch. xxxiv. (the episode of the Shechemites) is a mixture of Iahveist and Elohist.

DEFINITE CONSTITUTION OF IAHVEISM.

family, had it performed upon their children so as to spare them being afterwards placed in an embarrassing position, just as we have our children vaccinated in the present day. It was understood that Iahveh wished it to be so, and that one of His precepts was disregarded if a child was not circumcised soon after birth. The Jewish festivals developed, but they did not attain anything universal or national.* The passover, fused with the feast of unleavened bread, became the great annual festival. It was inaugurated at night, and was accompanied by rejoicing and song.† The pious even already believed that this festival was the memorial of the miraculous exodus from Egypt.‡ But for the great majority it was merely the great spring feast of Iahveh. The idea that all religious acts gained in importance by being celebrated in the temple at Jerusalem became more and more prevalent.§ The petty size of the kingdom of Judah rendered such an idea practicable. The worshippers who were the furthest away from Jerusalem had not more than twenty-five miles to come. There was already in formation around the temple a group of very ardent devotees, who became the residents, the *gerim*, of it.‖ These *gerim* of Iahveh had not

---

* See vol. i. p. 46 and following; vol. ii. p. 298 and following.
† Compare Isaiah, ch. xxx. v. 29.
‡ Exodus, ch. xii.
§ Isaiah, ch. xxx. v. 29; compare Psalm cxxii. v. 1-4.
‖ See vol. ii. pp. 44, 45.

up to that time been anything better than parasites, living upon the sacrifices and the junketings which went on around the temple, but a moral spirit was introduced into this institution, which, moreover, never produced anything that was good. It was thought that, to be the neighbour of Iahveh, great moral purity was requisite.* The virtuous man consoled himself by saying to God, "The foolish shall not stand in Thy sight."†

* Psalm xv.
† Psalm v. v. 5.

CHAPTER IV.

THE ANAVIM.

THUS was constituted an excellent type of morality already in germ in the writings of the earlier prophets, and now represented by a party and forming a school. It was a morality for the lower and the middle classes, who were hungering for justice and uprightness, who detested the haughty bearing of the aristocrats, who understood but little as to the necessities of the State, and who affected a gentle and humble bearing. Preached with fervour by the prophets and their disciples up to the time of the definite constitution of Judaism, practised by the pious Jews during the centuries immediately preceding the Christian era, propagated by Christianity, this morality became that of the human race; thanks to it, the rights of the poor, or, to be more accurate, of the weak, have everywhere prevailed, at least, up to the time when Christianity, with its original nature becoming completely warped, formed an alliance with the military and aristocratic classes, and simply preached to the poor resignation.

In the ideal distribution which he had made to His people of worldly goods, Iahveh had not foreseen that there would be rich and poor. The rich, in the eyes of the consistent Iahvist, are an obstacle to progress. The constant objective of Iahveist policy is to protect the weak against the strong and to reduce to a minimum the advantages of the rich over the poor.* The king is the king of the poor.† To lend money at usury is a crime. The rich is, as a rule, represented as a man of violence, bent solely upon despoiling the weak. In the mind of the Israelite pietists the origin of a large fortune is always bad. They were of St. Jerome's opinion: *Omnis dives iniquus aut hæres iniqui*. It is the prevailing idea in the East. The poor man is there regarded *a priori* as good, the rich man as wicked. Upon one occasion when I was speaking in eulogistic terms to my dragoman of the inhabitants of a village which we had just passed through, he replied, "It is not surprising, they are all poor people."

The poor man is the friend of Iahveh, and some singular synonyms proceed from this idea. The word *anav*, "gentle," and the word *ani*, "poor, afflicted," both derived from a root which means humility, come to be used indiscriminately for each

---
* See vol. ii. p. 358 and following.
† Isaiah, ch. xi. v. 4. Compare xiv. v. 30, 32; ch. xxii. v. 19.

THE ANAVIM.

other.* "Poor, afflicted, unfortunate, oppressed, gentle, resigned, pious. humble" were not distinguishable the one from the other. The words which signified, strictly speaking, "poor" (*dal*, *ébion*) became the equivalents of holy men, friends of God. The expressions "the poor of God or the poor of Iahveh, the humble of the land, the weak of the earth, the gentle among the people," were names by which the pure Iahveists were designated.† All this was due to a sentiment analogous to that which in the Middle Ages created the names of minors, minims, the poor of God, humiliati, etc. The feeling of resigned melancholy which fills the heart of the poor is in some of its aspects akin to piety, and humility of feeling predisposes in some degree to devotion.‡ Upon

---

* Let me add that, owing to the paleographical confusion of *iod* and of *vav*, צנוים, צנוי׳, and עניי עניים, were treated as practically the same by the copyists.

† See Gesenius at the words ענו and עני. The words *ani, anav,* as designating the pious, are to be found in the oldest of the prophets, with *ébion* and *dal* as their synonyms. Amos, ch. ii., v. 6 and 7 (synonym of *saddiq, ébion. dal, anav*); compare v. 11 (see vol. ii. p. 428): Zachariah, ch. ix. v. 9; Psalm x. v. 2; xiv. v. 5-6; cxii. v. 9-10; cxl. v. 13-14. We find this use made of them at nearly every page of Isaiah, and of the later prophets, even in reference to the well-to-do. In Jeremiah, ch. xx. v. 13, אביון is taken in the religious sense. The use of these words in the Psalms is very frequent, but in these cases the date is nearly always uncertain. In the book of the Alliance (Exodus, ch. xxii. v. 24), in Agur (Proverbs, ch. xxx. v. 14), in the Strong Woman (Proverbs, ch. xxxi. v. 20), ענו bears its natural meaning.

‡ In certain Arab proverbs, مسكين has a complimentary signification.

the other hand, the Hebrew words which mean
"rich, great, strong" (*asir, gadol, aris*) are nearly
always to be taken as the reverse of complimentary.*

From the time of Hezekiah these associations of
ideas become irrevocably fixed.† The true servant
of Iahveh is a poor man, persecuted by the rich,
worried by the great. Iahveh loves him because
he is humble, because he does not cast umbrage
upon his greatness. Iahveh is his protector, his
justiciary; He will in the end give him the victory.
The enemies of Iahveh are the enemies of the poor;
the enemies of the poor are those of Iahveh. It is
easy to see how such a frame of mind would easily
degenerate into lurking hypocrisy and factitious
humility, especially with a creed which did not
admit that the just man should defer until another
world his revenge and his compensations. These
people were all terribly in earnest. Those who
indulged in raillery (the *lécim*) are always represented as impious. The *léç* is the frivolous, the
bold man, the jester; he is the Voltairian of that
age, the man of fashion, the man who girds at the
poor. These *lécim* were left to themselves; they
had their separate seat, which was called "the
seat of the scornful." From this seat proceeded

* Compare Isaiah, ch. liii. v. 9; Proverbs, ch. xviii. v. 23;
Micah, ch. vi. v. 12; St. Matthew, ch. xix. v. 23, 24. The same
remark applies to *Nadib*, Isaiah, chap. xiii. v. 2.

† Isaiah, from his earliest epoch, ch. xiv. v. 32. See above,
pages 6-7.

THE ANAVIM. 35

many a gibe at the holy people; the latter, upon their part, regarding this group with as much loathing as if they were plague-stricken.*

A theocratic democracy, a religion residing nearly altogether in social questions, such was the Judaism of the eighth century—the true Judaism —of which Christianity was but the full development and application. The *anavim* or *hasidim*† form an élite among humanity; they are the gentle of the earth; they are above all the just, the upright (*isarim*), the just generation (*dor saddiq*), the faithful of the land (*néemné érès*), the quiet people (*rigée érès*), the upright hearts (*isré leb*), the followers of the perfect way (*temimé dérek*), the men who fear God, who love Him, who have trust in Him, who seek Iahveh.‡ This is the point at which one must stand to see the dividing of the two lines which, at first parallel to each other, afterwards diverge *ad infinitum*. Constituting a sort of fraternity or pious association,§ the *anavim* keep up relations only among one another, so that they may not suffer defilement.‖ When the name of Pharisees was applied to these pietists about the

* Psalm i. v. i.

† *Hasidim* is the favourite word used in the Psalms; it appears in Micah, ch. vii. v. 2. Compare Proverbs, ch. ii. v. 8.

‡ These expressions are very frequent in the Psalms.

§ Psalm xxii. v. 23. Compare the expressions סוד ,עדת עריקים
דור עריקים, דור דרשי יהזה, ישרים.

‖ Constant declamations against the רשעים, which form the staple of the Psalms of this period.

Asmonean epoch, the only real innovation was in regard to the words.

The *Anavim* foreshadowed the Pharisees of the Gospel. Upon the other hand, what a future is reserved for this *ébion*, brother of the *anav* and of the *hasid*, who will be the first Christian (Ebionite),* and whose name will constitute the first beatitude: " Blessed are the *ébionim;*" It is impossible to describe in words to what an extent the whole of budding Christianity is in Isaiah, in his contemporaries, and in whatever there was of original working at this critical moment in the conscience of Israel.

One thing is from the very first clear, and that is that Israel will found neither a republic, nor a kingdom, nor a civil state, nor a *polis*. Israel will found the synagogue, the pious coterie, the Church, Pharisaism, and Christianity. Pietism, in the long run, is destructive of citizenship. It is not Israel as a whole which is the people of Iahveh, it is the *anavim* and the *hasidim* alone who are the flock of Iahveh. Israel is but an élite of saints, the profane are the soil which serves to produce the chosen plants, the vine which serves to produce the wine. All this bears a strong resemblance to Islam. These *hasidim* are Mussulmans who have handed

* See *Histoire des Origines du Christianisme*, vol. i. p. 132-138 185 and following; 189-190, 376; vol. ii. p. 115 and following vol. iii. p. 511; vol. v. p. 44-45, 48 and following; 73-74, 195-196 275-277; vol. vi. p. 280 and following.

over their affairs to God.* God is their *vékil*, and what a vékil! He will assuredly avenge them. With such a course of reasoning you give an example of great moral discipline to the world, but you suppress all idea of nationality.

The State and even the *polis* (especially the latter) imply classes, hereditary privileges, injustices, abuses, liberty accorded to certain vices, a severe elimination of social questions. Israel, upon the contrary, was only bent upon securing social justice. A court, a military caste, an aristocracy of birth were all repugnant to it. The *ébion* accepted his poverty, but upon the condition that he was the friend of God and the pivot of the nation. Of the sacrifices which must be made for the country, he exaggerated some and would not hear of others. He was not willing to take upon himself the austere duties which consist in the acceptance of inequality, resignation to injustice. Thus he worked more in the interests of humanity than of his native land; he lost the country which was supposed to be given him. Israel was destined to be rather a universal ferment than a special nation, tied down to one country. His dispersal was inevitable from the very outset; it was when scattered that he was destined to accomplish his principal vocation.

King Hezekiah presided over these transforma-

---

* Psalm xxii. v. 9; xxxvii. v. 5; Proverbs, ch. xvi. v. 3.

tions with a sort of benevolent impartiality. His piety was in his sentiments, in an ardent faith, in an absolute trust in Iahveh. He was almost ostentatious in his contempt for human means, affecting to expect no succour except from God. Like David, he hoped that Iahveh, in recompense for what he had done for Him, would have blessed all his undertakings. If, at times, Iahveh seemed to abandon him, he reproached Him half apologetically; but he did not lose heart.* His objective was the present life only. When Iahveh communicated to him his grandiose dreams of a boundless future, what did he answer? It would be idle to seek to guess. The special feature of the conscience of Israel, the secret of his force and his inconsistencies, was to keep latent reserves of ideas which were destined to unfold themselves in due time, and with which, during whole centuries, he had seemed to have nothing in common.

Hezekiah is entitled, therefore, to take his place on the first pages of the history, no longer mythical but henceforward positive, of Judaism. The ideal of the *anavim* was not, in fact, complete without a king entirely at their service. The pious poets had, perhaps, already composed those Psalms in which the perfection of the theocratic king is traced in such glowing colours.† In Psalm xx., one can hear, as it were, the prayer with which the *hasidim*

* Song, in Isaiah, ch. xxxviii.
† Psalm lxxii.

THE ANAVIM.

greeted the king when he came to offer sacrifice; while Psalm xxi., which closes as usual with threats against the aristocracy hostile to reforms, is pervaded by an accent of victory. The king will not be at a loss to seek out these wicked men in their hiding places and exterminate them.

In other passages, the king sketches out for himself, by the pen of his pious advisers, the perfect plan of a theocratic sovereign.* This Psalm may as well have been contemporary with Josiah as with Hezekiah. We see how old the Pharisaic spirit is in Israel. The question of social relations was an important one for the pious man. Our moral principle that there is no fear of contagion for the high-minded man, that he may see and touch everything without contracting the least defilement, was contrary to the genius of the holy men of Israel. It was necessary to select one's company, to so arrange matters as to avoid relations except with people of one's own sect. This principle, dividing the world into small sects and coteries, made anything like what we call society impossible in the East. The necessary outcome of this was the most odious iniquity. The king who was to put in practice the maxims of the perfect King of Israel would be a formidable tyrant. It is dangerous to take as a rule of conduct the purging of the

* Psalm ci. There are at the beginning of this Psalm certain superfetations due to errors of the copyists. Compare Psalm xlii. v. 3 and Psalm cv. v. 2.

enemies of God, that is to say, of those supposed to be such, out of the city; for God does not take any one into His confidence and does not communicate the list of His friends. Philip II., in obedience to this precept, signed his lists of extermination and had them carried into execution the next morning. Israel founded morality rather than liberty. In fact, seven centuries B.C., no one had any idea of liberty as we understand the word, and Greece herself scarcely began to get a glimmer of it. According to the Iahveist compiler of Genesis, the thoughts of man are by nature evil; the main function of the king, as representative of God, is to repress. Our "large-hearted" liberalism would have produced the same effect upon these ancient believers as it produces upon the Mussulmans and the Protestant Puritans; it seems to them the very incarnation of impiety, the absolute negation of the rights of Iahveh. The bench from which we expound this benignant philosophy would have seemed to them the pulpit of evil, and they would assuredly have called it the *mosab lécim*, "the seat of the scornful."

CHAPTER V.

FUSION OF THE TWO NARRATIVES OF SACRED HISTORY.

The two kingdoms, as we have seen, had each their account of the primitive history of the Beni-Israel, dating from the creation to the theocratical division of the country by Joshua. The plan of the two books was the same, and so, too, was the religion of the two authors; but the spirit was very different. The book of the North, called Iahveist, possessed an amplitude, a candour, and a manner of conceiving the rôle of Iahveh which would be calculated to please the pious Iahveists, whether of Samaria or Jerusalem. Long before the destruction of the kingdom of the North, the Iahveist version was accepted in the pious but as yet in no wise narrow-minded world of Jerusalem. The beautiful passages which it contained caused certain others to be condoned. Several parts of this ancient text would assuredly have been written differently from what they are if the book had been composed subsequently to the preachings of Amos, Hosea, and

Isaiah. There was nothing, however, in the lofty ingenuousness of the narrative calculated to shock the pietists. The pride of Ephraim and of the northern tribes was very marked in it, but did not find expression in a manner offensive for Judah. The history of Joseph, bringing out so clearly the superiority of the Josephites over their brethren, ceased to be galling when Joseph was no longer alive. The Book of the Alliance, which was the only legislative part of the old Israelite book, contained many precepts aimed at the form of worship prevalent in Jerusalem, but nothing of that was in the nature of a direct attack. These parts might be taken as referring to the time of the sojourn in the desert. The gravest critical error would be to suppose that there was at that time any conception of a sacred text. It was believed that there had been revelations by Iahveh; the principal ones were supposed to have been made to Moses on Mount Sinai; but no book claimed to give an exclusive account of these revelations. There was no one volume which was the *Thorat Iahveh* solely and *par excellence*. The divine word was accepted from whatever source it came, and it is probable that the oral tradition was regarded as a source very preferable to the written texts.

The only difficulties which stand in the way of such a conception are when we imagine the legislative parts of these ancient books, especially the Book of the Alliance, as having legal force as soon

FUSION OF THE TWO NARRATIVES. 43

as the book had secured acceptance.* It would be readily imagined, for instance, that Hezekiah, having fully adopted Iahveism, must have put in force the clauses contained in the small code which summarises them. But there can be no doubt that he did nothing of the kind. Several of these clauses were probably part of the common law, and put in force as such; but never before Josiah, or even before the captivity, was the Jewish State governed by an absolutely theocratic and revealed law, and these codes constituted models of perfection which it was hoped the State would one day approach. But the ardent utopists who wrote them knew very well that their work would not forthwith force itself upon the judges nor be embodied in their judgments. The views adopted in this respect were very much the same as among Christian peoples, which, while admitting the Pentateuch as a revealed code, have rarely been tempted to apply its legislation. It needed all the rigorism of Scotch Protestantism to designate, in the enunciation of judgments to be carried into force, passages from Exodus and Deuteronomy as articles having the force of law.

The best proof, moreover, that no text had as yet the pretension to embody the revelations of Iahveh is that, side by side with the narrative that we call Iahveist, was preserved that which we call Elohist,

* See vol. ii. p. 314.

the product of a more modern compilation. This represented the Book of the Alliance under a form better in harmony with the Jerusalemite idea, under the form of the Decalogue. It did not contain anything which could offend the susceptibilities of Judah, as it had been compiled at Jerusalem. And yet this book was less read than the Iahveist version,* doubtless because it was regarded as less pious, less calculated to teach the strict duties of Israel to Iahveh. The number of copies must have been very limited. The Elohist version, the principal object of which was the enumeration of genealogies, may have been contained in only one or two copies. People read very little in those days; the spoken word took the place of the book, and that is why the words took such vivid forms, which were conceived with a view to strike the memory and impress themselves upon it.

This duplicity in the compilation of a book which day by day grew in authority, was not, however, without serious drawbacks. It had had its use in the time of the two kingdoms, but it had ceased to possess any since the house of Israel had been reduced to a small territory. If the dispersal of the Jews had not been so great in the Middle Ages, it is certain that the two Talmuds of Jerusalem and

---

* The prophets and Deuteronomy make little use of it; and yet it cannot be said that they are ignorant of its existense. See vol. ii. p. 319, 320, note. Hezekiah makes use of the tenth chapter (Elohist) of Genesis.

FUSION OF THE TWO NARRATIVES.

of Babylon would eventually have been fused into one. The idea of thus fusing the two narratives of sacred history must have been conceived at a very early date, and if it is only guesswork to fix the date of it in the reign of Hezekiah, I believe that it would be difficult to find a period which corresponds better than his to a condition of mind in which such an enterprise could be conceived and carried out.*

This fusion, in fact, necessitated such frank and candid views that it is difficult to conceive it at an epoch of pious scribes who superstitiously regarded the old books as sacred writings. It is not possible to hack about so freely a text admitted to be inspired. Holy bodies must not be anatomised. The divergences between the conversions were very marked. The rules which the unifier followed were pretty much as follows: 1st, when the two narratives were identical or nearly so, to give only one, sacrificing the details which the other might contain; † 2nd, when the two versions were parallel, without being quite the same, as was the case with

* To take the formula in use with certain schools, R had B to refer to; now B was lost long before the captivity; so R must have done his work at an ancient epoch.

† Thus the narrative of the death of the patriarchs is nearly always taken from the Elohist. In following his ordinary methods, subject to many repetitions, the author would have ended by making his characters die twice. Many times one can feel that a topic only to be found in the Iahveist was originally also in the Elohist version.

the deluge, the history of Israel, or the episode of Dinah, to combine the two narratives, at the risk of producing an incoherent text, full of zigzags and tautology; 3rd, in case of formal contradictions, to sacrifice one of the two narratives outright, or, when the possibility presented itself, to make two stories with one.* If the unifier of the two texts had believed that both of them were sacred, it is not possible to admit that he would have discarded such important facts, and especially that he would have left standing contradictions so pronounced as those which subsist, the most elementary principle of the human mind being that a fact cannot have occurred in several different ways at the same time.

The method of the unifier was that of most of the Oriental compilers.† In most cases he made no change in the words of the text which he copied, aiming chiefly at the utilising of all the fragments cut off, and at losing as little as possible of his originals. The Arab historians read the same result in a more convenient manner by relating in succession the different opinions: " there are some who

* Thus we have the numerous alliances of the patriarchs with Iahveh and the consecrations of Bethel constantly recurring. It will be seen how analogous these methods are with those which attended the compilation of the Gospels, especially of that attributed to St. Matthew. See *Histoire des Orig. du Christ.*, vol. v. p. 173 and following.

† It may also be compared to the method of Tillemont, minus the sidenotes and brackets.

say," "there are others who say," and who terminate with the customary phrase *Allah alam* ("God knows best what is the truth"). The Bible narrator never leaves an option open between the different parties; but he often places side by side, or not far apart, details which contradict each other; and the consequence is that certain narratives are only intelligible if printed in parallel columns, or by distinguishing the various compilations by means of different characters.* There was nothing like preciseness of mind in the unifier, and he was not swayed by any artistic preoccupation.

The sacred history as it was formed from these cuttings and these rough-and-ready sutures was unquestionably a badly executed and incoherent work, a compilation. It must be added that if the unifier had made his fusion more skilfully, we should no longer see the diversity of the sources. The plane would have effaced all these irregularities. The text would offer us a perfectly homogeneous surface upon which criticism would have had no hold, as is the case with the well-ordered work of the Greek historians. These great artists consider it an unpardonable fault to let the different characters of their documents be visible. In the Hebraic work, upon the contrary, such as we have it, the fragments are seen in their entire and undigested

---

* See vol. ii. p. 279, note. See also the essay of Messrs. Kautzsch and Socin (Freiburg in Brisgau, 1888).

form;* we are able to discover them again, and then, up to a certain point, compare them and so re-establish the primitive components.† The additions and the modifications of the unifier appear to have been of trifling importance; they are the most prominent in the history of Joseph.

Therein resides the essential difference between the Greek and the Hebrew *epos*. The Greeks had genius even in compilation. Their Homer, despite more than one *hiatus*, is a prodigy of harmony. The sacred history of the Hebrews contains admirable pages, but it is laborious reading in the detail. The Middle Ages showed their good sense when they carved out of it subjects for their imageries and their moralities. The two component parts were masterpieces of simple and natural narrative; the unified text is a piece of marqueterie, a piecing together of badly mortised cuttings; a heap of diamonds cut with a view to a different arrangement of the stones.

One cannot help asking whether, in order to

---

* It is the same in some Greek compilations of the decadence, for instance, in the Chronicle of Antioch by John Malalas.

† All the Oriental compilations are in this case. The last absorbs those that precede it, without assimilating them; so much so that the most recent compilation always has in its stomach, so to speak, morsels of previous works quite raw. Thus Mar Ibas Cadine is to be found whole in Moses of Khorenus; Tabari was devoured by those who succeeded him; Firdussi has absorbed whole books of the earlier kings; once he had the honesty to notify the fact.

arrange a sacred history which would advantageously have taken the place of the two parallel versions, the unifier had not some other documents of which he thought it necessary to take account in his work of harmonisation. We have seen that the Iahveist, in composing his book, had before him older writings, the patriarchal legends of the tribes of the North and the Iasar or book of the wars of Iahveh. It is almost certain that the unifier, and most of the learned men in Hezekiah's time, still possessed these two books; in other words, that the Iahveist version had not made away with its sources of information, as has so often happened in history. We shall presently have a proof of this in respect to the *Iasar*. As regards the patriarchal legends of the North, it is scarcely possible to doubt that the unifier had them in his hands at the same time as he had the Iahveist version.

For it is a very remarkable fact that the unifier appears, in several instances, to reproduce the text of the patriarchal Legends of the North, even when he reproduces the Iahveist text. The Legends of the North, for instance, gave a narrative which was very much in favour with those who related patriarchal stories. Abraham, when sojourning with Abimelech, king of Gerar, was led to pass off his wife as his sister. This subject had furnished the Iahveist with two distinct narratives, one attributed to Abraham in Egypt, the other to Isaac at Gerar. The unifier has borrowed these two narratives from the Iahveist,* but that was not enough for him. In the 20th chapter of Genesis he has preserved for us the primitive text of the Legends of the North. The same observation may be made with regard to several other episodes, specially as to the sacrifice of Isaac, the political economy of Joseph, the legends concerning Ishmael, Caleb, and the family of Moses. It may also be assumed that, in the portion called the Book of Numbers,† certain passages of the *Iasar*, or the Book of the Wars of Iahveh, which the Iahveist had passed over, were taken up by the unifier. The rôle of the latter, in short, did not consist simply in fusing two texts together; his task was a more complicated one; being anxious to make a complete sweep of the older versions, he took care to transcribe into his own version all that seemed to be interesting. He knew that the book of the Legends of the North would not outlive the use he was putting it to, so he was determined to exhaust it, so to speak.‡

It is the law of Oriental history writing, in fact, that one book should annihilate its predecessor. The sources of a compilation rarely survive the compilation itself. A book in the East is rarely recopied just as it stands. It is brought up to date by the addition to it of what is known, or supposed

---

* Genesis, ch. xii. and xxvi.

† Ch. xxi.

‡ This is especially noticeable in the narratives about Jacob. Genesis, ch. xxx. xxxi. For Ishmael, note Genesis, ch. xxi. v. 8-21,

to be known, from other sources. The individuality of the historical book does not exist in the East; it is the substance, not the form, which is held of importance, and no scruple is felt about mixing up authors and styles. The end sought is to be complete, and that is all.

The volume which was the outcome of this work of unification formed about half of the existing Hexateuch. There were wanting Deuteronomy, all the Levitical laws, and several narratives of the life of Moses, which were repetitions of the narratives already adopted by the unifier, and which were afterwards borrowed from the Lives of the Prophets. It is owing to the preference given them by the unifier that these ancient stories of Israel have come down to posterity, and been the admiration of all ages. The Elohist text, nevertheless, secured upon one point the most complete triumph. We do not know how the Iahveist text treated the narrative of the creation, but it was doubtless less beautiful and complete than that of the Elohist. This was what led the unifier to commence his work with the solemn page which served as a *début* for the Elohist: " In the beginning, God created the heaven and the earth." As regards all the history of the origin of humanity, the unifier preserves the framework of the Elohist, introducing into it long fragments of the Iahveist, so that we may say that the first pages of the Elohist, up to the appearance of Abraham upon the scene, have been preserved to us in their entirety. The six first Elohist fragments, indeed, if made to follow one another, form a continuous narrative, which is not the case with the Iahveist fragments, between which considerable gaps may clearly be perceived. It seems that in the mind of the unifier, the Elohist version had a certain preference as a peculiarly Jewish and Jerusalemite version, his plan being to complete it by means of the other version, only it happened that the supplements exceeded in extent and importance the text which he was intent upon amplifying.

The legislative part was represented, in the unified text, by the Book of the Alliance preserved in its integrity, and by the Decalogue as it is in Exodus. It is assuredly not impossible that some of the prescriptions introduced by the formula, "And God said unto Moses," which now form part of the Levitical prescriptions, were already in existence. It is probable that the temple had, from an early period, its written rules. The code of the lepers,* the list of the things which are impure,†

* Deuteronomy, ch. xxiv. v. 8, refers to a code of the lepers which, as a matter of fact, may be found in ch. xiii. and xiv. of Leviticus.

† Of the two lists of impure things given in Leviticus xi. and Deuteronomy xiv. that of Leviticus is the older and the more simple. It is likely that in a list of this kind that prohibitions calculated to raise a smile may have been omitted; it is less likely that there should have been added the names of unclean animals which no one, at a more or less civilised epoch, would be tempted to eat.

FUSION OF THE TWO NARRATIVES. 53

perhaps the code of the sacrifices,* the articles upon the offerings, the vows and the legal impurities; but these small codes formed pamphlets apart, not fused in sacred history. They were only collated later, doubtless after the captivity, to form the body of laws which may be called Levitical.† In fine, the first fifteen chapters of Leviticus, together with the twenty-seventh,‡ may very possibly have been in existence, at all events as to their substance, in the time of the ancient temple. At a later date these sacerdotal prescriptions must have been utilised anew by adapting them to the time of the restoration, and warping them by strange hypotheses, such as the Levitical cities, the *ohel moëd*. Those who were animated by a lofty religious sentiment, like Isaiah, were not at all inclined towards ritualist practices. But this was not the case with everybody. Piety, as a rule, impels people to be scrupulous in their observance of forms and ceremonies. When the scoffers, in order

* Leviticus i.-vii. It seems, nevertheless, as if this small treatise on sacrifices refers to a state of worship posterior to that brought out by Deuteronomy. As to the heterogeneous combinations, and as to some other points in which Leviticus appears to be anterior to Deuteronomy, see below, p. 213, note 2, and p. 232, note 1.

† These Pandects are disseminated from Exodus xxiv. to Numbers xx., absorbing the whole of Leviticus. Several chapters of this part of the Pentateuch are old; but large additions were made to it after the restoration of worship following upon the return from captivity.

‡ All the passages in which the Deuteronomy seems to be based upon anterior Levitical texts are to be found in these chapters.

to make much of the prophets, went about repeating wherever they met them in a nasal tone, "*Qav laqav, sav lasav*" (precept upon precept, line upon line),* they marked the commencement of the ritualist casuistry, which was destined in the end to consume Israel. A constantly-repeated saying was—

> For out of Sion shall go forth the law,
> And the word of the Lord from Jerusalem.†

The password of the prophets was *Iahvé mehoqénou*" (Iahveh is our lawgiver).‡ The tendency of mind which will make itself manifest a century later in Deuteronomy was already in germ in the school of Isaiah. In addition to the Book of the Alliance, some parts of which had grown old, and the Decalogue, always young, there were, perhaps, small Thoras, if I may so call them, such as the 15th Psalm,§ in which were enumerated in a few telling lines the duties of the servant of Iahveh. Isaiah was very partial to resumés of this kind.‖ There was no consecrated text or stereotyped version for these commandments of God, but the substance was always the same; and when "the law of God" was mentioned everybody knew what was meant. We shall see further on how this legislative nucleus underwent enormous developments;

* Isaiah, ch. xxviii. v. 10.
† Isaiah, ch. ii. v. 3; and Micah, chap. iv. v. 3.
‡ Isaiah, ch. xxxiii. v. 22.
§ Compare Psalm ci.
‖ Isaiah, ch. xxxiii. v. 15.

and how, thanks to successive additions, the book of the sacred legends, having become in the main a book of laws, eventually, by a far-fetched substitution, got to be called the Thora.

It may be admitted that the ancient book, in the time of Hezekiah, ended with the hymn attributed to Moses which now forms chapter xxxii. of Deuteronomy, a passage the rhetoric of which recalls that of the prophets of the classic epoch. One sole idea pervades it: the happiness or the misfortunes of Israel will always be in proportion to their fidelity to the law of Iahveh. This passage seems to have originated in the kingdom of the North, and we seem to find the echo of it in Hosea and Isaiah. It is doubtful, however, whether it had a place in the Iahveist version. It is a specimen, and there were no doubt many others, of these sporadic fragments which the unifier utilised concurrently with more extensive documents. Science cannot pretend, in such difficult matters as this, to indicate more than the general outline. Much indulgence is due to the savants who were the first to wear out their eyesight in this work. Those who deciphered the papyri of Herculaneum had not a more difficult task. In these small calcined blocks all the letters were visible; but the pages were so embedded and stuck together, that it was impossible to say if such and such a letter belonged to this page or that. By careful and patient unrolling, something like order was introduced into what appeared to be utter confusion. The modern hypotheses as to the composition of the Hexateuch have been sometimes condemned as being too complicated. The probability is that they are not sufficiently so, and that there are in the reality a number of special incidents which have escaped us. The simple hypotheses are nearly always false, and, if we could see the facts as they actually occurred, we should recognise that, upon a number of points, we had conceived things as taking place in a much more regular order than they really did.

CHAPTER VI.

LITERATURE IN THE REIGN OF HEZEKIAH.

THE reign of Hezekiah was an epoch of great literary activity; it may, indeed, be called the classic epoch of Hebrew literature. Each human development has, in this way, its hour of perfect harmony, in which all the parts of the national genius sound their highest note in unison. The Hebrew language attained perfection. Besides Isaiah and his school, who were in full possession of the tradition of ancient eloquence, many writers of rare talent kept up the standard of the language and produced masterpieces by its use. A body of men, who were afterwards styled "the men of Hezekiah,"* sprang up around the king, bent mainly upon making extracts and compilations;† but they formed, no doubt, as well a sort of literary academy, in which style was the chief object of concern. The king himself cultivated with success lyrical and parabolic

---

* אנשי חוקיה, Proverbs, ch. xxv. v. 1.
† It is the meaning of the word העתיקו.

poetry.* The rapid decline which was observed in the course of a century, from Isaiah to Jeremiah, in the style of writing Hebrew shows that this was one of those epochs during which, in order to preserve the language, certain precautions, a sort of State supervision, were necessary.

Writing had become quite a common usage in Judæa. The judicial decisions were given in writing,† people were proud to wear them affixed to the shoulder when they were favourable.‡ The specimen we possess of the writing in Jerusalem eight centuries B.C. § shows us characters already more or less the worse for wear, with a good many of curves in them and a running hand. The substance used was probably the prepared papyrus, or *charta*, imported from Egypt. The form of the book or of the more or less lengthy document (*sépher*) was the roll.‖

The time when writing thus becomes very common, and when the substance used for writing upon ceases to be expensive, is nearly always an important literary epoch. A number of topics which had not yet been definitely fixed are put into concrete form, and matters for which oral tradition

* Isaiah, ch. xxxviii. v. 10 and following.
† Isaiah, ch. x. v. 1.
‡ Job, ch. xxxi. v. 36.
§ Inscription of Siloé. See vol. ii. p. 509, note 6.
‖ The word מגלה does not occur before Jermiah, ch. xxxvi. v. 2 and following. The passage in Psalm xl. v. 8 is doubtful. Septante: χάρτης, χαρτίον.

had so far sufficed are codified. It is the period for compilations and collections. In the East, as I have said, to recopy is as a rule to do a thing anew. Most of the documents of the ancient Hebraic literature thus underwent, in or about the time of Hezekiah, very thorough remodelling.

Many of the lettered men from the North had taken refuge in Jerusalem after the destruction of the kingdom of Israel. They brought with them texts of great literary beauty, scarcely known in Judah. The work to be done was to perpetuate all this part of the tradition, which was in a fair way of being lost. We have seen the process that occurred in regard to sacred history. The combined narrative stopped, like the two separate narratives, at the supposed conquest of Palestine by Joshua and at the division of the land among the tribes. This history had an essentially religious character, and it always kept its own separate framework. But a very natural curiosity caused several reflecting persons to desire to know what happened afterwards. From the conquest of Palestine to the establishment of royalty there was a long interval, during which Israel had only intermittent *sofetim;* this was the heroic age of the nation, the commencement of history properly so called. The *Iasar* or book of the wars of Iahveh contained invaluable information as to these times, songs of a very primitive kind, adventures of rare and singular interest. Retailed from a profane point of view, and without any aim at edification, these old stories had a charm which captivated the whole world. They had merely to be taken out of the collection. This was what the author of the Book of Judges did. He touched up but very slightly the text as he found it,* only added the reflections required to show the misfortunes of the people as the consequence of their unfaithfulness, and doubtless cut out but very little. Thus we have acquired a real treasure, a text of the ninth or tenth century B.C. still to be traced athwart the corrections of later scribes.

The narratives of the wars of Iahveh and the songs of *Iasar* extended, in my opinion, down to the final accession of David to the royalty of Jerusalem. These narratives of the time of Saul and of the youth of David formed the groundwork of the so-called Books of Samuel, but in this case elements of other origin have been mixed or added: upon the one hand pieces and fragments of *mazkirim* of David's time; upon the other pages of little value drawn from the lives of the prophets and from entirely legendary writings.

In this way the essential parts of the great narrative compositions of the tenth century entered into more recent compositions. The *Iasar*, the wars of Iahveh, the patriarchal legends of the North were cut up, so to speak, to suit more

* First of all, no doubt, many stories, like that of Sampson, had been modified.

LITERATURE IN THE REIGN OF HEZEKIAH. 61

modern arrangements of the facts. In ancient times, a literature put to use in this way not only was not made a copy of, but rapidly disappeared. It was considered to have done its share towards the common work, and no further attention was bestowed upon it; thus the ancient books of the North perished while in the heyday of their success. It may be that this exquisite literature inspired the lettered men in Hezekiah's reign with a few imitations. The charming book of Ruth has come down to us as a doubtful remnant of the idyllic literature which dated the ideal age of all poesy from the time of the Judges.*

For the epoch of Solomon, Rehoboam, Jeroboam, and their successors there were extant trustworthy annals from which was drawn a history of the kings of Judah and of Israel, which was continued up to date. Hence we have those *Books of the Kings*, which assuredly had not in Hezekiah's time the dry and scanty aspect they now bear. After the captivity, a clumsy abbreviator, connected closely with Baruch and Jeremiah's school, composed by cuttings the book which we now possess— a poor extract, carried out in a most partial spirit from a vast mass of documents, and mixed up with weak parts borrowed from the prophetic agadas.

From Hezekiah's time probably commenced those lives of the prophets which were intimately con-

---

* The book is certainly Judaic; it gives the idea of Sacred History as being in the state which it is at present (ch. iv. v. 11).

nected with the history of the kings. Certain narratives concerning Elijah and Elisha have a grandeur which brings them very close to the most striking pages of the Iahveist; others, upon the contrary, contain exaggerated, puerile, and almost odious details, introduced, no doubt, at the epoch when it was the custom to imagine the prophets confounding the kings and dominating the people by fear. The prophecy of Elijah and Elisha was of so grand a character that the idea of their being schismatics never suggested itself at Jerusalem.

The literary work of the "Men of Hezekiah" assumed several different characteristics. One of the kinds most in favour with Semitic people of all epochs was that of the *mesalim*, proverbs, maxims expressed in a terse form, small fragments of an enigmatic and far-fetched turn. It is a constant practice with literature of this order that a real or imaginary personage, celebrated rightly or wrongly for his wisdom, should get the credit of all the anonymous sayings and centralise the maxims of the most divergent ages. Among the Hebrews, from the time of Hezekiah, it was Solomon who played this part of the paremiographical and gnomical author. The Men of Hezekiah compiled a collection of proverbs, which were, even at that period, attributed to the son of David,* and supplemented them

---

* Proverbs, ch. xxv. and following. The other two collections (i. and following; x. and following) appear to be not so old. The repetitions which exist between the collection of the Men of Hezekiah

LITERATURE IN THE REIGN OF HEZEKIAH.

with several other small collections of very ancient wisdom, attributed to enigmatic personages — Lemuel,* Agur, and Ithiel.† There, too, is found the charming alphabetical poem of the Strong Woman, a little chef-d'œuvre which is only paralleled by the portrait of the foolish woman.‡

The spirit of poems like these is often more than half profane. It was almost that of free philosophy. Yet God is therein spoken of as Iahveh.§ A sort of compromise had been arrived at between Iahveh and the wisdom common to all the nations. Religion had not as yet enfolded man completely; the view of the world had not been intercepted; fanaticism scarcely existed, or at all events did not prevent the individual exercise of the mind

This sort of profane culture was not, moreover, an isolated fact in the Semitic East. The tribes

and the collection ch. **x.** and following forbid the supposition that the Men of Hezekiah merely continued the collection x. and following.

* This name is probably symbolical. See vol. ii. p. 440-441, note. Possibly למואל is a mistake for למראל, the "disciple of El" Compare למדי יהוה, Isaiah, ch. viii. v. 16; ch. l. v. 4; ch. liv. v. 13. See, however, Genesis, ch. xlvi. v. 10, and Numbers, ch. xxvi. v. 12 (*lamed* abbreviated becoming *iod*).

† *Agour-ben Iake* (Proverbs, xxx. v. i.) is also symbolical. לאיתיאל repeated by dittography is probably a gloss introduced into the text. Ithiel would in that case be the author's true name.

‡ Proverbs, ch. ix. v. 13-18.

§ יהוה is used in all parts of the Proverbs, even in Agur and the Virtuous Woman. קדשים (the Saints), for God, occurs twice in the Proverbs (ch. ix v. 10; ch. xxx. v. 3). Compare Hosea, ch. xii. v. 1.

bordering upon Palestine, such as the *Beni-Kedem* or the *Orientals*, shared the same philosophy.* The Idumean tribe of Teman, more especially, was celebrated for its wise men.† The place occupied by king Lemuel or Libbudel,‡ the opening fragment of whose gnomical poem we are supposed to possess, is not, in all probability, to be sought for in an Arab or Aramean dynasty any more than it was in the series of Palestinean kings. It seems, nevertheless, that there was a kind of intellectual culture, finding expression in parabolic form, of which the Jewish people alone have transmitted to us the recollection, but which was not exclusively its own. It is even possible that, among the monuments of Hebraic wisdom, is to be found more than one fragment of the wisdom of the neighbouring tribes, characterised, like that of Israel, by the sententious form, the parallelism, and the fanciful fashion of beginning each strophe with the letters of the alphabet in their Cadmean order.§

An extraordinary book has been preserved to us as the expression of that one period during which, despite the burden of their religious vocation, Israel

* I. Kings, ch. v. v. 10.

† Jeremiah, ch. xlix. v. 7; Obadiah, ch. ix.; Baruch, chap. iii. v. 22-23. Compare Job, chap. xv. v. 10, 18, 19.

‡ Proverbs, ch. xxxi. v. 1-9. The idea that that *massa* (Proverbs, ch. xxx and xxxi. v. 1) might have been an Arab kingdom is a most improbable one.

§ The short poem of the Strong or Virtuous Woman and Psalm xxxvii. (rather old) are among the first which are notable for this.

LITERATURE IN THE REIGN OF HEZEKIAH.

raised their eyes boldly to heaven.* The book of Job is one of the most astonishing monuments of the human mind handed down to us by the past. This admirable composition, which was assuredly written by an Israelite, but which might just as well have been the work either of a Temanite or of a Saracen,† stands out upon the summit of the two slopes of the Hebrew genius, that which rises and that which descends. It treats of the question which lies at the very heart of Judaism. It is the Hebrew book *par excellence*, and, what shows how free and large-minded was the age of which Hezekiah is the centre, it is quite a book of philosophy; it does not teach, it discusses.

How comes it that, under the empire of a just God, the wicked often succeeds, while the just man is often overwhelmed by undeserved misfortunes? This question was for the Israelite a capital one. It

---

* The literary equivalents of the book of Job are: Amos, Joel, Hosea, Isaiah, the Song of Hezekiah, and the Psalms of the *anavim*. See below, p. 130 and following. It would seem as if the book had been composed by an *anav*. Compare also Isaiah, ch. xix. v. 5, and Job. ch. xiv. v. 11. For further details, see the essay prefacing my translation of the *Book of Job*. (Paris, Lévy, 1858.)

† The care taken not to use the word Iahveh in the philosophical discussion clearly implies that Job and his friends are, in the eyes of the author, strangers to Iahveism. In the same way the sacred narrators avoid putting the name of Iahveh in the mouth of the non-Israelites, and the Elohist narrator keeps from using this name up to the revelation of Sinai. The book of Job and the sapiential books also avoid the use of Sabaoth.

may be said that the struggle against this autonomy is the entire history of Judaism. The history of Judaism is a long effort of 600 years to arrive at the solutions which belief in the immortality of the individual furnished first of all to the Aryan races. More advanced in certain respects than the other peoples, the Beni-Israel saw very clearly that the rewards and punishments of the other world are a vain thing devoid of reality. It is within the circle of real life that must be sought the equilibrium of supreme justice. Set out in this way, the problem is absolutely insoluble, or rather it implies a false major, viz. that the world is governed by a clear and determined conscience, by a reflecting Providence, careful of doing justice to the individual. The exaggeration of the dogma of Providence is the great error of Judaism and of Islam. If Iahveh is the just God *par excellence*, and if everything which occurs in the world is done by Iahveh, or at least with His knowledge, it is necessary that the final liquidation of accounts between the Creator and his creature should result in an exact balance between merit and reward. Crime and punishment are synonymous. He who has sown good things will reap good things; he who has sown evil things will reap evil things.* What can be more opposed to the daily experience of the facts of this world? Eliphaz seeks in vain for a reply to the objection

* Hosea, ch. viii. v. 7; ch. x. v. 13; Job, *passim*. See vol. i. . 132.

of those who say, "How doth God know?"* A more extensive knowledge of the universe, and above all the habit of distinguishing between conscious and unconscious reason, have almost suppressed for us, leaving in the place a fearful, gaping wound, the problem which perplexed these wise men of old. There was not a cure, but an extirpation, and the extirpation will perhaps be mortal for humanity. For the Hebrew, to whom the idea of the infinity of the universe was unknown, and who had not the least notion of the inconscience of supreme reason, the situation was an inextricable one. Up to a certain point it was tenable for the prophets—for Isaiah, to take an instance—considering, as they did, only the race and the nation, being content for the ordinary current of affairs with a summary kind of justice, and living in the expectation of a day of absolute reparation, when all the things distorted by man would be put straight. The fall of the kingdom of the North was explained by the fact that it had not followed a sufficiently pure Iahveism†; but it was difficult to prove that, in these terrible Assyrian inroads, there was the shadow of a discernment between the just and the unjust. Poor Hezekiah, good man as he was, passed his life, at all events previous to the catastrophe of Sennacherib, like a bird upon a twig, watching to catch the direction of the wind.

* Job, ch. xxii. v. 13-14.
† 2 Kings, ch. xvii.

And what, above all, is to be said of divine justice in regard to individuals? Not only is virtue here below not rewarded; one may almost say that it is punished. It is baseness which is rewarded; the advantages are all upon its side; otherwise the sharp-witted would turn their backs upon it. Heroic virtue—the virtue even unto death—finds in its very heroism the exclusion from all possible remuneration.

Thus we see the problem of morality, of virtue, of duty stated, even in the eighth century B.C., in the most absolute form. The author of the book of Job does not solve it, and no wonder. Kant solves it by suppressing it; the categorical imperative, which is his Iahveh, breaks his word to man in the most discreditable manner. The extreme concern which Israel shows for the honour of his God does not permit of his believing Him capable of such a failure. Hence arises an endless struggle against reality.

The excellence of the book of Job consists in its representing this struggle in a framework of admirable grandeur. A man without reproach is struck down by misfortunes which are all due to fatalities of nature or of humanity, but which, according to the idea of the day, are attributed to the direct action of Iahveh. Job submits to the divine will, but curses the condition of humanity exposed to such trials. Less enlightened than he, his three friends, more especially Eliphaz, who belonged to the school of the wise men of Teman, seek to discover the cause of his misfortunes, and think they have found that it resides in secret sins he must have committed. The human conscience is so obscure! No one can tell if he deserves love or hatred. One is often impure in the eyes of God without being aware of the fact. Job, who is certain of his innocence, protests, and, in order to defend himself, is tempted to strong utterances which seem to incriminate the justice of God. His friends regard him as impious.* Iahveh then appears upon the whirlwind, and, reproaching Job's friends for their hardness and Job for his rashness, crushes the pride of the man who pretends to understand anything of the works of God. Job humbles himself; God re-establishes him in his former state and doubles his former blessings; instead of seven sons, he has fourteen; instead of three thousand camels, he has six; and he dies old and full of days.

The stroke of genius in this poem is the indecision of the author, in a subject where indecision is the truth. All possible solutions are attempted by the different speakers; no one is definitely selected. At one time justice is considered to reside in the totality of the tribe; at another the family is the unity which explains everything. A

* The speech of Elihu (ch. xxxii.-xxxvii.) is certainly an interpolation. It is, moreover, an insignificant fragment, with no doctrinal importance.

wicked man may prosper, it is true; but his children are little thought of after him; the ill-acquired riches of their father are drawn from their belly with hooks. To which Job replies that this is of very little importance, for in hell there is neither feeling, nor sight, nor memory.*

It may even be doubted whether the author is entirely satisfied with the *dénoument* which he has chosen. But this *dénoument* is quite that which the Hebraic conception required. The book of Tobias, the companion one to that of Job, at an interval of eight centuries, does not go beyond the same solution.† Tobias is struck with blindness while performing a pious act, so that the case is still more strange than that of Job. Tobias is firm in his trust in God. He is healed, he lives to a great age, sees his children well provided for, and Nineveh, the enemy of his people, brought to ruin. What could he desire more? Judith is also rewarded by living to the age of 120, and by dying surrounded by honour, amid her people, which has been saved and made happy by her.‡ The misfortunes which befall Iahveh's faithful servants are a passing trial. Iahveh owes it to himself to extricate them, and even to compensate them for their sufferings. This compensation always occurs in this life. Death has nothing of which man can complain when he dies

* Job, ch. xiv. v. 21-22.
† *Hist. des orig. du Christ.*, vol vi. p. 228-237.
‡ *Hist. des orig. du Christ.*, vol. v. p. 29 and following.

old, leaving behind him a numerous family to keep his name alive.

This childish theory was day by day more shaken; another six centuries and many martyrs were needed for Israel to get quit of those two irreconcilable dogmas, " God is just ; man is but a fleeting shadow," by means of the desperate expedient of the resurrection and of the millennium.* Ancient Israel never admitted the idea of absolute immortality; that would have been to make a man a god. A thousand years is really a very long time, and assuredly a martyr who had lived for that period, in the midst of a Jerusalem which has become the capital of the world, ought to be satisfied.

It is in the book of Job that the force, the beauty, the depth of the Hebrew genius are seen at their best. The Pentateuch, Isaiah, the Psalms have all exercised a greater influence upon the world. *Job* has excited surprise and terror; the Middle Ages did not dare to translate it;† it is astonishing that it should have been allowed to remain among the canon books. If the Song of Songs proves that Israel was young in his day, the book of Job proves also that in his day he displayed great freedom of thought. No doubt the limits of the philosophical development which was

* This is what I shall explain in vol. iv. if I have life and strength to write it. See *Hist. des orig. du Christ.*, vol. i. p. 56-57, 290 and following; vol. ii. p. 97-98; vol. iii. p. 196-197, 379, 413, 529-530; vol. iv. p. 446-447, 468.

† See Guyart des Moulins, *Histoire Littéraire de la France*, vol. xxviii. p. 449.

capable of emerging from such a condition of mind are clearly defined. The immensity of the God of Job did not admit of the whole *cosmos* being embraced. The analytic study of the reality was impossible under the sway of such a master. The fundamental theory of our system of the world, the fixity of the laws of nature, could not be conciliated with so absolute a will, extending to all the details of the universe. The author of the book of Job, had he lived thousands of years, would never have arrived at science as conceived by the Greeks and as definitely created by modern genius. But he would have arrived at a very refined philosophy. He would have felt the necessity of introducing distinctions into his haughty and trenchant affirmations. He would have seen that an Iahveh, as he imagines Him, could not be just ; that things do not happen at all as he imagines them; that no special will governs the world, and that what happens is the result of a blind effort tending upon the whole towards good.

From this fresh point of view he would have understood that no man has ever been, like his hero, the butt of systematic blows from fate ; that Job is very wrong to curse the day he was born, inasmuch as this day has been for him the cause of more good than evil; that God no more took his riches away from him than He gave them to him; and, in short, that to close the mouths of his superficial friends he had only one observation to make, viz., that moral evil exercises no appreciable action upon the course of physical facts, so much so, that in the name of morality itself all idea of reward and punishments should be dismissed from the order of contingent facts. Justice would have appeared to him as a thing in the future; he would have seen that it makes default in the present, that it is the slow work of reason, not a sort of immanent law of the world. This intelligent Israelite would, in the seventeenth century, have been Spinoza; in our day he would have been one of those Jews, lovers of the truth, who resign themselves to the tardy coming of the kingdom of justice, knowing very well that the impatience of man will do nothing to advance its progress. In reality, the *beni-elohim* are right; the creation is good, and does great credit to the Almighty; the objections of Satan against the work of God are quite out of place, but thousands of millions of years will probably have to elapse before the just God is a reality. Let us wait.

The work accomplished under Hezekiah consisted, in the main, as we have seen, in saving from among the wreck of the kingdom of Israel the Hebrew texts written in the North. Was the book of Job among the number, and is its breadth of tone the outcome of the purer air which was breathed by the tribes which had remained in closer contact with the nomad life? That is quite possible. At the same time, another work, the

Israelite origin of which can with greater certainty be affirmed, is the Song of Songs.* This charming poem was assuredly conceived in the North. The opposition of Jerusalem and of Tirzah,† capital of the kingdom of Israel before Samaria, and also the almost ridiculous part assigned to Solomon in it, would be sufficient to prove this. At all marriages it was customary to recite and to sing love dialogues, the theme of which, varied by means of different episodes, always harped upon the same string; a young shepherdess of the North, carried off by the men who supplied Solomon's harem, remains true to her lover despite the seductions of the court. All the scenes which went to represent this one idea wound up with the same tableau, the young girl asleep in the arms of her lover.‡ This was all known by heart; the plan of the work being very elastic, and the prosody of certain fragments not being hard and fast, any changes which might be desired were easily made, as is the case with the Italian improvisatore. After the destruction of the kingdom of Israel there was every reason to fear that such a *scenario* might be lost. I am quite prepared to admit that the *Sir has-sirim* was written first of all by the men of letters in Hezekiah's reign, without being certain that the

* See the notice heading my translation (Paris, Lévy, 1860).
† Solomon's Song, ch. vi. v. 4.
‡ It was what was called קול חתן וקול כלה, Jeremiah, ch. vii. v 34; ch. xvi. v. 9; ch. xxv. v. 10.

very defective text which we possess is the one which was then fixed by the *Kalam*.

A style which was, upon the contrary, peculiar to Jerusalem began to develop very fast under Hezekiah. The *sir*, or song, was as old as the Semitic peoples themselves; but the ancient ages, with little mysticism about them, had quite overlooked the refinements which can be imported into the modulation of sentiment. About the time of Hezekiah, the *sir* became diversified *ad infinitum*. It was no longer, as formerly, the poetic echo of an external fact; it is the meditation of the soul upon the situation to which it finds itself brought by the injustice of man and by its own weakness. Thus the *sir* had a great resemblance to the *masal*, and it was sometimes difficult to discern the one from the other. The short poem of this kind was called *mizmor*, and it generally had a musical accompaniment. It is doubtful whether, in the time of Hezekiah, the *mizmor* had its place in the liturgy; but the tendency was already in this direction. Even thus early many pious men would have liked the sacrifice to have been abolished, and replaced by praise (*toda*). In any event the *mizmor*, sung upon one of the varieties of the lyre or the guitar (*nébel*, *cinnor*, *negina*), was the manner of speaking to God, of holding converse with Him. We shall find Hezekiah praying to Him in this manner. It is in the following generation that the *mizmor* will produce its masterpieces; yet it is already flourishing in the time of which I am writing. In two or three instances, Isaiah expresses himself after the manner of an accomplished psalmist.*

Then was inaugurated the psalm, perhaps the most beautiful and certainly the most fruitful creation of the genius of Israel. The ancient prayer, accompanied by dances and by shouts, to attract the attention of the god, took rank among the ridiculous conceptions of a gross and uninstructed age. The prayer of the heart came into being. The sober and steady pietism of the *anavim* showed in this its great originality. From a style coldly patriotic and starchly official, it created the pure hymn; from a confused noise it evolved a harmonious lyre, adapting itself to all the subjective effusions of a soul bruised by the rigours of life. The pious man had, henceforth, a consolation, an *alibi*, in the midst of his troubles; a private chapel in which he could indulge in secret dialogues with his benevolent Creator. Before being too hard upon these dreams of the past, we must bear in mind to what a marvellous use the Church has succeeded in putting the music of the Psalms, and reckon up the number of good and gentle spirits whom the harp of Israel has consoled.

With regard to the question whether, from the reign of Hezekiah, the collection into one book of the lyrical pieces dating from earlier epochs was begun, it may be said that this would have been in con-

* Isaiah, ch. xii. v. 1 and following; v. 4 and following.

formity with the spirit of the age, and the academy of Hezekiah would have found therein a natural outlet for its activity. But such a selection, had it been made, would have come down to us, in a separate form, in the general collection of the Psalms, as was the case with the Proverbs. But none of the five books which now compose the Psalms can be the collection which might have been formed in Hezekiah's time.

The phrase, "the age of Hezekiah," would not be out of place to designate the remarkable literary *ensemble* which the Hebrew genius produced towards the close of the eighth and the beginning of the seventh century B.C. Usage, led astray by the false chronological ideas of orthodox criticism, has not adopted it. Such an expression would imply, moreover, in this petty world of Palestine, an amplitude of life to which Greece, Italy, and modern Europe have alone attained. There were powerful causes at work to prevent the framework of Israelite society from becoming, like Greece, the complete model of a civilised society. All-powerful Assyria placed Palestine in the same position in which Hellas would have been if Persia had conquered her two hundred years later. The much more general use of writing gave to the Syria of the eighth century an enormous start against the Greece of that time;* but civic freedom has advan-

* About 700 B.C. only certain islands of Greece used the Cadmean alphabet.

tages for which nothing can make up. The Greek genius, enfolded as it was within the narrow circle of Homer's and Hesiod's songs, already gave indications of being more comprehensive, more extensive, more laic, if I may so say. The Greek genius will prevail in the intellectual, philosophical, and political order; but religious and social questions will be outside the radius of its childlike serenity. Isaiah planted the standard of the religion of the future ere Solon and Thales of Miletus had been born. People were athirst for justice in Jerusalem when at Athens and at Sparta no protest was raised against slavery, when the Greek conscience, in any embarrassing conjuncture, is satisfied with the peremptory reason: Διὸς δ' ἐτελείετο βουλή.

CHAPTER VII.

INVASION OF SENNACHERIB.

THE Assyrian sway was a purely military one, and the work of the conquest stood constantly in need of being done over again. The passage of the armies was not followed, as in the case of the dominion of Rome, by a kind of administrative and civil conquest. Sargon, who at the beginning of his reign had appeared so terrible to Syria, was little heard of during the fifteen following years.

The clouds which obscured the close of his reign * seemed to encourage the revolt. Hezekiah ceased paying tribute,† and thus broke the bonds of vassaldom which attached him to Nineveh. At the same time he opened up negotiations with Egypt, more especially with Ethiopia, which was at that time at the height ‡ of its power, and which maintained very regular relations with Syria.

* Maspero, *Histoire Ancienne*, p. 431-432, 4th edition.
† 2 Kings, ch. xviii. v. 7.
‡ Isaiah, ch. xviii., implying a wonderful knowledge of Central Africa. Compare Maspero's *Histoire Ancienne*, p. 410 and following.

It seems that in all this Hezekiah followed the advice of Shebna,* who had, as it appears, preserved his credit at court under another name.† Isaiah continued his intrigues and declamations against him, and the manifesto in which Jerusalem is designated by the symbolic name of Ariel ‡ may be attributed to this period.

Ariel will be crushed in a year by the serried masses which are drawing near to it. That will be its own fault; Ariel does not hearken to the prophets, practising only the external forms of worship, and no one thinking of the true worship, which is that of the heart. Justice is not truly rendered.§

Ethiopia has sent messengers into Judæa, but the prophet protests against their being listened to. So long as Iahveh wills it so the Assyrians will prevail. When it is Iahveh's pleasure the Assyrians will be crushed; their corpses will cover Judæa and be a prey to the birds. Then the Ethiopians will return to make offerings to Iahveh.‖ The triumph of the *anavim* and of the *ebionim* will be complete.

---

* See above, p. 9 and following.

† In Isaiah, ch. xxii. v. 15, Shebna is *soken*, in other passages he is only *sopher*.

‡ Isaiah, ch. xxix. The passage in Isaiah, from ch. xvii. v. 12 to ch. xviii. v. 7, appears to refer to the same state of things.

§ Isaiah, ch. xxix. v. 13-15.

‖ It is remarkable that the Ethiopians are always represented by the prophets as having a propensity for the worship of Iahveh, and that they for this reason were treated more favourably than the other *goïm*.

INVASION OF SENNACHERIB.

This will be the end of the reign of the violent (*anavim*), of the scoffers (*lécim*), of the unjust judges, of the perverters of right. Those who have gone astray will return to wisdom; the rebellious will submit themselves to instruction.

The assassination of Sargon in his palace at Khorsabad, about 704 B.C., served to further accentuate in the provinces the tendency to revolt against the Ninevite power. Sennacherib, the son and successor of Sargon, had to reconquer nearly the whole of what his father had held by force.* Eulœus, king of Sidon, refused to pay the tribute, and his example was followed by the king of Ascalon. The inhabitants of Ekron, discontented with Padi,† whom Sargon had given them for king, seized him and sent him captive to Hezekiah. This was equivalent to making him a gift of their town; but Hezekiah, while accepting this, instead of putting Padi to death, as the Ekronites desired, merely retained him prisoner. More prudent than Eulœus, Hezekiah, the petty princes of Arvad, of Gebal, and of Asdod, the kings of Moab and of Ammon, remained neutral until fortune had declared itself upon one side or the other.

In Jerusalem, the military and patriotic party urged that an opportunity which they regarded as

---

* Schrader, *Die Kiel. und das A. T.* p. 285 and following; G. Smith, *History of Sennacherib* (London, 1878); Maspero, p. 433 and following.

† מדה]אל[.

excellent should not be lost for crushing the standing danger of the freedom of the East. This military party appears to have been almost indifferent in matters of religion; they were not, at all events, Iahveists of the reformed school; they had no great objection to graven images;* they were hard, perhaps unjust, towards the people, as aristocrats so often are. In striking contrast to them, like white upon black, stood out the party of democratic theocracy and of religious puritanism, opposed to a lay state and to military precautions, being intent solely upon social and religious reforms. In a year, they said,† the city will be destroyed; it will become a refuge for the wild beasts, until a spirit from on high shall be poured out upon it, and until there is a complete transformation. Then the desert will blossom like the rose; universal peace will reign amid unalloyed prosperity. This will be the fruit of justice, itself the fruit of the attention paid to the utterances of the prophets inspired by Iahveh.

Women, it appears, were upon the side of the politicians, rather than of the prophets.‡ Isaiah regards them as being in general opposed to reforms, and is very severe upon them.§ In one of his most violent passages he apostrophises the careless ones,

* Isaiah, ch. xxx. v. 22.
† Isaiah, ch. xxxii. v. 9 and following.
‡ Isaiah, ch. xxxii. v. 9-20.
§ See vol. ii. pp. 418, 419, and below, pp. 104, 105, 119, 147.

who, thinking only of their attire, will not believe in the woes to come. They were probably ladies of the royal family whom the rugged prophet had in his mind, for we shall see presently * that the women about Hezekiah were not at all favourable to the austere doctrines of the reformers.

It is a rare thing for a man to serve several causes at the same time, even when they are good. The man of faith is always a political danger, for he puts his faith before the interests of his country. The party of the prophets gained the day in history. They were in favour of the submission to Assyria, and, taking into account the impossibility of conquering so strong a power, it cannot be said that they were wrong. If Shebna had not been counteracted by Isaiah, it is probable that Jerusalem would have had, in Hezekiah's time, the same fate as Samaria when Hoshea was king. But the rôle of a preacher of the counsels of despair is a melancholy one; he must be very sure that he is uttering the words of Iahveh to feel it his duty to say to a conquered people: "Submit; do nothing in the way of revenge; you will infallibly be defeated."

Yet this was the idea which pervaded the manifestoes of Isaiah at the time of which I am speaking. All the resources of his virulent and popular talents were called into requisition in order to declaim against the diplomacy and military preparations,

---

* See below, pp. 104, 105.

against the Egyptian alliance more especially.*
This alliance was concluded without consulting
Isaiah, who would not hear of it.† The system of
sending messengers with presents through Arabia
Petræa will end in disaster. There are superficial
people who would have the preacher speak to
them after their illusions and not according to
the truth, who become impatient when they are
spoken to about Iahveh. Woe unto them! Salvation must come by conversion, by the reform of
society.‡

The prophet closes by foreshadowing a perspective
of happiness. The Assyrian shall be exterminated
without the intervention of a sword wielded by man.
The people shall renounce their graven images and
the fragments be cast upon the dunghill. Upon
the morrow of each crisis it was thought that a
social golden age was dawning in which the king
would be just, and in which those who conducted
affairs would be perfect, in which the prophets
would be listened to, and in which the impious
would be reduced to impotence. Then even the
foolish will understand, the churl shall no longer
be called bountiful, nor the crafty man liberal.

Does one not seem to be reading the words of a
rabid socialist of our own day, declaiming against

* Isaiah, ch. xxx.-xxxii., three distinct *surates*.
† Isaiah, ch. xxxi. v. 1-3. Compare ch. xxx. v. 16; Psalm xx. v. 8; xxxiii. v. 17; lxxvi. v. 7.
‡ Isaiah, ch. xxx. v. 16-17.

the army, making mock at patriotism, predicting with a kind of savage joy future disaster, and summing up his views much as follows: " Justice for the people, that is the true vengeance; reform society, and you will be victorious over your enemies; wherever the poor are victimised, wherever the rich enjoy privileges, there can be no country." Isaiah, it is fair to add, gives to these dangerous truths a brilliancy which they have never possessed since. The beautiful political fragment which I have been analysing concludes with a theophany of Iahveh which breathes the old naturalist spirit and melts, as in the fifth act of an opera, into the flickering flame of Ashur's funeral pile.*

It was only after a lapse of three years that Sennacherib, having vanquished his enemies in the region of the Tigris and the Euphrates, could turn his attention to Syria and Egypt.† He took the valley of the Orontes and the coast, wrote his stela upon the rocks of the river of the Dog to the north of Beyrout, as Rameses II. had already done, crushed all the small Phœnician royalties, Tyre excepted, and was only stopped when he came to Ekron. There he met a first Egyptian army, which he cut to pieces; he captured the city, and

* Isaiah, ch. xxx. v. 27-33. See also vol. i. p. 238.

† For the chronological difficulties arising from 2 Kings, ch. xviii. v. 13, and Isaiah, ch. xxxvi. v. 1, see Dillman, *Der Proph. Jes.*, pp. 312-313. The hypothesis substituting Sargon for Sennacherib, is open to serious objections.

directed all his forces against Lachish, to the south of the Philistines.

How came it to pass that Hezekiah, who had entered into the league against Assyria, did not join forces with Egypt and the Philistine cities to arrest Sennacherib's advance at Ekron? The reason doubtless was due to the indecision which the turbulence of the prophets caused to reign in his counsels. Isaiah was not strong enough to prevent the Israelite patriots from turning their eyes towards Egypt and Ethiopia; but his continual declamations against all human precautions and against anything which seemed like a policy of precaution paralysed any action Hezekiah might have taken. The natural common sense and the piety of the king neutralized each other.

The Assyrian army ravaged Judæa to a most terrible degree.* The emotion at Jerusalem was very profound, as no preparation for resistance had been made. The wall of the city had several breaches in it; no steps had been taken for protecting the water supply from the enemy,† as the prophets would have regarded this as a species of insult to Iahveh. To those who talked of horses and war-chariots they replied with their everlasting refrain: " Some trust in chariots and some in

---

* 2 Kings, ch. xviii. v. 13 and following; ch. xix. v. 29 and following; Schrader, *Die Kiel.*, p. 285 and following; Maspero, *Hist. anc.*, p. 433 and following.

† Isaiah, ch. xxii. v. 24-27.

horses; but we will remember the name of the Lord our God."*

When the terror became uncontrollable, brief oracles were put into circulation, announcing that Iahveh had resolved to destroy the Assyrian army in Palestine itself.† The manifestoes—the articles as we should now call them—of Isaiah at this solemn moment come one upon the other. He does not seem to be the least affected by a state of affairs for which he is in fact responsible. "What aileth thee now, that thou art wholly gone upon the housetops?‡ Thou that art full of stirs, a tumultuous city."§ He does not reproach the unhappy Jerusalemites with anything beyond not fasting and weeping enough. All the tribe of Judah takes refuge in Jerusalem. That will not save any of them; they will all be taken together. Elam, Qir, the most remote provinces of Assyria, are drawing nigh. The cavalry is at the gates; the siege is about to begin.∥

Hezekiah took the only step which his previous tergiversations left him the choice of. He sent to the camp of Lachish to make his submission to the

---

* Psalm xx. v. 8, and 2 Chronicles, ch. xxxii. v. 6-8, expresses the same idea. For the expression שם יהזה, compare Isaiah, ch. xxx. v. 27. See above, p. 185.

† Isaiah, ch. xiv. v. 24-27.

‡ To get a good view of what was happening.

§ Isaiah, ch. xxii. v. 1-14.

∥ Isaiah, ch. xxii. v. 8-14.

King of Assyria.* Sennacherib imposed a contribution of three hundred talents of silver and thirty talents of gold. For this Hezekiah had to deliver up all the money that was in the temple and in the palace treasury, and even that was not sufficient. In order to complete the sum, it was necessary to take off the gold which covered the gates of the temple and from the pillars which Hezekiah had overlaid. Padi was re-established in his kingdom of Ekron, and received, by way of compensation for his imprisonment by Hezekiah, certain cities of Judah. The kings of Ashdod and of Gaza were also recompensed for their fidelity to Assyria at the cost of Hezekiah.

If the campaign had terminated in this way, the triumph of Iahveism would have been but a poor one. The national conscience needed something more striking. Whether it was that the legend, by means of the historiographical combinations which are customary with it, ran riot,† or that the campaign of Sennacherib really finished disastrously for the Assyrians, the prophetic party related the event as a complete victory for Iahveh. Sennacherib, as it appears, thought that Hezekiah had committed an act of treachery and made a fresh

---

* Layard, *Monuments of Nineveh*, 2nd series, plate xxiii.

† The inconsistency of the original narratives is manifest, 2 Kings, ch. xviii., between the verses 16 and 17. It would seem as if the data relating to two Assyrian expeditions had been mixed up.

attack upon Jerusalem. An Egyptian army was formed at Pelusium, and Tahraqa hurried from Ethiopia to support the coalition.

Sennacherib, we are told, sent from Lachish the three principal persons of his government, the tartan, the chief of the eunuchs, and the great cupbearer, with a large force to obtain the full submission of Jerusalem.* The Assyrian army encamped near the conduit of the upper pool, in the plain which is to the north-west of Jerusalem.† The three Assyrian chiefs expressed a desire to negotiate, and the king sent out to parley with them Eliakim, the son of Hilkiah, Shebna,‡ and Joab, the son of Asaph the recorder (*mazkir*). The grand cupbearer

---

* All the episode which follows (Isaiah, ch. xxxvi.-xxxix.; 2 Kings, ch. xviii.-xix.) was taken by the compiler of Isaiah from a book which contained fragments written by Isaiah. It is from this, too, that it was taken by the latest compiler of the books of the Kings. The compiler of Isaiah did not borrow from the books of the Kings, for he had the Song of Hezekiah as well.

† The topographical particulars are here repeated word for word from Isaiah, ch. vii. v. 3. This is surprising; *à priori*, it is almost certain that the camp of the Assyrians must have been near what is now the Russian settlement, a point at which they could intercept the water coming into the besieged city from Mamillah. This was what was called the $\pi\alpha\rho\epsilon\mu\beta\upsilon\lambda\grave{\eta}\ \tau\tilde{\omega}\nu\ \text{'}A\sigma\sigma\upsilon\rho\acute{\iota}\omega\nu$. It was there also that the camps of Titus, of the crusaders, etc. were. In the valley of Kedron the camp could not well have existed. So that the reference here must be to the conduits of the water from the north-west supplying the pool of Hezekiah. The episode of Achaz, upon the contrary, appears to have occurred near the fountain of the Virgin. See V. ii. p. 509.

‡ A very unlikely association of persons.

explained to the Jews how presumptuous the conduct of Hezekiah had been, and how vain was the alliance with Egypt, that crushed reed which pierces the hand that leans upon it.* Their God Iahveh had been angered by the king, who had conceived the unfortunate idea of abolishing His worship elsewhere than in Jerusalem.† Iahveh himself protects the Assyrians, seeing that He has given them the land. The negotiators are said to have closed the discussion by scoffing, while the Jews built their hopes on the chariots and horsemen of Egypt.‡ The Assyrians will give them, if they like, two thousand horses, upon condition that they find horsemen to ride them.§

The people, according to the traditional narrative, were on the walls and heard the whole of what passed. The three Jewish functionaries were terrified at the effect which such a speech might have upon the crowd, and they entreated the grand cupbearer to speak in Aramean, which they understood, and not in Hebrew. But the latter continued to address himself to the multitude. He would not disguise from the Jerusalemites that the plan of his master, after his victorious return from Egypt, was to transplant

* A familiar phrase with the prophets (see Ezekiel, ch. xxix. v. 6), very improbable in the mouth of the Assyrian.

† See above, p. 2, note 26.

‡ Another of the ideas of the prophets put into the mouth o Rabshakeh.

§ Perhaps an allusion to Isaiah, ch. xxx. v. 16 and following.

them, in order to remove them from the vicinity of their natural ally, promising them that the land given them should equal Judæa in fertility. Iahveh is a powerless God; He will not save them; Iahveh is, in reality, with the Assyrians. The gods of other peoples have not saved any of them from the hands of the Assyrians.

The conduct of Isaiah in this difficult conjuncture appears to have been most correct.* The prophet assured the people that Iahveh would be at no loss to avenge His honour, that the Assyrians might by their presence once more prevent the harvest, but that the year after the seeds would be sown, that in no event would the enemy besiege Jerusalem. Iahveh will prevail; the just will be saved.† There was but one cry in the mouths of the pietists during these days of anguish,‡ and, as a matter of fact, the position of Sennacherib became more and more embarrassing. Tarhaqa, who had just conquered Egypt, was advancing to the attack, and it was soon learnt that the Assyrian army was quitting Judæa and the land of the Philistines to go and meet the Ethiopian.§ Jerusalem breathed again; the fangs of the monster which held the city within his jaws began to relax.

* Isaiah, ch. xxxiii.
† Isaiah, ch. xxxiii. v. 15-16.
‡ Isaiah, ch. xxxiii. v. 22.
§ The order of the day by Isaiah, preserved in the legend, 2 Kings, ch. xix., and in Isaiah, ch. xxxvii., is of doubtful authenticity.

There was an outburst of joy a few weeks later. The Assyrian army had ceased to exist; it had been destroyed in lower Egypt, more, as it would appear, by disease than by the sword of the enemy,* and Sennachereb fled back to Nineveh.

What a triumph for Iahveh! The prophecies of Isaiah had been fulfilled in every particular. Hezekiah had been victorious because he had put trust in Iahveh alone. The legend was formed very quickly. The oracles of Isaiah, predicting that the army of Sennacherib would be exterminated in Judæa without the succour of man, were recalled.† The plague in ancient days was always attributed to a deity or to a destroying angel.‡ It soon got to be related that the *maleak Iahveh* had, in one night, slain 185,000 Assyrians, and that the next morning the plain was strewn with corpses. The Egyptians also explained the disappearance of the Assyrian army by a miracle.§

The reign of Sennacherib was prolonged for a considerable period, being brilliant and prosperous.‖ Later, it was said, he was assassinated by two of his officers, Adrammeleck and Sharezer, while he was praying in the temple. This was considered as a sequel to the divine vengence. The Jewish

---

* Herodotus, ii. 141.
† See above, p. 87.
‡ Note the angel of Arauna.
§ Herodotus, book c.; Maspero, p. 440.
‖ Maspero, pp. 440 and following.

annalists brought forward the date in order to draw it nearer to the alleged extermination and render the vengeance of Iahveh more complete. The enemies of theocracy cannot die without their death being a punishment from heaven.

CHAPTER VIII.

THE LAST YEARS OF HEZEKIAH.—TRIUMPH OF THE
THEOCRATIC DEMOCRACY.

WITH the disappearance of Sennacherib, Hezekiah found himself raised to a higher degree of power than he possessed in the early part of his reign. The petty neighbouring princes who had been enriched at his expense lost no time in making themselves friendly with him. Presents came in to him from all directions. His treasure-house, which he had been obliged to empty in order to pay for his ransom, was soon refilled.* There was absolute security from Assyria, for, as is always the case with a two-headed state, the empire founded upon the momentary union of Nineveh and Babylon, menaced disruption. Merodoch-Baladan, who had for a considerable period already represented the protest of Babylon against Nineveh,† sought to

---

* Isaiah, ch. xxxix. v. 2; 2 Chronicles, ch. xxxii. v. 27-29.

† G. Smith's *History of Sennacherib*, p. 129 and following, and Schrader's discussions. The Assyrian texts would lead one to date

THE LAST YEARS OF HEZEKIAH.

form an alliance with the king of Judah.* No such prosperity had been seen at Jerusalem since the time of Jehosaphat.

The party of reform at that time enjoyed a few years of undivided power. The unsuccessful attempt of Sennacherib was, in fact, a decisive event in the history of Judaism. The recollection of this terrible episode of the famine, perhaps of the plague which accompanied it, was long treasured up. The proclamations of Isaiah during this crisis were nearly all preserved. Even if we admit that the legend of the destroying angel found its way in long afterwards, the deliverance announced by the prophets, accomplished without horses or chariots, without any of the means foreign to the tactics of Israel, was not that the greatest of miracles? The national god had secured an unparalleled victory.

At first sight that appeared to be but a very poor gain for humanity. The national god of Israel is very proud and very jealous. He wishes all the glory to be ascribed to Him. He likes to be praised and to be flattered: He does not object to being told a falsehood,† when it comes from a vanquished foe who is compelled to humble himself before Him.

---

all that relates to Merodach-Boladan from before the death of Sennacherib. But I am loth to modify the fairly logical order of the Hebrew historiographer.

* 2 Kings, ch. xx. v. 12. בן בלאדן, variation introduced into the text. The Assyrian name *Binbaliddina* does, as a matter of fact, exist.

† Meaning of מְחַשׁ Psalm lxvi. v. 3; lxxxi. v. 16.

One does not see why, fashioned in this way, he should be so passionately in favour of right and goodness. But it is here that comes in the masterpiece of the Israelite prophets. Their ideal God was at the same time the god of the nation. Therein was the secret of their strength. A patriotic cause has more chance of success than an abstract one.* Religions in their maturity are too strong for politics, but budding religions have often been dependent upon political circumstances now forgotten. The epoch of Sennacherib was, like that of Antiochus Epiphanes, like that of the return from captivity, one of those moments when the future of humanity was staked on the cast of a die. Isaiah had, so to speak, staked his whole credit upon a tangible fact, the deliverance of Jerusalem. He had laid a wager, and he had won it. If Sennacherib had come back victorious from Egypt and had taken Jerusalem, Judaism and consequently Christianity would not exist.

During the remainder of Hezekiah's reign, that is to say for five or six years, the prophets were all-powerful. Isaiah was the soul of the king's counsels, for Hezekiah, convinced of the prophet's superior gifts, submitted to his advice, and it is possible that during this latter period, the moderation which had characterised the first part of his reign was not always observed. There were con-

* Babism, for instance, will only succeed when it has identified itself with some national cause in Persia.

THE LAST YEARS OF HEZEKIAH. 97

spiracies and plots. The *anavim* assured the king that he would triumph over the perverse, and urged him to exterminate them and their seed.* The king does not appear to have followed the bad advice which they offered him, but he gave satisfaction to the aspirations of the good. Internal reforms were carried actively forward in the direction defined by the *anavim;* the party of the scornful was abased, and authority passed almost entirely into the hands of the pious. Justice was probably better administered to the poor; but the higher classes, the men of intelligence, were annoyed, and the women were highly irritated. The strength of the reaction which ensued, under Manasseh, seems to indicate that the saintly party, while it had the upper hand, more than once abused its power.

One of the finest lyrical fragments of Hebraic literature, the Psalm *Quare fremuerunt gentes,*† probably refers to that period. The triumph of the *anavim* is associated therein with a defeat of the kings of the earth, who had sworn to compass the ruin of the holy people. The King of Zion is the anointed of Iahveh; God has said to him, "Thou art my son; this day have I begotten thee." The plots formed against him come to naught. The wicked are desirous of throwing off the yoke which weighs upon them, but Iahveh laughs them to scorn. The king will rule them with a rod of iron and

* Psalm, xxi. v. 9 and following.
† Psalm ii. at v. 12, instead of בר read בו.

break them in pieces like a potter's vessel. A great lesson this for those who judge the earth. To serve Iahveh with fear, that is what will save a man in the day of wrath. Like Isaiah, the psalmist's ideal is a world converted to Iahveism and the dominion of the Messianic king extending to the ends of the earth.*

An illness which fell upon Hezekiah† demonstrated in a very striking way the singular distinctions of the piety of that day. Isaiah, aware of the serious nature of the illness, said to him, "Set thine house in order, for thou shalt die and not live." Hezekiah turned his face to the wall and addressed the following prayer to God: "I beseech thee, O Lord, remember now how I have walked before thee in truth and with a perfect heart, and have done that which is good in thy sight." And he wept sore. Isaiah had not yet got out of the middle court when the word of Iahveh came to him, saying, "Turn again and tell Hezekiah, the captain of my people, thus saith the Lord, the God of David thy father, I have heard thy prayer, I have

* Thus, for instance, the conversion of Aram and of Hamath was anticipated with especial confidence. Compare Psalm lxvi., taking into account Grætz's corrections and comparing Zechariah, ch. ix. v. 1.

† Isaiah, ch. xxxviii. According to v. 6, Sennacherib had not yet evacuated Palestine, and the fifteen years of verse 5 are probably calculated in view of this. But in that case the treasure of Hezekiah (ch. xxxix. v. 2) is quite inexplicable. All these historical appendices of Isaiah teem with artificial comparisons, which smack very much of legend.

THE LAST YEARS OF HEZEKIAH.

seen thy tears; behold, I will heal thee; on the third day, thou shalt go up unto the house of the Lord. And I will add unto thy days fifteen years." Hezekiah asked for a sign that he might be more sure of the prophecy. The prodigy chosen by Isaiah remains an enigma to us. It consisted, apparently, in putting back by ten degrees the shadow on the sundial set up in the courtyard of the palace by Ahaz. Isaiah also had a plaster of figs placed upon the boil, and the king composed a song upon his recovery, which is preserved to us in Isaiah.* Merodach-Baladan was upon such intimate terms with Hezekiah that he deemed it incumbent on him to send ambassadors to congratulate him upon his recovery.† It is probable, moreover, that the Babylonian king was also desirous of inducing him to join in a league against Nineveh. Hezekiah treated the envoys with great ceremony, and showed them all the precious things he possessed: gold, silver, perfumes, arms, and utensils of all kinds. Isaiah, who foresaw, no doubt, the consequences of such an alliance, was very displeased at this imprudent display. He reprimanded the king severely, and told him, it is said, that all these beautiful things would be one day carried off to Babylon. According to comparatively recent narratives, he added that more than

* Isaiah, ch. xxxviii. v. 10-20.

† There are traces here of some artificial combination of Hebraic historiography, influenced by the prophets.

one of his descendants would be an eunuch in the palace of the King of Babel. Hezekiah, at first much moved, is said to have reconciled himself to this with the remark, "Good is the word of the Lord. He said, moreover, there shall be peace and truth in my days." In this conjuncture Isaiah seems again to have been actuated by a very wise policy. The attempt at Babylonian independence to which the name of Merodach-Baladan is attached does not appear to have succeeded.[*]

The reign of Hezekiah left very profound traces behind it, and it saw what may be called the definite foundation of Judaism by means of the sort of precipitant which was brought about between the diverse elements up till then floating in the Israelite conscience. There were, in a way, two Iahveisms, as in our day there are in reality two Catholicisms, the moderate Catholicism, which is neither more nor less than a traditional adherence to the established worship, and the exalted Catholicism, which grows feverish when reflecting upon the future of the Church and of the Papacy, which carries on a propaganda, which regards it as a bounden duty to have no relations with those who think evil. One may belong to the Catholic faith, and even attend mass, without being the adept of the Catholic party, which regards Catholicism as destined to transform the world and to solve all the social problems.

[*] Winckler, *Untersuchungen zur altorientalischen Geschichte* (Leipsic, 1889), pp. 55 and following

THE LAST YEARS OF HEZEKIAH.

Under the Restoration, when the Jesuits had the upper hand, a man might be very attached to the religion of his country without belonging to what was called "the congregation." In the sixteenth century a man might describe himself as sincerely Christian without following the reformers in their theological mania, and without sharing their hatred of the very much abused religious state which had been consecrated by ages of use.

There were, even among the worshippers of Iahveh, some very sensible people, and quite honest in their way, who did not like the external attitude of austere affectation and the mixture of charlatanism which the prophets mingled with their pious activity. The feeling was much the same as in regard to the *frérots* and *papelards* in the time of St. Louis. They were like a "Salvation Army," importunate, proud in their humility, the masters of power, and without pleasing whom it was hopeless to expect success. Very deep was the indignation of serious people when they saw affiliated persons of the prophetic sect taken out of their hovels, and being raised in an hour out of the dust to the highest functions of State.* Whenever a devout coterie gets hold of the reigns of government in this way it provokes a strong reaction. A whole store of hatred was being held in reserve against the *anavim* for the day when their royal protector should no longer be there to befriend them.

* 1 Samuel, ch. ii. v. 8 (an inserted Psalm).

Pietists are by their essence given to persecution; they complain bitterly when they are persecuted, and yet they think it very hard when they are not allowed to persecute others; they are so sure of being right! The king was wiser than his pious friends; but his complete devotion to the cause of the *anavim* had excited among the aristocratic classes a discontent which was destined one day to break forth with great violence. The worldly and the poor of Iahveh became irreconcilable enemies.

CHAPTER IX.

REACTION AGAINST THE ANAVIM.—MANASSEH AND AMON.

HEZEKIAH died at the age of fifty-four, after twenty-nine years' reign, but we do not know where he was buried, for, from his day, the old burial-place of the kings of Judah, at the foot of Ophel, was abandoned. Perhaps these burial-places offered more than one trace of paganism, and the Puritans thought it their duty to conceal the entrance to it.*

Isaiah had probably preceded to the grave the king of whom he had been the trusted counsellor. According to Iahveist ideas, Hezekiah had not had the full number of days to which he was entitled, and if the Scheol had not been as devoid of intelligence as Hezekiah himself thought, Isaiah would assuredly have found it difficult to explain why this life, so much in conformity with the ways of Iahveh, had not lasted one hundred and twenty years.

---

* The large fires which were formerly lighted at the funerals of the kings (2 Chron. ch. xvi. v. 14; ch. xxi. v. 19; Jeremiah, ch. xxxiv. v. 5) were perhaps connected with some Pagan usage.

What must have been more inexplicable still, in the eyes of the Iahveists, was that the reign of the perfect king was followed by a much longer reign (the longest known in Jerusalem), which was in every respect the counterpart of Hezekiah's.

Menassé, whom it is customary to call Manasseh, was only twelve when he began to reign. His mother's name was Hephzibah, that is to say, "My desire is in her." He reigned fifty-five years at Jerusalem (696-641), without our knowing anything more of him than that his conduct was the very opposite of his father's. The hatred accumulated by the absolute reign of the *anavim* bore its fruit, and the party of the worldly, of the *lecim*, who, without being impious, had been offended, perhaps annoyed by the hypocrites, again had the upper hand. The absence of documents does not admit of our forming so much as a conjecture as to how this revolution, quite in keeping moreover with the general laws of history, was brought about. The youth of Manasseh was, no doubt, the principal cause, and the influence of his mother became preponderant. Now women, a queen more especially, would naturally not be favourable to the movement of the prophets. These sordid wearers of the *saq* could scarcely attract the sympathy of well-bred people. The prophets, for their part, were very much opposed to women's idle vanities. Isaiah, as we have seen, treated women very harshly. These great organised Semitic religions are made for men not for women. The old Judaism,* like the old Islamism,† made very scant room for women, so that women were not at first at all favourable to it.‡

The governing classes, upon the other hand, the military more especially, recovered their influence. The zealous sectarians who had curried favour with Hezekiah, and who, moreover, no longer had their leader Isaiah, found themselves, after the king's death, exposed to the hostility of those whom they had ill-treated. The wind veered round very suddenly. The party opposed to the *anavim* assumed power in a body, and the judicial institutions of the time, or rather the absence of judicial institutions, opened the door to a terrible degree of arbitrary dealing. The trials at the gate of the city were, like the accusations before the agora in the Greek cities, a threat held over everybody's head.§ The

* The superstitions of women were not of much consequence. See nevertheless Proverbs, xxxi. v. 30. Take note also of the prophetess Huldah.

† In the early Islamism woman has no religion, not even a soul. One of the compliments an old Arab poet pays his mistress is that she does not read the Koran. It is only quite recently that women have a place given them in the galleries of the mosques. The Mussulmans do not like their women to be devout. With the Shiites, who are less Semitic than the Sunnites, the women are more pious.

‡ We shall find the same thing occurring at the death of Josiah (see below, p. 302, 303, 313).

§ The metaphors taken from trials are continually occurring in the Psalms and the book of Job. Psalm xxxvii. v. 33; cix. v. 7; cxxvii. v. 5, etc.

great duty of Iahveh was to save his servants when they appeal to the law. The administration of justice was the great scourge of the time. Every man ran a risk of being dragged before the bar of the tribunal of his adversary. The bearing of false witness was an every-day occurrence; the party in power thus holding the lives of their adversaries in their hands. Fanatics did not stick at this method of getting rid of their enemies; the liberals, having become all-powerful, paid back their former oppressors with interest.

We have no precise information as to how far these acts of violence went. It is very possible that certain zealots expiated the domineering acts done by them during Hezekiah's reign, and that a few saintly personages fell victims to their intemperate zeal. But we know how quick fanatics are to complain when their fanaticism meets with resistance. The accusation of having "filled Jerusalem with innocent blood,"* is assuredly an exaggerated one. Jeremiah, a century later, only makes vague allusions to this.† Fanatics are in the habit of calling themselves oppressed when they are no longer the masters; toleration is what they detest above all things. They prefer being harried to

* 2 Kings, ch. xxi. v. 16; ch. xxiii. v. 26; ch. xxiv. v. 3-4.

† See ch. ii. Jeremiah, in which all the misdeeds of Manasseh's reign are grouped together. The misdeed relating to אביונים נקיים, Jeremiah, chap. ii. v. 34, is not clear. The passage of Jeremiah, ch. ii. v. 30, is general; nevertheless, if it is not special to Manasseh, it implies Manasseh.

being placed by common law upon a footing of equality with what they regard as error. It is always a mistake to persecute them; but, as a rule, whenever they are subjected to the buffets of fortune, they have in a measure brought it upon themselves. What appears true is, that the violent language of the prophetic school was severely checked, and that Manasseh in reality practised toleration, granting no exclusive privilege to the worship of Iahveh, and allowing the pagan rites which his father had proscribed to be freely practised. The places devoted to pagan forms of worship were re-established; Manasseh did not merely allow each of his subjects to worship after his own fashion, for he himself appears to have been eclectic in matters of religion. Within the temple of Iahveh he erected altars to Baal and to the strange gods. He made *aseroth* for himself as Ahaz had done, one of these graven images being in the temple itself.* The Monotheistic Jews were quite under the impression that the gods of the nations were neither more nor less than stars; it was asserted that the two courts of the temple had altars for all the host of heaven, and that the king worshipped alternately before these *stellæ*.

A much graver accusation, if not a calumny, was that of having made his son (the eldest) pass through the fire, that is to say, of having sacrificed him by burning him in honour of Iahveh or Moloch,

* פסל האשרה

doubtless at the time of some extreme peril. It appears that the seventh century B.C. witnessed a certain recrudescence among the Jews of that hideous usage of the old Semitic peoples.* The valley of Hinnom, to the south of Jerusalem,† was the theatre of it, there being at this place, close to the Potters' Gate,‡ *bamoths*, or earthen platforms, upon which the fire offered up to Moloch was almost always alight; the shrieks of children making the vicinity very sinister. People with any respect for themselves kept well away from this spot, or if they had to pass by spat upon it, so that it soon came to be called the *Topheth*, or "spittle."§ The Iahveists of the reform held these rites in horror, and attested that it was false that Iahveh had ever ordered anything of the kind.‖

Manasseh offended the orthodox not less sorely by his leaning for divination and sorcery. He consulted familiar spirits and ventriloquist wizards, all things which the pure Iahveist regarded as most reprehensible. The Iahveist nabi, being thus over-

---

* The oldest Bible texts never mention this crime. Compare vol. ii. p. 516-517, note. That there was a regular cremation, not a mere purifying by a rapid passage through the flame, is proved by 2 Kings, ch. xvii. v. 31; Ezekiel, ch. xvi. v. 20; ch. xxiii. v. 37; Jeremiah, ch. xix. v. 5; ch. xxxii. v. 35. Compare ch. vii. v. 31. See below p. 138.

† *Gé-hinnom*, or Gehenne.

‡ חדסות or הדסית. Jeremiah, ch. xix. v. 2. That must have been near the Chaudemar of the crusaders (*Haceldama*).

§ 2 Kings, ch. xxiii. v. 10; Jeremiah, ch. vii. v. 31-32; ch. xix. v. 6, 11, 14.   ‖ Jeremiah, ch. vii. v. 31; ch. xix. v. 5.

shadowed by his rival, the *qosem*, was put into the background. We do not read, during Manasseh's reign, of a single prophet mixing himself up in home affairs, as Isaiah, Micah, Hosea, and Amos had done. Nahum, the only prophet of that reign, is more or less of a profane writer, without any Messianic or moral tendency.

What rendered this crisis really cruel for the conscience of the true Israelite was that it lasted nearly seventy-five years, the reign of Amon and the first part of Josiah's reign having the same characteristics as that of Manasseh. Prophetism, during this period, seems to have held its peace; and it needed all the tenacity of the Hebrew spirit not to yield to a temptation which struck at the very roots of the faith. What, in short, can be said about a god who has only this present life to reward his faithful followers, and who abandons them to their enemies, who so neglects his honour as to allow himself to be outrageously mocked by those who deny Him? Evidently, he must be asleep; he must be forgetting himself. "Arise, awake, Iahveh," is the cry of that day.* The concentrated mass of sadness and hatred which the prolongation of this unnatural situation created was the inspiring motive of a series of psalms conceived in a new spirit.† The author always repre-

* קומה, עוּר.

† All these Psalms are characterised by numerous errors in transcription. They have a critical destiny of their own.

sents himself as being in distress, abandoned by God, surrounded by wicked men, exposed to the jeering of triumphant impiety. These psalms take the place, as it were, of the prophets, who are not associated with this period. We can perceive in them, as clearly as in no matter which prophet, the rage of the humiliated *anavim*, their wrath against the worldly.

Thus, in Psalm xciv. verse 20, there is a direct allusion to Manasseh as a government "which frameth mischief by a law" (*hoq*). The impunity of the wicked often inspires the persecuted *anav* with thoughts very analogous to those in the book of Job.* At other times he is overcome by despair, and, without ever failing in his declaration of innocence, regards himself as abandoned by the God who should avenge him.† The trial would have been too severe a one for any other race. A god who fails so much as this in all his promises would with any other people have been given up. The great waiting power of Israel was displayed perhaps more strikingly in this circumstance than in any other. The principle of the intermittent justice of Iahveh proved the saving clause. Iahveh is generally asleep; His justice is only exercised on set occasions, by some sudden revolution which repairs everything. If there were really martyrs

* Psalm lxxiii. Compare this and also Psalm xlix. with Job. See above, p. 67.

† Psalm xxii. very much altered.

under the reign of Manasseh they must have died of impotent rage. For we do not, as a matter of fact, find appearing from this epoch the ideas of resurrection and of a reign of martyrs which, in the time of Antiochus Epiphanes were the outlet of a desperate situation. The poor *anav*, despised by the mighty of the earth, consoled himself by recapitulating the motives he had for not being envious of his successful adversaries. Their prosperity will not last. And then the just man is much happier in his peaceful mediocrity. He will in the end possess the earth. No just man was ever known to be quite poor.* Under a variety of forms the proud Israelite thus makes Iahveh feel that His true interest is not to abandon His servants. God is not praised in Scheol; the dead have no feeling. In leaving one of His servants to descend into Scheol, Iahveh deprives himself of an eulogist.† There is no torture that Israel did not put itself to in order to avoid the idea which all other religions have accepted with singular facility, the idea of life beyond the grave. The recompenses of another world seemed to Israel mere chimeras until the fate of the martyrs imposed the idea as a necessity in the time of the Maccabees. The anguish endured during the reign of Manasseh, terrible as it

* Psalm xxxvii. This is a very good specimen of the sort of canticle which these pious men delighted in. Compare Proverbs, ch. xxiv. v. 1.

† See Isaiah, ch. xxxviii. v. 10-20.

was, was not strong enough to move the faith of Israel in what it regarded as unshakable evidence.

It is, perhaps, to this period of extreme difficulties that must be ascribed the book which cast the first foundations of the legend of Daniel. Ezekiel, about 590 B.C., classes Daniel among the men of mark, with Noah and Job.* The book which has made this person celebrated was not the one which now figures in the Canon.† The primitive Daniel, as his name, coupled with passages from Ezekiel, indicates, was a wise man who displayed in his judgments the sagacity of God himself.‡ Stories like that of Susannah, inferring that it is impossible that God should allow an innocent person to be condemned, are quite in keeping with the time of Manasseh.§ The argument drawn from contradiction in trifling details (so defective in itself, and one which has, in England especially, caused such very unjust judgments to be passed) is just one of those which were wont to defray the stories of celebrated trials. The principle that God has means

* Ezekiel, ch. xiv. v. 14, 20; ch. xxviii. v. 3.

† Daniel would have been twelve years old at the outside when Ezekiel cites him as a venerable sage.

‡ It may have been surmised that the original Daniel went through the captivity of Nineveh, while maintaining intact his dignity as an Israelite and his faith. But we never find the Judaites concerning themselves with the Israelites led into captivity, or imagining they had remained true to the worship of Iaveh. The book of Tobias, conceived under this impression, is quite modern.

§ See above, pp. 105, 106.

REACTION AGAINST THE ANAVIM.

of preventing the innocent from being made victims is quite in keeping with the taste of Job and of the Anavite Psalms. The books soon got lost, but the anecdotes of judicial sagacity were preserved orally.* At the time of the Maccabees the ancient framework was taken up again, and within it were placed all the ideas of the time.

* The Palestinian book of Daniel, composed 163 B.C., did not exhaust the oral tradition. Other anecdotes, such as that of Susannah, that of Bel and the Dragon, were added to it, but never succeeded in securing a very definite place.

CHAPTER X.

THE REVOLUTIONS IN ASIA DURING THE SEVENTH CENTURY.—NAHUM.

The great power possessed by the Sargonides at the beginning of the seventh century, reduced, as it were, to silence the small kingdoms, or free towns, of Syria, Judah more especially keeping quite in the background. It is true that the events of the reign of Manasseh are unknown to us in detail; it would seem as if the orthodox annalists, holding this reign in abhorrence, were desirous of suppressing the history of it. What we read in the books of the Chronicles as to an asserted captivity of Manasseh in Assyria is purely fabulous,* for the Assyrian documents, which give

---

* 2 Chronicles, ch. xxxiii. v. 11 and following. The vague character of this narrative, the erroneous mention of Babel, the allegation of an entirely apocryphal document (v. 18, 19), all prove this to be an *agada*, taken not from serious historiography, but from the quite legendary book of the *Hozim* or Prophets. If such a circumstance were true, one would not understand how the latest compiler of the books of Kings could have suppressed it. It was

THE REVOLUTIONS IN ASIA.

us long accounts as to the struggles of Esar-haddon and of Assherbanipal with Egypt, as to their devastating campaigns against Phœnicia, especially against Sidon, are silent as to Jerusalem, and represent Manasseh as the vassal of Assyria.* The state of affairs mutually accepted appears, therefore, to have been one of peace upon payment of a tribute, leaving to the local king his freedom of action within his own dominions. The political status of the prophets having been null under Manasseh, the policy of the king and of the governing classes was less hampered, more exempt from disturbing causes. Now the good sense of the nation, abandoned to itself, could not fail to see that peace with Assyria was imperatively called for. All the small kingdoms of Syria had already realised that there was no longer any existence possible for them except as members of a vast feudal empire embracing the whole Eastern world. Asia Minor itself

---

so much in harmony with his object to demonstrate that the impious king had been punished! The reflections which he makes (2 Kings, ch. xxiii. v. 26; ch. xxiv. v. 3-4) prove that he was unaware of this alleged conversion. The Assyrian texts do not speak of a war against Judæa, and it would be natural that they should speak of it if it took place. They merely mention Manasseh as being subject to Assyria. The legendary nature of the passage, taken as a whole, does not prevent verse 14, relating to the works executed by Manasseh, from being historical. The author of the Chronicles was well informed as to the works at Jerusalem.

* Schrader, *Die Kiel. und das A. T.*, p. 306 and following; Menant, *Ann. des rois d'Ass.*, p. 245. The allusion in Ezra, ch. iv. v. 2, is inaccurate at all points.

entered into this sort of confederation,* which preceded that ruled over by the Persians and the Greeks, and later by the Byzantines, the Caliphs, the Mongolians, and the Turks.

The result of this era of peace was a great increase of material well-being for Judæa. The reigns of Manasseh and of Amon appear to have been very prosperous. The court, more especially, and the upper classes, emancipated from the censorship of the pietists, furthered the development of luxury, and of the new fashions,† derived from Egypt and Phœnicia. The ardent Iahveists had an inward revenge in hugging the idea that Nineveh was reserved for early destruction.

As a matter of fact, the violence of the military masses of that day did not admit of any long sustained construction. Nineveh, powerful as she was, was incessantly being harried. First came the invasion of the Scythians; then the Medes began to organise themselves; the Assyrian power, divided against itself, inspired little confidence. The monarchies which have two capitals have an inevitable tendency to become dislocated. So much strength and weakness astonished the Iahveists.

* The Lydian kingdom, the last king of which was Crœsus, seems to be a dependency of Assyria. It is for that reason that Lud (Genesis, ch. x. v. 22) is coupled with Aram and Arphaxad. All the region of the Upper Meander has received a deep Semitic impression. I have collected the elements for a treatise on this subject.

† Zephaniah, ch. i. v. 8.

The sight of these empires tumbling one over the other pleased and stirred their imagination.* Israel, therefore, took up the attitude which it was to maintain for centuries, viz. that of a petty ill-disposed people amid other peoples, able to predict their fall with astonishing sagacity and rejoicing at it. A certain Nahum, probably from Judæa,† appears, in these troubled times,‡ to have been gifted with singular foresight. The capture of No-Ammon (Thebes in Egypt) by Asshur-banipal (about 663)§ directs his thoughts to the ruin of Nineveh, which was not to occur until long afterwards, but which in his passion he was led to believe was close at hand.‖ Nineveh will be destroyed, because it has done evil to Israel; and the Israelite patriot thrills with joy: " Behold upon the mountains the feet of Him that bringeth good tidings, that publisheth peace! O Judah, keep thy solemn feasts, perform thy vows; for the wicked shall no more pass through thee; he is utterly cut off."¶

---

* See the terrible picture drawn in Ezekiel, ch. xxxii. v. 17 and following.

† The ethnic *Elkosi* has no sense. The hypothesis of his being an Oriental Israelite is upset by ch. i. v. 4, ch. ii. v. 1, and by ch. iii. v. 14, more of a Jerusalemite than of a Ninevite character.

‡ The oracle of Nahum is assuredly posterior to the episode of Sennacherib. See ch. i. v. 9; ch. ii. v. 1, 12-14.

§ Schrader, p. 449 and following. Maspero, p. 460.

‖ Nahum, ch. i. v. 2-6.

¶ Nahum, ch. i. v. 15. See also Nahum, ch. iii. v. 5-7.

In an age so agitated as the seventh century B.C., there was never much risk in making sombre predictions. Perhaps the pressure of the Medes and of the Scythians already began to be felt. Hatred, moreover, sufficed to inspire such anticipations. Nahum distinguished himself from among all the other prophets in that he did not mingle with his sinister announcements any hope of conversion, any moral preaching. He has not the love of a persecuted *anav;* * he is a nationalist, who rejoices to foresee the misfortunes of the enemies of his country. So much moderation surprises one during the reign of Manasseh, so odious to the prophets, and here we have a proof that what is told as to the tribulations undergone by the *anavim* is marked by great exaggeration. There was probably nothing beyond certain reprisals which the worldly people inflicted upon an intolerant coterie. It is not certain that in the time of Manasseh there were not prophets understanding Iahveism in the old-fashioned manner, simply as the religion of a provincial or a tribal god.†

Manasseh died at the age of sixty-seven, and his memory was execrated by the advanced party. For more than fifty years all the evils which befell the nation were, in the eyes of the pietists, the punishment of the inexpiable crimes of Manasseh.‡

---

* He does not once employ the words *anav, ani, anvè areç.*

† Nahum, we have seen, does not vary much from this type of prophet.

‡ 2 Kings, ch. xxi. v. 11-12; ch. xxiii. v. 26; ch. xxiv. v. 3-4; Jeremiah, ch. xv. v. 4.

He was buried in a garden, called the garden of Uzza, near the palace. Amon, son of Manasseh and of Meshullemeth, the daughter of Haruz of Jothah, reigned only two years. He followed the example of his father and left an execrable memory behind him in *anavite* circles. He was assassinated in his palace by his officers; yet he appears to have been popular, for the people massacred the conspirators and proclaimed in his stead his son Josiah, a child of eight (639 B.C.). The regency, which at first governed in his name, appears to have continued the principles which prevailed during the reigns of Manasseh and of Amon. The *sarim*, or princes of the blood, more attached than ever to foreign fashions, showed a deplorable tendency to sacrifice the ancient customs to what was then regarded as the progress of civilisation.* Jedidah, the daughter of Adaiah of Boscath, mother of the young king, doubtless presided over the council, and women of her class, belonging to the aristocracy of Judah, were not much given to the ideas of the *anavites*, which they must have regarded as dangerous innovations. At the age of thirteen the young king was married to Zebudah, the daughter of Pedaiah of Rumah, and, about two years afterwards, to Hamutal, the daughter of Jeremiah of Libnah, both of whom were the mothers of kings.†

* Zephaniah, ch. i.
† 2 Kings, chap xxiii. v. 31, 36.

CHAPTER XI.

RECRUDESCENCE OF ANAVITE PROPHETISM.—SOPHONIUS, JEREMIAH.

THE anavite was only apparently dead. For the fifth or sixth time a vanquished pietism reared its head again and endeavoured to regain possession of power. The excesses of the fanatics in Hezekiah's reign were forgotten. The regency which governed in Josiah's name gave popular movements free scope to declare themselves, and about 630 B.C. the old spirit which appeared to have become extinct with Isaiah was resuscitated.

The signal for this renaissance of messianic and anavite prophetism appears to have been given by a certain Zephaniah, son of Cushi, son of Gedaliah, son of Amariah, son of Hizkiah, known by the name of Sophonius. The brief fragment handed down to us under the name of this prophet is excessively sombre; and we find in it a repetition of the fierce anger of the Iahveist compiler of the Thora of Jerusalem against civilisation.* Jerusalem † is a

---

* See vol ii. pp. 285, 286.   † Zephaniah, ch. iii.

worldly city, full of horrible things. The worship of Baal is formally recognised in it; there are people who prostrate themselves upon their roofs before the stars of heaven, and who swear as readily by Iahveh and by Moloch. This heedless city does not hearken to any of the premonitory warnings. Its chiefs, its judges, its priests, are all unjust and prevaricating. Its prophets utter lies. In the name of his personal inspiration, Zephaniah rises up to announce the near approach of the day of divine vengeance upon Judah and the Gentiles.*

This day presents itself to the eye of Zephaniah under the likeness of a great festival, a superb sacrifice. First of all there are the princes of the blood, the ministers,† fond of foreign fashions, clothed in strange apparel, the courtiers who favour the bad conduct of the royal household; then the Canaanites, the merchants in the bazaar, with their hoards of silver; then the impious, who do not believe that Iahveh concerns himself with human affairs, either to do good or to do evil.‡ Only the *anavim*,§ who have followed the rules of Iahveh, will be saved in that day, thanks to their justice and their humility.

* The author appears to have read Joel. Kuenen, p. 454, note 2.

† Zephaniah, ch. i. v. 8. With regard to בני המלך, see above, p. 45, note 2.

‡ See above, pp. 67 and 110.

§ Ch. ii. v. 3.

Zephaniah would certainly have invented the deluge, if that myth had not already appeared in the sacred code. Iahveh, very wroth, is bent upon destroying everything. The coming day of Iahveh will be the end of the world.* The prophet announces, more especially, the ruin of the Philistines (*Krétim*), whose land will be for the time adjudged to Judah. Moab and Ammon have been hostile to Israel; woe unto them! The Cushites will be struck down. Nineveh in its turn will be destroyed.† In nearly every case, the Israelite prophet, in announcing the wrath of Iahveh, has in view the force which is to serve as the minister of Isaiah. In the view of Isaiah and the prophets of his time, the dark spectre was always Assyria. About the middle of the seventh century, the empire of Assyria being shaken, the executioners of the decrees of Iahveh are the nameless barbarians (Medes and Scythians) who threatened Asshur from the north and the east. The Scythians, during Josiah's minority, exercised, throughout all the interior of Asia, a supremacy which the petty kingdom of Judah could not fail to feel.‡ This supremacy, however, not

* Zephaniah, ch. i. v. 2, 3, 15, 16, 17, 18.

† Zephaniah, ch. ii. v. 14-15. This passage has been altered.

‡ Herodotus i. pp. 103-106; Justinus, ii. pp. 3 and following; Strabo, i. iii. p. 21. A vague souvenir of the Scythian invasions is to be found in ch. xxxviii. and xxxix. of Ezekiel. Ch. i. iv. v. and vi. of Jeremiah have been applied, but without there being any decisive proof upon the point, to the same event. A great point is made of the fact that, in these passages, the invaders are represented as coming from the North; but any invader of Judæa, even

having left any positive trace* in the history of Israel, it scarcely seems in conformity with the rules of sound historical criticism to base too ambitious hypotheses upon so fragile a foundation.† The predictions of the prophets had often a rather vague objective. Their descriptions of the end of the world were a sort of commonplace quite incapable of any precise application. Nahum and Zephaniah may very possibly have launched their threats without having in their mind anything beyond the general views as supplied by the earlier prophetism. The Messianic reign, as Zephaniah conceived it, resembles in every respect the Messianic reign of Amos, or of Joel, of Hosea, Micah, and Isaiah. From beyond the rivers of Cush, from all parts, the dispersed people of the true God will bring offerings. All the earth will invoke Iahveh with pure lips. The Pagan gods will disappear; men will come from the distant isles to prostrate themselves before Iahveh. In Jerusalem the triumph of the anavites ‡ over the proud and the

if he came from Babylon, being compelled to make the circuit of the Bekaa, entered the country from the north.

* The evidence afforded by the name of Scythopolis has no weight. This name, like that of Pella, Areopolis, Philadelphia, &c., is posterior to Alexander.

† The ethnical designation of the Scythians, among the Hebrew writers, is Mések-Tubal. Ezekiel (ch. xxxii. v. 26) includes the armies of Mések-Tubal (Meshed-Tubal in the English Bible) among the great armies destroyed in his time. But he does not connect them in any way with Palestine.

‡ צם צני זדל.

worldly * will be complete. The *ani* and the *dal* will henceforth be all powerful; Iahveh will be King of Israel, and will have His capital in Jerusalem. An era in which the ills of an earlier date shall be healed will open, and Israel, brought back from its exile † and restored, will taste at last the fruits of its fidelity.‡ Zephaniah does not seem to have made a very strong impression upon the society of his day, but a much more powerful individuality soon made his appearance in the prophetic world and decided the fate of Israel. This was Jeremiah, who was, under Josiah, what Isaiah had been under Hezekiah. Very inferior to his predecessor in point of talent, he surpassed him in tragic seriousness and downright pertinacity. He was the first saint, in the narrow acceptation of the word. In him the sombre sectaries of holiness, whom the thirteenth and sixteenth centuries produced, were to have their ancestor, their celestial patron, and their model, often a bad one to copy.

Jeremiah may be reckoned as among the men of the greatest importance in history. If not the founder of Judaism, he is the great martyr of it. But for this extraordinary man, the religious history of humanity would have taken another course; there would not have been any Christianity.

For Jewish prophetism enters with Jeremiah upon quite a new path. Its religious character

* צלויי נאזה.   † See vol. ii. pp. 359, 360, 376, 388
‡ Sophonius, iii. pp. 11 and following, p. 15.

becomes much more pronounced; the tribune makes way for the priest. Amos and Hosea, like Isaiah at certain moments, astonish us by their boldness, their love of the people, their indifference in regard to theological and liturgical questions. Their indignation does us good. When they see how unjust the world is, they would like to crush it. They reason much after the fashion of the anarchists of our day: "If the world cannot be mended, it must be ended." Jeremiah is not nearly so much concerned with the social question and the triumph of the *anavim*.* He is above all a pious man, and of a very strict morality. He is, it must be added, a fanatic, full of hatred against his adversaries; at once classing all those who do not admit his prophetic mission among the wicked, desiring their death, and foretelling it. This is very far removed from our highest virtue, politeness. But the seventh century B.C. was also very far off from ours. The moral code had at that time need of being affirmed and founded, and the Jew had not at his disposal the terrors of a chimerical hell. The moral rigorism of our day does almost as much harm as good to humanity; yet it was useful in its time. We of the nineteenth century may well take sides with Mary Queen of Scots against Knox; but in the sixteenth century fanatical Protestantism did more service to the cause of progress than Catholicism, even when it was rather easy going.

* Jeremiah and Ezekiel do not employ this word; very rarely they use the words *ebion* or *dal*. See Jeremiah, ch. xx. v. 13.

Jeremiah must therefore be classed with those great reactionists whom we do not like, but whose part in history it would be unjust to disregard. From the literary point of view there is a distinct decadence. His style has not the classical solidity of the writers in Hezekiah's age; it is clear, prolix, and flabby; it savours of imitation, it teems with reminiscences of earlier writers. But the religious genius of Jeremiah was without a parallel; three-fourths of the rays of glory which encircle Moses should be credited to him. Even the sixteenth century has no giant to compare to this man possessed, as one may say, of the pietist idea. Rarely has a moral tendency so seized upon a human conscience and filled it with concentrated passion; and this with a minimum of motives for action quite surprising. Jeremiah is neither a prophet nor a superstitious man, nor a priest, nor a soldier, nor a politician. He has no worldly science; his theology is of the simplest; his ideas as to another life are null. And yet what tenacity in this belief in good! What courage in failure! How great he is in his solitude, how heroic in his captivity, how sublime in his desolation! He is an Elijah of reality, an Elijah whose pages are before us and whom we can touch. He does not doubt for a moment his Iahveh, even when Iahveh most outrageously violates his mandate as administrator of justice. Job, a century earlier, insults God openly for failing in his duties. Jeremiah sits down and weeps. In these supreme temptations of faith, he firmly believes that it is man who is wrong. When God inflicts a blow upon his servant it is the latter who is in fault. A grand and chivalrous affirmation this, a sublime act of faith which covers all the faults of the Israelite, and makes of him in truth the confessor of God upon earth. The hero of this desperate effort to defend Providence against the weight of appearance is the Rabbi of Mayence in the thirteenth century, who, led to the stake, invented as against himself all sorts of crimes in order not to let it seem that Iahveh could allow an innocent man to perish.

Jeremiah was son of a priest of Anathoth, a small town about three miles north of Jerusalem. Anathoth was an ancient priestly town of the Benjamites, like Nob,* the residence of several families which, from the earliest antiquity, were privileged to offer sacrifices to Iahveh. Hilkiah, the father of Jeremiah, belonged to one of these families, the social status and the calling of which it is difficult for us to fix. The centralisation of the worship at Jerusalem was not yet effected; nevertheless, there was a strong tendency that way. It is doubtful whether Hilkiah still offered sacrifices upon the ancient altar which Anathoth doubtless still possessed. These priestly families, which had scarcely any further reason for lasting, furnished perhaps ready-made matter for the ideas of "the poor of the earth." Jeremiah, however, does not appear

* 1 Kings, ch. ii. v. 26.

to have been in want. It is from the depths of Iahveism, and not from external circumstances, that he appears to have derived the intense fanaticism which plunged him while still very young* into the fiery furnace of the passions of Israel.

In the thirteenth year of Josiah, when he was only twenty (627 B. C.), Jeremiah entered upon the prophetic career. His circle of action was at first confined to his compatriots. His language was hard, imperious, and austere. The love of exaggerated authority with which he spoke turned his hearers against him. The people of Anathoth denied his prophetic vocation, and sought to kill him. The ideas which seem to represent Jeremiah's mental condition at this epoch † remind one of the Book of Job, and there are many indications that the prophet read this book very regularly.

Jeremiah, even at this early period, appears as what he remained all his life, a man of very extreme views, an inquisitor, drawing down upon himself universal hatred by his scathing invective. What shocks us most about him is the hypocrisy of his moderation and his affectation of weakness. Like a true Iahveist, he remits his vengeance to Iahveh, in the assurance that he is leaving it in safe hands. A revelation ‡ tells him of the dangers he is

* Jeremiah, ch. i. v. 5-7.
† Jeremiah, end of ch. xi. and beginning of ch. xii. See also ch. xix. and xx.
‡ Ch. xii. v. 6.

RECRUDESCENCE OF ANAVITE PROPHETISM. 129

in from his relatives. In conformity with that intimation, he leaves his village of Anathoth, predicting its extermination, and comes to Jerusalem, where his ardent preaching will find a field more worthy of it. From this moment Jeremiah becomes the chief of a vast reaction which will never cease, and which will lead first to the Maccabees, and then, with singular variations of degrees, to John the Baptist, to Jesus, to James, a brother of the Saviour, to the Ebionite section of the founders of Christianity, to Rabbi Aquiba, to Judah the Holy.

The style of preaching of the new mouthpiece of Iahveh is well represented by the first chapters of the Scriptural book bearing his name. The constant self-affirmation to which the prophet resorts has a very fatiguing effect. The great moral defect of Jewish prophetism is the obligation under which the prophet is to affirm his mission without proofs, or with proofs transparently unreal. This gratuitous affirmation is all the more persistent in the case of Jeremiah, because he never appeals to tangible miracles, to *signs*, as Isaiah says.*

Isaiah would not have written the verses in chapter i. of Jeremiah,† who regards a prophet as being a sort of infallible Pope, whose duty it is to discern things,‡ and who is clothed with full powers from Iahveh. He is the intimate confidant of

---

* See vol ii. p. 412.
† Ch. i. v. 4-10.
‡ Jeremiah, ch. vi. v. 29 and following.

Iahveh, who establishes him as a wall against the kings, the princes, the priests, and the people.* The word of God is, in his mouth, a devouring fire.† Is it a democrat, or is it a theocratic sovereign who speaks in this way?

This theory of a spontaneous mission has a certain grandeur of its own; but, applied to political institutions, it could only lead to anarchy. How, in fact, can a distinction be made between those who also claimed to be inspired by Iahveh and who announced or advised contradictory things. The miracles, employed as diacritical signs, began to fall into disuse. The rivalries between the prophets were very fierce, each trying to ruin the other's reputation, and to lay violent hands upon his prophecies.‡ Each one related his own dream, and these dreams were in many cases homicidal calumnies. The fashion of adducing natural calamities as proofs, a deplorable paralogism which Jeremiah is constantly employing, might be made to mean anything. Jeremiah uses sarcasm against his fellow prophets.§ This was a vicious circle from which there was no issue. The principal adversaries of Jeremiah are prophets like himself.∥ He does not hesitate to say that it is from the prophets of

---

* Jeremiah, ch. i. v. 18.
† Jeremiah, ch. v. v. 14.
‡ Jeremiah, ch. xxiii. v. 16 and following.
§ Jeremiah, ch. xxiii. v. 16 and following.
∥ Jeremiah, ch. xxiii.

RECRUDESCENCE OF ANAVITE PROPHETISM. 131

Jerusalem that all the impiety of the country comes.*
The prophets of Samaria prophesied in the name of
Baal; the prophets of Jerusalem encourage the
evildoers and prevent them from repenting.

Jeremiah is, above all, an exclusive Iahveist.
Idolatry, the worship of the stars, and the pagan
rites are, in his eyes, the greatest of evils. Imitation
of the stranger is the source of it all. Jeremiah
complains of these acts of infidelity like a lover
who has been betrayed.†

The jealousy of Iahveh extends even to the
political alliances of his people. Confidence in
Iahveh is the only means of salvation; cleverness,
strength, riches, will be of no avail.‡ The prophet makes mock of the coming and going of those
who negotiate between nations, as when he says,
"What hast thou to do in the way of Egypt . . .
or what hast thou to do in the way of Assyria?§

In many respects, as we see, the Iahveh of
Jeremiah has been almost reduced to the rank of
a national god. Jeremiah finds it quite natural
that other nations should have their god; he does
not blame them for it. But what seems to him
monstrous is that people should abandon their god
when he has not failed in his promises. The fundamental idea among the prophets of the eighth

---

* Jeremiah, ch. xxiii. v. 15.

† Jeremiah, ch. ii. v. 10-37. Compare the gentle reproaches in ch. iii. and iv. v. 1-4.

‡ Jeremiah, ch. ix. v. 22-23.   § Jeremiah, ch. ii. v. 18.

century, that foreign nations should come to the worship of Iahveh, is very rarely found in Jeremiah. If driven into a corner he might be got to say that these peoples, in abandoning their god, would behave as badly as Israelites in being unfaithful to theirs. When the Israelites, carried into exile, shall say, "Why doth Iahveh thus treat us?" they shall be answered, "Like as ye have forsaken me, and served strange gods in your land, so shall ye serve strangers in a land that is not yours." * In other places, it is true, Jeremiah depicts Iahveh as the God who has made heaven and earth. He frequently borrows the grandiose descriptions of Job, in which Iahveh is represented as the immediate factor of the great natural, more especially of the atmospheric phenomena.† His logic, which was not his forte, made the best use which circumstances admitted of these forced combinations.

A difficulty which often presented itself to his mind, and which arose from his contradictory notions about Iahveh, was the severity of God for Israel, and His surprising indulgence for the Gentiles, who, after all, were much more guilty than Israel.‡ The objection which perplexed Jeremiah will haunt Israel until the very last; it fills the Apocalypses coming at the end of the first

---

* Jeremiah, ch. v. v. 19.
† Jeremiah, ch. x. v. 10 and following.
‡ Jeremiah, ch. x. v. 24–25.

RECRUDESCENCE OF ANAVITE PROPHETISM.

century of the Christian era.* Just as the fathers and the bishops of the fifth century often seem friends of the barbarians and have the appearance of inviting their inroad because they predict it, in the same way Jeremiah appears to be the secret ally of the northern hordes and, later on, of the *Casdim*. These terrible bands, these irresistible cyclones, are in his eyes the executors of the will of Iahveh. What concerns him in the first years of his apostolate † is an invasion coming from the most remote lands of the north.‡ The people whom Iahveh will bring is an ancient one, whose language Israel does not understand.§ They are a very numerous people, and cruel, mounted upon war horses (regular cavalry, not chariots), armed with bow and spear, laying all waste before them.‖ At the period when Jeremiah wrote these forewarnings, Nineveh was probably still in existence. The redoubled attacks of the Medes and of the Scythians had weakened but not ruined it. It was probably

---

* The books of Esdras, Baruch. See *Hist. des Orig. du Christ.*, v. 352 and following, 519 and following.

† Jeremiah, ch. iv. v. 16 ; ch. v. 15.

‡ Jeremiah, ch. i. v. 13 and following; ch. vi. v. 22; ch. x. v. 17-25. See above, p. 151, note 2. Special signs indicate that the reference here is to truly Northern peoples, not to the *Casdim*. Note מארץ צפון, ch. vi. v. 22, and ch. x. v. 22 ; ממלכת צפונה, ch. i. v. 15.

§ Jeremiah, ch. v. v. 15. This does not apply to Asshur, which there would be no need to design enigmatically. There is some novel feature here.

‖ Ch. vi. v. 22 and following.

these Iran and Tarter hordes whom Jeremiah saw upon the horizon as the scourges of God.*

One of the most finished extracts from Jeremiah † is the description of this invasion, which doubtless existed only in his visions. The panic is universal; everybody loses his self-control; Iahveh, to punish the people, allows the false prophets to deceive them. Bad news arrive apace from Dan and Ephraim. The anguish of Jerusalem is at its height. This harlot, who has abandoned herself to all the strangers (foreign fashions, foreign alliances), is at the end of her devices. "When thou art spoiled what wilt thou do? Though thou clothest thyself with crimson, though thou deckest thyself with ornaments of gold, though thou rentest thy face with painting, thy lovers ‡ will despise thee; they seek thy life."

A general transportation, such as that which befel Israel and so many other nations, will come upon Judah. The mass of the people will be exterminated. The temple and Jerusalem will be treated like Shiloh.§ Judah will be rejected of God like Ephraim, and Iahveh will have no more of the sacrifices of his people.∥ It is obedience which he requires, and that is withheld from him. The tombs of the kings of Judah will be desecrated

* The *Casdim* do not enter upon the scene before ch. xxi.

† Ch. iv. from v. 5. Compare ch. v. with threat of a siege.

‡ The foreigners, to alliance with and imitation of whom Jerusalem had sacrificed everything.

§ Ch. vii. and viii., forming a long sermon.

∥ Ch. viii. v. 1 and following.

as well as the great burial-places of the *sarim*, of the *cohanim*, and of the *nebiim*, at the gates of the city.* These catastrophes† were destined to occur, but at a later date and at other hands than the prophet believed. It needed sagacity to foretell the ruin of Jerusalem forty years in advance. The great forces which were at work in Egypt left no room for so small an individuality as Judah. The situation of the people of Israel in the seventh century B.C. was very much what it was in the first century of the Christian era, when confronted by the growing mass of the Roman empire. The predictions ascribed to Jesus concerning the events of the year 70 are of the same order as those of Jeremiah. The Jewish spirit has always had a great tendency to predict general evolutions. Jeremiah sees very clearly that the small kingdom of Jerusalem will be destroyed root and branch, like that of Samaria. The future of Israel is not necessarily compromised on that account. The tree will be cut down, but the roots will not be pulled up; it will grow again.‡ There will then be an Israel formed by the reuniting of the two families, docile to the prophets, which will observe the precepts of Iahveh.§ Jeremiah does not go much beyond this; like all the prophets he sets little store by

* Ch. viii. v. 1 and following.
† Ch. vii. v. 30-34. Repeated in ch. xix.
‡ Ch. v.
§ Fragments, ch. iii. and iv. v. 1-4.

rites,* he only esteems the worship of the heart.† But the brilliant dreams of the prophets of the eighth century as to the future conversion of the world to the religion of Israel do not seem to please him.‡ In one instance only does the great Israelite ideal raise him to the conception of the pure worship: "In those days, they shall say no more, The ark of the covenant of the Lord: neither shall it come to mind: neither shall they remember it; neither shall they visit it; neither shall it be done any more. At that time they shall call Jerusalem the throne of the Lord, and all the nations shall be gathered unto it, to the name of the Lord." §

---

* Jeremiah, ch. vi. v. 20 ; ch. ix. v. 23 ; ch. xi. v. 15; ch. xiv. v. 12, &c., especially ch. vii. v. 21 and following.

† Ch. iii. v. 16 ; ch. iv. v. 1 ; ch. vii. v. 6 ; ch. xxxi. v. 33, &c.

‡ The conversion of the tribes bordering upon Israel is of much less importance.

§ Ch. iii. v. 16 and following. V. 18 in ch. xxiii., which expresses a directly opposite idea, is of doubtful authenticity; it is missing in the Greek.

CHAPTER XII.

JEREMIAH AND THE CIVIL POWER.

It could not but follow that such passionate declamations* must produce a violent reaction. At various conjunctures, private individuals, injured by his furious diatribes, and the government, made responsible for all the mischief which ensued, took steps to close his mouth, so full of venom. In this way the impassioned man of Anathoth was given the best opportunity for displaying his qualities of courage and dauntless energy. The power of martyrdom was inaugurated; for when the authorities are not resolved to carry matters to an extreme against its thorough-paced opponents, mere vexatious prosecutions only give them force.

One of the places where Jeremiah was very fond of giving utterance to his predictions and threats†

* Jeremiah, ch. ix., ch. xxiii. v. 9 and following.

† The date of this episode, related in ch. xix. and xx. (compare ch. vii.) of Jeremiah, is very uncertain. The mention of the King of Babylon and the threat of being carried away into Babylon would incline one to make it posterior to 605. It is hard, however, to conceive of Jeremiah being exposed at this date to treatments

138   *HISTORY OF THE PEOPLE OF ISRAEL.*

was the place called *Tophet*, in the valley of Hinnom, a revolting and impure spot, with a worse reputation than any in Jerusalem. It was there that were offered the holocausts of the first-born to Baal-Moloch,* or, it may be said, to Iahveh; the *bama* to be seen there, near the Potters' Gate, was the place of the great whoredom of Judah, to use the language of the time. Jeremiah asserted that Iahveh ordered him to sit in this place, in order to deliver his most terrible oracle. He announced, more particularly, a siege during which the Jerusalemites would be reduced to eating the flesh of their own fellows.† The whole city would become a *Tophet*, a funeral pile. Upon one occasion, when Jeremiah had accentuated these prophecies, accompanying them by the breaking of a vessel, he went up from Tophet to the court of the temple, and spake in still more violent terms. Then Pashur, the son of Immer, who was chief governor in the temple, heard him, smote him, and put him in the stocks, which were in the high gate of Benjamin, by the walls of the temple.‡ The next day, Pashur

such as Pashur inflicted upon him. There is less difficulty in supposing that the biographer of Jeremiah, writing during the captivity, has confused the dates.

* שרף.....באש צולות לבצל (ch. xix. v. 5) proves that the reference was to holocausts. Compare Deuteronomy, ch. xii. v. 31.

† Ch. xix. v. 9.

‡ These kinds of stocks, in which either the head or the feet, sometimes both, were fastened, are still to be seen in the East, at the gates of cities or in a tower over the gate.

JEREMIAH AND THE CIVIL POWER.   139

took him out of the stocks, and Jeremiah went away, launching sinister predictions at him.

A sort of private prayer which Jeremiah uttered upon this occasion testifies very plainly to the depth of the conviction by which he was animated. His mission is a burden to him; he would like to escape from it; but there is no getting away from the cunning devices of Iahveh.* Then he delivers himself up to lamentation at having been born, this being taken from the great malediction of a like kind in the book of Job. As a literary composition it is poor, but the sentiments which it expresses are exquisite. The struggle against the fatal burden of the divine mission has never been expressed with more sincerity. The part of Cassandra is a difficult one to sustain; and he to whom it falls is always led to complain of his lot.†

Iahveh consoles him by promising him that the efforts of a whole nation shall not suffice to break down his wall. Let him only have patience, and he shall be victorious.

In another place,‡ Iahveh forbids him to marry or to have children. All that are born in Judæa are destined to be as dung upon the face of the earth. Judah, who so loves idolatry, will be satisfied. He will be exiled to a country where he will be able to serve strange gods at his will. Even the

---
* Ch. xx. v. 7 and following.
† Ch. xv. v. 10 and following.
‡ Ch. xvi.

Temple of Zion will be destroyed.* In order to sweep away the high places, Iahveh will sweep away everything.

The struggle became one to the death. The official world was at its wit's end, and sought for the means to rid itself of this implacable censor. A plot was formed against Jeremiah; and, by means of calumnious denunciations, it was thought that he could be ruined:† and, though the intrigue failed, the implacable soul of the prophet did not forgive its authors. The terrible prayer in which he supplicates Iahveh never to forget the crimes of his enemies, and to exterminate their wives and children,‡ reads like that of an inquisitor, identifying his cause with that of his god. Among the errors which Jeremiah followed up with his fiery utterances there was one so abominable that any degree of violence in regard to it was justified, and that was the horrible practice of human sacrifices. But, so strange is the irony of things, we shall soon find Jeremiah the promoter, more or less directly, of a code which decreed death as a punishment for heresy in belief. The one is as bad as the other. The Spanish *auto da fés* are every whit as deplorable as the monstrosities of the valley of Hinnom. Jeremiah only suppressed Moloch to resuscitate him. What a long time it has taken the human

---

* Jeremiah, ch. xvii. v. 3 and following.
† Jeremiah, ch. xviii. v. 18 and following.
‡ Jeremiah, ch. xviii. v. 19-23.

mind to arrive at this very simple truth, that theoretical opinions sincerely held cannot be deserving of punishment, inasmuch as they are involuntary, and that the sincerity of opinions cannot be legally tested. Jeremiah would have been very much astonished if he had been told that the sins of others were no concern of his. Our liberal principle, which is not to concern ourselves with our neighbour, would have seemed to these fanatics to be the most dangerous impiety.

CHAPTER XIII.

THE REFORMS OF JOSIAH.

THE preachings of Jeremiah were not a solitary instance, for Jerusalem contained a whole group of men who carried the spirit of reform to its most extreme consequences: pure theocracy, the prohibition of idols, and religious unity. Not much philosophy was needed to see the absurdity of idolatry. The foolishness of saying to a piece of wood, "Thou art my father;" to the stone, "Thou hast brought me forth;" was too marked not to be readily perceived. The loud shouts and the wild dances with which the simple accompanied their prayers and their sacrifices, moved the Puritans to jests, such as, "Take care that you do not get hoarse;"* or else, "Cry aloud; your god is hard of hearing!" The details of the fashioning of the idols were also made much of,† while a certain man, called Habakkuk,‡ who appears to have been

* Jeremiah, ch. ii. v. 25; 1 Kings, ch. xviii. v. 27.

† Jeremiah, ch. x. v. 3-15. Compare Isaiah, ch. xl., xli., xliv.

‡ The form (Habacum) is perhaps the true one. The פ of the writing of a certain epoch very much resembles a final ם.

one of the pillars of the devout party, was as severe as the most austere Mussulman upon the sculptors.*

Phidias would have found it difficult to struggle against objections such as Habakkuk raises in this passage. As a matter of fact, Jeremiah and Habakkuk were as much astray in theology as the idolaters whom they held up to ridicule. They imagined that the scourges originated from a god who punished mankind, that death is due to a decree pronounced by the same god against those whom he wishes to destroy at a given moment, and they enjoined prayers being offered to the selfsame god accordingly. This is as false as to believe that a wooden, an earthen, a stone, or a metal image can have any effect upon the weather. It is less superstitious in appearance; but it is much more capable of inspiring fanaticism. The one god has had his fanatics; the idols of wood or metal can scarcely be said to have had. This theology after the fashion of Jeremiah has, moreover, a still graver drawback—that of allowing men to believe that they are in the secret of the ways of Providence, and of leading them to form a number of false opinions, especially to regard the unfortunate man as being always deservedly punished, which is at once unjust and cruel. The *lécim* would have been right if they had confined themselves to saying that no special will presides over the government of this world; but the distinction between

* Habakkuk, ch. ii. v. 18-20.

the conscious and the unconscious in the development of the universe could not then be made, seeing that, in our day, it is scarcely understood by the great majority of even educated men.

It may be asked whether more light existed, in any part of the world, about 625 B.C., as to these contradictions of the religious and moral world? Most probably not. China, no doubt, was already at rest, with that absence of theological and teleological requirements, which is the cause of its remarkably conservative spirit, which may almost be compared to that of the bees and the ants. India already indulged in metaphysics, but had got no further than a jangle of ill-assorted tenets, and a conflict of schools leading to no result. Babylon, from a very remote period, had been in possession of positive science, especially in regard to mathematics and astronomy; and from an early epoch Babylon had its theory for explaining the origin of the world without gods, these theories being more or less known in Phœnicia, in Aramea, and in Haran. But true science appears to have been extinguished at various times by the science of charlatanism. There occurred, it would seem, in Babylon, what would occur in our days if the scientific charlatans, backed up by the fashionable world and the newspapers, were to invade the Institute, the College de France, and the faculties. With us certain requirements superior to the caprices of the fashionable world, such as artillery,

THE REFORMS OF JOSIAH. 145

the manufacture of explosive materials, and industry based upon science will uphold the true science. In Babylon, the charlatans had the upper land.

Already, it is true, the genius of Greece was making its appearance in the rational order, and was in process of creating reason, as it had created beauty. The great principle of the fixity of the laws of nature was dimly seen by a few élite minds, such as Thales of Miletus, Pherecydes of Syrus, who probably derived their inspiration from Phœnicia, itself in turn the intermediary of Babylonia. The superiority of Greece over the East was an indicated if not accomplished fact. The germ from which science and philosophy will issue for the whole of humanity is clearly visible. Solon and the seven sages, as they are disclosed to us athwart the delightful anecdotes of their legend, have much more wit about them than Jeremiah. But as regards social questions, and the question of life beyond the grave, the Jewish sages enjoyed an immense advantage. In no Greek city had the struggle against idolatry, against the mercenary priests, against the rich oppressors, so much originality as at Jerusalem. In short, the battle of humanity was, for the time being, fought in that small city, the name of which was not destined to be borne throughout the world for another thousand years.

The religious spirit of Jerusalem was concentrated in a very small minority; but the great religious movements are nearly always brought about by a handful of extremists, who take possession of the head of the State, borrowing from him his authority, and, in return, placing their own ascendancy at his disposal. This is what happened with Buddhism and Asoka, with Christianity and Constantine, with Protestantism and the princes of the sixteenth century. Already in Israel Hezekiah's power was doubled by that of an Isaiah. The same thing occurred again seventy-five years later, but upon a much more considerable scale, and with a prospect of lasting which upon this occasion was fulfilled.

Owing to circumstances of which we are ignorant, Josiah, at about the time he attained his majority, became converted to, or at all events declared himself in favour of, the party of reform, of which Zephaniah, Jeremiah, Habakkuk, and a prophetess named Huldah were the most ardent champions. Everything tends to prove that this conversion, carrying with it consequences of such import for the history of humanity, was brought about by feelings of religious terror.* The prophets possessed a hold upon the laity similar to that which the monks of St. Martin of Tours secured for themselves over the Franks. It was supposed that the threats of the man of God were always carried out. The sovereign who fell in with this

* 2 Kings, ch. xxii. and xxiii.

idea was lost, for the prophet led him by terror. The sombre pictures with which the pages of the *nebiim* teem were not then what they are for us, mere literary fragments. They were very nightmares, and the prophet was regarded as having more or less at his disposal the phenomena which he announced. The unfortunate king, scared and dazed, esteemed himself only too fortunate when the prophet consented to adjourn the realisation of his threats until the next generation.* He sought by all possible means to satisfy the man who held in a measure the decrees of heaven in his hand.

What proves clearly the conversion of Josiah, like that of Asoka, to have been a personal fact is that his family does not appear to have become subject to the influence which the pietists gained over him. His three sons and his grandson, who reigned after him, did not at all share his ideas, and we shall see that they withdrew themselves completely from the influence of Jeremiah. Queen Hamutal, more particularly, the mother of two kings, appears to have been, like most of the queens, anti-pietist. Now the influence of the mother over the children is, in the East, much greater than that of the father. The influence of the husband over the wife is small, and it is not rare to find strong antipathies set up, thanks to polygamy, between them.

What Hezekiah had done, without resorting, as

* The case of Hezekiah; Isaiah, ch. xxxix. v. 7-8.

it seems, to violent means, and while taking care not to make the measure too general, Josiah did as an oriental sovereign, believing himself to have absolute rights over the creed of his subjects. The ideal theocratic sovereign was found; for here, at last, was a prince who admitted holding his power from Iahveh, and who was resolved only to exercise it according to the will and for the greater glory of Iahveh.

Religious eclecticism had, since the accession of Manasseh, been the constant practice of Jerusalem and of the cities of Judah. The insignia of the Phœnician form of worship were displayed even in the temple, which at certain times was used at one and the same time for the sacrifices of Baal and those of Iahveh. The provincial *bamoth* were exposed to still greater promiscuity; and the *astarteia* were numerous, to the great detriment of public morality. The worship of the stars (*seba hassamaïm*) was performed upon the roofs of the houses, and specially upon the roof of the royal palace, whence long spiral columns of incense were seen rising to the heavens.* The people, who were always ready to find a fault, asserted that the gods of Judah were as numerous as its cities, and that there was not a street in Jerusalem but had its altar to Baal.† Human sacrifices must have been rare; but the odious apparatus for them was to be seen at Topheth,

---

* Jeremiah, ch. xix. v. 13.
† Jeremiah, ch. xi. v. 12-13.

THE REFORMS OF JOSIAH.

and it would seem that, in certain circumstances, the kings had resorted to them.

Josiah reformed all this; * for first the temple, then the city of Jerusalem, and then the cities of Judah, were cleansed of all the religious impurities which, since the reign of Hezekiah, had accumulated in them. The king ordered the chief priest, Hilkiah, the priests under him, and the keepers of the door to clear from out the temple of Iahveh all the vessels that were made for Baal, and for Asera, and for all the host of heaven. He had these burned outside Jerusalem, in the fields of Kidron; and had the remnants of them carried to a refuse heap.† The priests who had offered incense to Baal, to the sun, to the moon, and to the signs of the zodiac were dismissed. The grove (Asera) which had been placed in the temple was taken out of it and burnt outside Jerusalem, in the bed of the torrent of Kidron, and the ashes were scattered upon the accursed ground of Ge-hinnom.‡ The king

* 2 Kings, ch. xxii. v. 1 and following.

† 2 Kings, ch. xxiii. v. 4. *Bethel* is undoubtedly an error. The correction of Thenius בֵּית אָלָה *locus exsecrationis*, is confirmed by the first graphic characters of the following verse. It is possibly Ge-hinnom which is thus indicated. No doubt some copyist thought this was a local ה, ביתאלה "towards Bethel," which would have led to the wrong meaning and the wrong reading.

‡ The author of the Chronicles (2 Chron., ch. xxxiv. v. 4) was right in hesitating to accept the meaning "cemetery of the common people," which the text of the book of Kings suggests. I believe that בני העם should be בני חנם. Note ἐν τῷ πολυανδρίῳ. Jeremiah, ch. ii. v. 23 (Sept.).

ordered the houses of the Sodomites which were in the temple, at the spot where the women wove hangings for the grove, to be pulled down. He broke down the *bamoth* of the gates,* that which stood at the gate of Joshua, the governor of the city (probably at the entrance to the citadel), and that which was to the left of the principal gate of the city, near the corner tower.† Lastly, the king ordered the destruction of the altars which his predecessors had raised upon the platform of the upper chamber of Ahaz, as well as the altars erected by Manasseh in the two courts of the temple; and, after having had them broken to pieces, threw the ashes of them into the brook of Kidron.

The last kings of Judah had consecrated horses to the sun, between which and Iahveh they drew such little distinction that these horses were placed in the temple of Iahveh, to the great dismay of the orthodox Iahveist. Josiah put an end to this scandal by transferring the horses to the pavilion of the chief eunuch,‡ situated in the *pomœrium* or *parbar*.§

* Probably the small altars or *sacella* seen in the walls of Assyrian cities. See *Mission de Phénicie*, p. 163.

† The present Jaffa gate.

‡ 2 Kings, ch. xxiii. v. 11. The text of this verse contains several errors. מבא is a variant brought in for מבת (compare the same error Isaiah, ch. ,xxiii. v. 1, and also 1 Samuel, ch. xvii. v. 52, נא for נת; Judges, ch. ix. v. 41, Aruma-Torma, &c.). The name of eunuch נתנמלך may also be a variant introduced from נתנו מלכי, at the line above.

§ *Parbur* or *parvar* is apparently derived from *péribolos*. See vol. ii. p. 22.

Josiah also caused the chariots of the sun, which had probably been used for some ceremonial, to be burnt.

The revolting Topheth was marked out most distinctively for expiation, and Josiah had it defiled,* that is to say, he had converted it into a dung-heap. At a later date it became a place of burial,† still keeping up the idea of impurity.

The *bamoth* which were before Jerusalem, upon the right hand of the mount of Corruption, did not fare any better.‡ Solomon, in his religious eclecticism, had had them built for the Ashtoreth of the Zidonians, for the Chemosh of the Moabites, and for the Milcom of the Ammonites. Josiah had them thoroughly profaned; he brake the *masséboth*, cut down the *aséroth*, and covered the place with the bones of men. Thus Jerusalem and its suburbs had nothing left which could offend the eyes of a puritan, so Jeremiah must have been satisfied, while within a century the aim of Isaiah and of Micah was attained.

In the country districts Josiah took measures quite as radical. The sacrificers of a lower grade,§ whom the kings of Judah, inclined to tolerance, had established to burn incense upon the high places in the different cities of Judah, and in the vicinity of

---

* 2 Kings, chap. xxiii. v. 10.
† See above, p. 108, note 1 ; p. 149, note 3.
‡ 2 Kings, ch. xxiii. v. 13-14.
§ נמרים.

Jerusalem, were recalled to the capital.* All these places, where prayer had been offered for generations, were defiled. Not a single *bama* was left from Geba to Beersheba, and by *bama* the compiler of the Books of Kings means worships opposed to that of Iahveh. But we shall see that even the worship of Iahveh was affected in its free and rural form.† This distinction between the worship of Iahveh upon the *bamoth* and the worship of strange gods upon the *bamoth*, which is to us of such capital importance, had scarcely any existence in that day. It is true that, to establish this distinction, the compiler of the Books of the Kings would have been compelled to admit that before Josiah's reign the worship of Iahveh was celebrated elsewhere than at Jerusalem—a fact which he strenuously denies, believing that the unity of the place of worship dates back from Moses.

In order to complete the reform, the king made stringent rules as to necromancy and ventriloquism. The teraphim, and all other objects of idolatry, were banished from Judah and Jerusalem, and superstition seemed to be almost entirely extirpated from the country.

The analogies between the history of Judaism and of Protestantism come out, it will be seen, more and more strongly. Reason is so weak that it has only the choice between the various degrees

---

* 2 Kings, ch. xxiii. v. 5.
† See below, p. 155.

of credulity. The puritan Israelites rejected the most foolish of the practices in vogue; they made fun of the people silly enough to seek for revelations in the voices supposed to come from the stomach, and yet they regarded as inspired the words of him who, without a shadow of proof, gave himself out to be a prophet of Iahveh. Protestants put down masses and indulgences, but maintained and even exaggerated the revelation of the Bible, the merits of the blood of Jesus Christ. These distinctions, which appear to us so unreal, are conditions of force in action. Poor humanity! How anxious it is to do good! But how little made it is, taking it as a whole, for the truth!

CHAPTER XIV.

CENTRALISATION OF JUDAISM AT JERUSALEM.

THE work of Josiah was not confined to purifying the places which had been defiled by idolatry and to restoring power to the *anavim*, who had been persecuted by Manasseh and Amon. The reforming pietists, who had acquired complete authority over him, were desirous of having institutions in keeping with the new tendencies. Judaism was like a lusty tree, full of sap; branches, which had hitherto been concealed beneath its bark and which were only in a potential stage of existence, were ready to spring forth. The boldness of the innovators was very great, stopping neither at impostures nor at historical falsehoods. Hence arose an organisation which lasted only a short period; but which, having its place in books that soon came to be regarded as sacred, remained an ideal type for the ages to come, and imported an element of great importance into the composition of humanity.

The principal cause of the religious abuses of which the prophets so bitterly complain was the

JUDAISM AT JERUSALEM.

lack of official regulations as to worship. The king made sacrifices to his God in the temple, which was in a measure an annex of the palace; the people of Jerusalem, and the personages of importance, obtained permission to sacrifice in it also. But sacrifices were also offered in a number of consecrated places in the territories of Judah and Benjamin, and as these local rites were not controlled, a great many impurities easily crept in. Some capital step was needed which would make Jerusalem the one centre of the worship.* The limited area of the territory of Judah made this possible, no locality being more than twelve leagues from the capital.

Josiah took this step with surprising decision. All the sanctuaries, except the temple of Jerusalem, were suppressed. This must have brought about a singular perturbation among the priestly families in the small provincial towns. Fancy, for instance, a regulation being made that the only masses said in the diocese of Paris should be at Notre-Dame Cathedral, and what would become of the clergy in the suburbs? Owing to the suppression of the *bamoth* or high places in the provinces, a number of levis were left without the means of

---

* 2 Kings, ch. xxii. v. 5, 8, 9, noting the pregnancy of the narrative. These כמרים or false priests are at the same time בחנים, admitted to some of the rights of the legitimate priests and sharing with them. Compare Jeremiah, ch. vii. v. 3-14; Deuteronomy, ch. xii.

livelihood, so they were mostly transferred to Jerusalem, to which place many came of their own accord, having first sold their patrimony.* They were not allowed to go up to the altar of Iahveh with the regular priests of the temple, who were supposed to be descended from Aaron, remaining mere assistants, or vestry clerks; but a share was allowed them in the distribution of gifts in kind, especially of the *massoth* or unleavened bread, which they ate "with their brethren," that is to say, altogether, without distinction.†

Thus the *personnel* of the temple was increased to an enormous extent. From this period the name of *Levitical priest* begins to be used to designate all the pure Iahveist priests.‡ The myth of a so-called tribe of Levi, taking toll of their brethren, then became fully developed. The germ of it exists in the ancient versions of sacred history, but it is not until after Josiah's time that the troop of priests massed in Jerusalem became an institution of Israel, and was, perhaps, the one which weighed heaviest upon its destinies.

The Levites were very poor, having little to live upon except the casual gifts of the temple. The people of the *anavim*, or the poor of God, thus

---

* Deuteronomy, ch. xviii. v. 6 and following.

† 2 Kings, ch. xxiii. v. 8-9. Compare Ezekiel, ch. xliv. v. 10 and following.

‡ Deuteronomy, ch. xvii. v. 9, 18; ch. xviii. v. 1; ch xxi. v. 5; ch. xxiv. v. 8, &c.

reached an enormous total. The temple was surrounded by a triple band of mendicants. Iahveh had an army of *fanatici* living by his altar, and spending their days in idleness under the shadow of his sanctuary. The poetry of the temple was created, for one always likes the places in which one has been poor. The enclosure which surrounded the sacred edifice was the point upon which a thousand varying sentiments converged. It was clear that if this temple came to be destroyed, it would be rebuilt by the affection which it had inspired. At this period Judaism had acquired a material existence; its roots will no more be disturbed; it will live on from age to age, putting forth, right and left, the most fertile branches. The ideal work, vaguely perceived by all the seers of Israel, is now realised in a house of stone, which may be regarded as indestructible to all time.

The revolution affected by these measures was not so much felt in the provinces as might be believed; for the centralising movement had begun since the destruction of the kingdom of Israel and since Ezekiel. Measures were taken so that the killing of animals, which had hitherto been inseparable from the sacrifices, should not be much interfered with. One central slaughter-house for Judah was really not enough. So that the killing of animals was, so to speak, made a lay occupation, and not confined to the religious order.*

* Deuteronomy, ch. xii. v. 15 and following.

It was at Jerusalem that the reformation was so profound and changed the whole face of religion. The temple assumed quite a fresh importance, and became what the temple of Melkarth was at Tyre, the one national sanctuary of a god who has but one temple and who is alone in that temple.* Absolute monotheism was founded upon an evident and tangible sign. The prophets, who had not hitherto set great store by the temple, began to group themselves around it, in the *liska*,† which formed a sort of gallery around the sacred building. The temple thus came to resemble in many respects a Mussulman mosque, with its *gobbé*, employed for educational work. Upon the other hand, a regular army of minor clerks was formed around the temple, and a long-sustained work of organisation began. Leviticism, which up to then had not been a serious rival for prophetism, became a power, or it should rather be said an obstacle, with which the untrammelled spirit of Israel had to reckon.

One of Josiah's first steps was to have the temple repaired. This combination of wood, metal, and stone stood in need of frequent restoration, and Josiah took up the regulations of Joash ‡ and had them carried out. The money which came in for the temple was collected by the keepers of the door, and then handed to the doers of the work, who

---

* Μονοῖκος. Compare *Hercules Monœcus*, Monaco.

† Compare the Greek Λέσχη.

‡ See vol. ii. p. 345 and following.

JUDAISM AT JERUSALEM. 159

made it over to the workmen and those who supplied the materials, without any regular accounts being kept and with perfect confidence in their good faith. Josiah instructed his *sofer* (scribe) Shaphan, the son of Azaliah, the son of Meshullam, to superintend the payment of the fund to the overseers and to see that the works were duly carried out.[*]

The festivals were, at the same time, fixed and made more general.[†] There were three in all: the passover, in the month of Abib (afterwards called Nisan); the feast of weeks, which was celebrated seven weeks after the beginning of harvest; and the feast of tabernacles, after the gathering in of all the crops. These feasts being only celebrated in Jerusalem, the pilgrimage thither thus became obligatory and assumed great importance. The passover, in particular, was arranged for, down to the smallest details.[‡] All naturalist associations were eliminated from it, and the passover became merely a souvenir of the deliverance out of Egypt, regarded as the great act of beneficence which attached Iahveh to his people.[§] The passover had

---

[*] 2 Kings, ch. xxii. v. 3 and following.

[†] Deuteronomy, ch. xvi.

[‡] 2 Kings, ch. xxiii. v. 21-23. We must be on our guard against the exaggerations of the Chronicles.

[§] The book of the Alliance and the ancient texts Exodus xiii., xxiii., xxxiv. have a mere rudimentary system. The system of Numbers, ch. ix. and xxviii., and of Leviticus, ch. xxiii., is later and more complicated.

for a long time been neglected, and the king, in the eighteenth year of his reign, celebrated a solemn passover which made a profound impression.*

These feasts, which had heretofore been of a very simple character, henceforth assumed a great solemnity. The host of Levites, as moreover that of the hieroduli or slaves of the temple, increased their lustre. The musical choirs, in particular, were organised with great care, and the liturgical Psalms, hitherto very few, became much more numerous. It is impossible to distinguish these hymns from those far more numerous ones which were composed—upon the re-establishment of worship—a century later, for the same forms of praise, "Praise Iahveh, celebrate his name, sing to Iahveh, &c.," recur in the two series; and the style of these pieces—of a light rhythm and of an easy composition—is always the same. The singing of these pieces, to the accompaniment of instruments, must have had a very charming effect. The songs of Sion were renowned; and, when in a strange land, the Israelites were asked to sing them as among the curiosities of their country.†

This well-planned method of embellishing life in a cycle of feasts and of practices having a

* 2 Kings, ch. xxiii. v. 12.

† Psalm cxxxvii. v. 3. Note *canticum novum* in the Psalms of the captivity and of the return. Isaiah, ch. xlii. v. 10 ; Psalm xxxiii. v. 3 ; xl. v. 4 ; xcvi. v. 1 ; xcviii. v. 1 ; cxliv. v. 9 ; cxlix. v. 1.

JUDAISM AT JERUSALEM.

spiritual meaning, the *chef-d'œuvre* of which was realised by Christianity in the Middle Ages, is quite the creation of Judaism. A pious Jew in the time of Josiah was almost as happy in his religion as a Christian in the time of St. Louis. All the difficult passages in life were made smooth or sweetened. We do not find that the Jewish marriage was accompanied by any religious ceremonies. Funerals were a painful necessity, like so many other things, which were not in any way sanctified. But circumcision, which at first was merely an operation preceding marriage, from an early period acquired a mystical meeting; it signified purification and consecration. It was applied to internal tendencies, and we read of the circumcision of the heart.[*] We are getting close to the epoch of the sacraments, and the essential conditions of that which constituted the charm of the Jewish and of the Christian life were already laid down.

Fasting, more especially, which had its root in the most remote Semitic antiquity,[†] became very much more general. The fundamental idea of Iahveism was that the pride of man is the greatest offence to God, and that consequently the humiliation of man is pleasing to the Almighty. Fasting, if it was accompanied by a garment made of breadths

---

[*] Jeremiah, ch. iv. v. 4; especially ch. ix. v. 24-25; Deuteronomy, ch. x. v. 16; Leviticus, ch. xxvi. v. 41; Ezekiel, ch. xliv. v. ~, 9.

[†] See vol. i. pp. 46-47.

of the coarse cloth called saq, roughly sewn together, was regarded as a very efficacious means of appeasing Iahveh, when it was supposed He was preparing to inflict punishment upon human pride. It is not certain that Josiah instituted an annual fast upon a fixed date,* but the time was at hand when this usage extended to an extraordinary extent and became linked with the anniversaries of national misfortunes. There were, moreover, extraordinary days of mourning or fasting to which the population of Jerusalem and of Judah were formally convoked.† These public manifestations gave rise to great exultation and to fanatical movements, over which the authorities could not always exercise a very effective surveillance. For the temple, like the large Mussulman mosques, was essentially a public meeting place, and one of great fermentation. The population of secondary priests and of people from the provinces, who thronged Jerusalem for the feasts, constituted around the sacred edifice a swarm of parasites, making a precarious living out of the sacrifices and attributing to themselves all the privileges of the gerim.‡ The temple thus began to become a powerful centre of religious action, which it had not hitherto been. The life which was led in it appeared to the

* This usage appears to be posterior to the captivity.
† Jeremiah, ch. xxxvi. v. 9. Compare Joel, ch. i. v. 14; ch. ii. v. 15; 1 Kings, ch. xxi. v. 9, 12.
‡ See above, pp. 29-30.

JUDAISM AT JERUSALEM. 163

inmates a happy one; and the delight of dwelling in it and participating in its abundance was extolled.* The pilgrimage, with its hymns,† became a very enchanting solemnity. The family rejoicings, from which the poor Levite and the stranger were not excluded, the humble good cheer of pilgrimage and pardon, recalled the patriarchal ideal in its idyllic and pastoral phase. All the joys of Israel are in reality an enlargement of the family life; their feast is a repast in common—the naturalist eucharist, to which the poor is admitted —the thanksgiving for life as it is, with its limits, which do not prevent it from being pleasant, under the eye of Iahveh, who dispenses good and evil.

Many psalms, which might be called Levitical, give the exquisite picture of the peaceful happiness which must have been tasted in the vicinity of the temple during the last years of its existence.‡

In thus becoming the panegyrical centre of the nation, the temple became the centre also of national movement. The gatherings of the masses in the temple for the fasts and for the feasts were the opportunities generally selected by agitators for their manifestations.§ It was at these gatherings

---

* Psalm xxxvi. v. 9; lxxxiv. v. 2, 11, etc. Compare Isaiah, ch. lvi. v. 7.

† Particularly those entitled *Sir ham-maaloth*.

‡ Psalms xxiii. and lxxxiv. In the latter, the verses 6-8 of which are too much altered for their meaning to be clear in a translation, we note at v. 10 the prayer for the king.

§ Jeremiah, ch. xxv. v. 2.

that Jeremiah recited or had read his most inflammatory pieces.* This was somewhat analogous to the anti-Islamite meetings in the valley of Mecca, upon which all the intellectual movement of Arabia converged. Jesus will, six hundred and fifty years later, be in that respect, as in so many others, his imitator. Judah had henceforth a common *sensorium*. This petty nation, so devoid of political institutions, was more richly endowed than any other for religious agitation. The fever which devoured it will never again be quenched.

The very fragmentary state in which the history of the kings of Judah has come down to us only enables us to see the main result of all these great things. Who inspired, who assisted Josiah in this great reform, his personal share in which was doubtless very small ? The name of Jeremiah suggests itself, for upon all points there is perfect harmony between the views of the prophet and the measures taken by the king. The prophets of the school of Amos, Micah, and Isaiah would never have advised this importance being given to the temple, for which they cared but little. But I have already observed that Jeremiah was more of the priest than any of the earlier prophets. It was natural that his tendency should be in the direction of the worship. His ideal implied a State religion and a king protecting with his sword the pure

* First manifesto against Jehoiakim, the scene of Baruch, and ch. vii.

worship of Iahveh. The measures of Josiah respond so completely to this programme that it is impossible to get away from the idea that behind all the acts of the king stood Jeremiah. If it be objected that a priest of Anathoth could scarcely have participated in the suppression of local worship, it may be answered that this priest of Anathoth was at open war with his family, which wanted to kill him. Who can tell whether this hatred did not originate in the sentiments which Jeremiah may have expressed as a youth regarding the abuses of these village forms of worship, into which must have crept so many details unworthy of the Divinity?

The zeal of Josiah extended to the territory of the ancient kingdom of Israel. There was little likelihood, in fact, of the ancient kingdom being forgotten, and of the alleged associations with Cuth, etc., obliterating Israelism in these parts.* The Israelite population was a numerous one, and the authority of Assyria was very little felt, while after the fall of Nineveh it may have ceased altogether. These countries fell entirely beneath the religious sway of Jerusalem,† the puritans of which had a special loathing for Bethel, which had been the principal centre of what they regarded as

* Jeremiah, ch. iii. and iv. v. 1-4.   Compare Ezekiel, ch. xx. v. 40.

† See 2 Chronicles, ch. xxxiv. v. 6, 9.

the infidelity of Israel.* The golden calf to represent Iahveh, which Jeroboam erected at this spot, had, it appears, been carried away into Assyria.† But the sanctuary still existed, and *aseroth* were to be seen there. Josiah had all these burnt and destroyed, and he even ordered the tombs upon the neighbouring heights to be ransacked, and the bones of those buried in them to be burnt upon the altar in order to pollute it.

The rest of Samaria was also visited and purified. The bamoth were swept away, and human bones burnt there. The priests who still attended these places of worship were slain and burnt upon the altars where they offered sacrifice.‡ In Judah, Josiah had shown much less severity, but in Judah he had to do with what was after all an irregular worship of Iahveh, whereas here it was sheer idolatry.

Acts of this kind lead one to suppose that the sovereignty of Josiah extended in some respects to the territory of the ancient kingdom of the North.§ Jeremiah is constantly harping upon a restoration of Israel, converted and brought back to the one sanctuary of Zion.‖ We must believe,

* See 2 Kings, ch. xvii. v. 28.
† Hosea, ch. x. v. 6.
‡ 2 Kings, ch. xxiii. v. 19-20. Compare 1 Kings, ch. xiii. v. 2
§ Ewald, *Gesch des V. I.*, iii. p. 690. See below, p. 224.
‖ Jeremiah, ch. iii. v. 12 and following; ch. xxxi. v. 1 and ollowing. Note particularly Jeremiah, ch. xli. v. 5.

JUDAISM AT JERUSALEM.

in fact, that, if the kingdom of Judah had lasted, he would have reconstituted Israelitish unity, with Jerusalem this time as capital. It is fortunate that this perspective was not realised. It is the programme carried out by the Asmoneans five hundred years later, and if Israel had no other title to glory than the existence of this small state, its place in the world would be a very small one. The ideal of the prophets of the old school, essentially humanitarian and cosmopolitan, was the true one. We have seen that Jeremiah remained partially a stranger to it. The movement over which Josiah presided, relating especially to the worship and the liturgy, would have carried Israel clean away from its true vocation, if Nebuchadnezzar had not come, like Titus at a later date, and made the direction of the great idealists absolutely preponderant. Twice it was the fate of Israel to owe its salvation to that which is the ruin of others, and to be recalled, by the crushing of its petty worldly hopes, to a sense of its great duties towards humanity

CHAPTER XV.

THE NEW THORA.

ALL these reforms of Josiah were effected in execution of a law of Iahveh, supposed to have been revealed to Moses. Before the reign of Josiah mention had frequently been made of a law or Thora of Iahveh, embodying the whole of His wishes, His compact, so to speak, with Israel. The compilation of the so-called Jehovist Sacred History contained a small code of this kind called the Book of the Alliance (Exodus, ch. xxi.-xxiii.),* conceived especially from the point of view of the kingdom of Israel, and supposed to have been revealed on Sinai. The Elohist version contained analogous moral directions (what is called the Decalogue, Exodus, ch. xx.),† of a more general character, also supposed to have been revealed on Sinai. The two brief religious codes were put together, and thus completed each other in the combined text which, as I believe, was compiled

---

* See vol. ii. p. 304 and following.
† See vol. ii. p. 334 and following.

in the reign of Hezekiah. In the temple also there were formed, probably in the time of Hezekiah, a species of decretals attributed from that time to Moses,* and relating to certain special points, for instance the regulations concerning lepers and the list of unclean animals. There were, moreover, moral poems, Psalms, for which it was claimed that they epitomised in a few sentences the moral teaching of Iahveh.

All this constituted an ensemble sufficient to justify such phrases as "to observe the law of Iahveh ... in conformity with the law, that is to say, the precepts of Iahveh." There was not, however, any book which could exactly be called the *Thora*. We must remember, moreover, that the ancient Sacred History had a very limited circulation, that perhaps only one copy of it was then in existence, that this book was at the period in question like the stela of stone, a thing without a duplicate. As I have already said, they did not know what it was to re-copy. When a book had to be re-copied a fresh book was produced by means of additions to, subtractions from, and combinations of the original text. Among the inscriptions of Asoka, which are what we should call posters, and which one would expect to find all the same, there are not two alike. Thus ancient Sacred History was almost unknown. The in-

* Deuteronomy, ch. xxiv. v. 8. See above, p. 63 and following.

tention of the pietist party being to effect a great change, their plan consisted not so much in drawing from obscurity the legislative portions of the ancient text, as in composing a fresh text into which the ancient precepts would be incorporated in a manner more suited to the ideas of the time.

The need for such a book had been particularly felt since the religious activity of those who surrounded Josiah had so perfected and completed religion. What was wanted was a book summing up all the legislative ideal of the theocratic school, the rules of a state perfect in the sight of Iahveh. Of course, the revelation of this code was attributed to Moses, in accordance with an idea which dated back from the time of the earliest traditions of Israel. But the revelation of Sinai (or of Horeb, as it was then called *) was regarded as complete and final.† So there came to be imagined a second revelation more comprehensive than the first, which Iahveh had made to Moses beyond Jordan, in the plain of Arboth Moab, before the solemn moment

* Horeb is foreign to the Jehovist and the Elohist. The passages Exodus, chap. iii. v. 1; ch. xvii. v. 6; ch. xxxiii. v. 6, seem to come from B. It is in the legend of Elijah (1 Kings, ch. xix. v. 8) that we find Horeb figuring as the "Mountain of God." After a certain epoch Horeb supplanted Sinai, and the Deuteronomist adopted this tradition. The name of Horeb in 1 Kings, ch. viii. v. 9, is a Deuteronomical correction. The modern compositions follow Deuteronomy.

† Deuteronomy, ch v. v. 2, 4; ch. ix. v. 8.

of entering the promised land. Very few persons were in a position to raise a capital objection which would have consisted in confronting the new text with the old. The new revelation was not, moreover, inconsistent with the ancient one; it was held to be only the conclusion and the summary of it.* In fine, the persons who were familiar with the ancient books and who might have challenged comparison with them were probably accomplices in the pious scheme from which the new text was evolved. Not to speak of Jeremiah, who appears to have been the moving spirit in the whole of this deception, we find among the prime actors, Hilkiah, the chief of the priests, the scribe Shaphan, son of Azaliah, son of Meshullam, two important personages, Ahikam, son of another Shaphan, and Achbor, son of Micaiah, a royal officer named Asaiah, and lastly Huldah the prophetess, wife of the keeper of the wardrobe, Shallum, the son of Tikvah, son of Harhas.

So upon a certain day in the eighteenth year of the reign of Josiah (622 B.C.),† the king being twenty-five years old, the scribe Shaphan, son of Azaliah, came to the temple to see after the ac-

* Deuteronomy, ch. i. v. 6; ch. iv. v. 10, 15; ch. v. v. 2, and especially ch. xxviii. v. 69. Deuteronomy presupposes the knowledge of the whole history of Moses, and even of patriarchal history as it is given in the most ancient books.

† 2 Kings, ch. xxii. v. 3 and following. Compare ch. xxiii. v. 23.

counts of the work being executed there, and to arrange upon this point with Hilkiah. When matters were settled, the priest confided to him in the most singular way: "I have found the book of the law in the house of the Lord."

Hilkiah at the same time gave the book to Shaphan, who read it. The latter, after he had made his report upon the works to the king, added that he had read a book given him by the priest Hilkiah, and he in turn read it to the king, who, when he heard the words of the book of the law and the threats which accompanied it, rent his garments, and said to Hilkiah, and to Ahikam, and to Achbor, and to Shaphan the scribe, and to Azaiah, "Go ye, enquire of the Lord for me, and for the people, and for all Judah, concerning the words of this book which is found; for great is the wrath of the Lord which is kindled against us, because our fathers have not hearkened unto the words of this book." The king had no doubts as to its authenticity, but as it is clear that since the accession of Manasseh, at all events, matters had not been treated quite so rigorously, he asked himself whether Iahveh would repent Him of His threats, and whether it was worth while to become converted, inasmuch as the mischief was done. The envoys of Josiah went to consult Huldah the prophetess, who lived at Jerusalem, in the quarter called Misné, and expounded the matter to her; the prophetess, at one with Jeremiah, replied that Iahveh was justly irritated,

THE NEW THORA. 173

but that He would be appeased by a return to the strict observation of the law.*

The new code was adopted as the programme of the reformed Iahveism, which the pietists of the new school desired to introduce. According to the narrative of the Book of Kings, Josiah assembled all the inhabitants of Jerusalem, and had the words of the book of the compact found in the temple read to them. The king, standing up on the platform, proclaimed the covenant with Iahveh, consisting in following His statutes, "with all their heart and all their soul, in keeping His commandments and His testimonies and His statutes, as they are written in this book." All the people made the covenant, and Israel was anew consecrated to Iahveh, as it was believed to have been in time of Moses and of Joshua.

We shall never know with the precision which our historical habits demand the details of this occurrence. The one thing certain is that we possess the volume so opportunely discovered by Hilkiah. It is the work, perfectly homogeneous and very well composed, which extends from verse 45 of chap. iv. of the section of Sacred History called

* This is assuredly what Jeremiah would have replied (Fragment, ch. iii. and iv. v. 1-4). The author of the book of Kings, persuaded that the decreed Iahveh has been pronounced since Manasseh's time (2 Kings, ch. xxiii. v. 26; ch. xxiv. v. 3, 4) gives another version. All the evil foretold will come to pass; but Josiah having humiliated himself before Iahveh, these evils will not occur till after his death.

Deuteronomy by the Greek translators, up to the end of chap. xxviii. of the same section.*

The code in question claims to be the supreme though not the only code of Israel. The covenant of Sinai or of Horeb still holds; † the law revealed at Arboth Moab is merely a new publication of it; but this new publication renders the first useless. The basis of the covenant of Iahveh with the people is the Decalogue, as the ancient text gave it.‡ This important document is reproduced with very trifling alterations. In respect to the laws, the new code makes very trifling innovations. In nearly all parts it merely repeats the prescriptions of the Book of the Alliance.§ It assuredly copied its list of clean and unclean animals from a more ancient text,‖ which it corrected and shortened. Upon a

* Compare 2 Kings, ch. xxiii. v. 24, and Deuteronomy, ch. xviii. v. 9 and following.

† Deuteronomy, ch. v. in several passages.

‡ Deuteronomy, ch. v. v. 6 and following; compare Exodus, ch. xx. v. 2 and following.

§ Thus the limitation of the right of pledging (Deuteronomy, ch. xxiv. v. 12; Exodus, ch. xxii. v. 25); the prohibition of usury among brothers (Deuteronomy, ch. xxiii. v. 20-21; Exodus, ch. xxii. v. 24); the right of freedom by purchase for the slave (Deuteronomy, ch. xv. v. 12-18; Exodus, ch. xxi. v. 1 and following); the right of asylum (Deuteronomy, ch. xix. v. 5; Exodus, ch. xxi. v. 13); the prohibition to cook the kid in the mother's milk (Deuteronomy, ch. xiv. v. 21; Exodus, ch. xxiii. v. 19); the motive of benevolence towards the stranger derived from the sojourn in Egypt (Deuteronomy, ch. x. v. 19; Exodus, ch. xxiii. v. 9). See below, pp. 186, 188.

‖ Leviticus, ch. xi. The prohibition of heterogeneous mixtures

THE NEW THORA. 175

mass of casuistical points it merely abridges earlier regulations, and in the case of lepers,* it refers back to a code which, as a matter of fact, is to be found elsewhere.†

What is entirely the author's own is the *Schema*, the corner stone of Judaism, the brief formula of his *Credo* all down the ages.‡

In taking this precept literally and in executing it from a purely material point of view, Judaism displayed a certain historical sagacity. The Thora discovered (that is to say, fabricated) under Josiah was the basis of the special religion which was founded in the eighth and seventh centuries B.C. in Palestine. This Thora was the worst enemy of the universal religion which the prophets of the eighth century had in their dreams; Jesus could only cause the spirit of the great prophets to triumph by crushing it and by denying it outright. But human things are a compound of matter and mind. Liberty and the chain, that which excites and that which restrains, the sublime and the commonplace, are equally necessary in the construction of a general whole which is to endure. But for the precision of the Thora, the ardent preachings of the prophets would have remained fruitless; they would

has also an older aspect in Leviticus (ch. xix. v. 19) than in Deuteronomy (ch. xxii. v. 9, 11).

* Deuteronomy, ch. xxiv. v 8.
† Leviticus, ch. xiii. and xiv.
‡ Deuteronomy, ch. vi. v. 4 and following. Compare Exodus, ch. xiii. v. 9-13.

have been like so many other manifestations of the human mind, which produced a great effect in their time, but of which the very trace is lost.

The Iahveh of the Thora conceived in the reign of Josiah is, like that of Jeremiah, at once the god of heaven and earth and the God of Israel. He is at once the universal God, and as such absolutely just, and a provincial God, immensely unjust.* When his people's interests are concerned, He is egotistical and immoral as a return for a fidelity which has little that is meritorious about it, seeing that it is interested, He promises Israel the height of human happiness, which happiness is to consist in possessing great and beautiful cities which he has not built, provisions which he has not stored up, cisterns which he has not dug, vineyards and olive groves which he has not planted.† These, the customary rewards of bravery and labour, are here the recompense of a theological virtue, the belief in a one God. Iahveh is faithful; He keeps his compact; He loves Israel; He has sworn it, and that is enough. It is not any merit of Israel which has won Him these favours; it is the free choice of Iahveh.

The great offence is to attribute anything to oneself. Whoso says, "It is by my own strength that I have got all this," is detracting from the glory of

---

* See especially Deuteronomy, ch. x. One might think one was reading Jeremiah.

† Deuteronomy, ch. vi. v. 10 and following.

Iahveh. This jealous God gives all things to those who serve Him except what is impossible; that is to say, immortality. They have life, the rapid multiplication of their race, perfect prosperity, rain in due season, all the good things of the earth;* the world exists for them alone: "And thou shalt consume all the people which the Lord thy God shall deliver thee; thine eye shall have no pity upon them."†

A legislation founded upon such premises as these could not be a tolerant one. The measures of precaution for maintaining Iahveist Monotheism bear the impress of extreme ferocity. In this respect the Deuteronomical code has not been exceeded even by that of the Dominican inquisition in the thirteenth and fourteenth centuries. Extermination of the unbelievers,‡ prohibition from having any contact with them, prohibition of mixed marriages upon the presumption that religious infidelity is the consequence of feminine seduction, the merciless crushing of every idolatrous object, absolute iconoclasm. "You must exterminate the evil from amongst you," such is the bloodthirsty formula in which these decrees are couched. The accusations for crime against Iahveism involve the most terrible responsibilities. A prophet, even if a

* Deuteronomy, ch. ix. v. 1 and following.
† Deuteronomy, ch. vii. v. 16. Numbers, ch. xiv. v. 9, is still more emphatic. Compare Numbers, ch. xxiv. v. 8.
‡ Deuteronomy, ch. vii.

worker of miracles, who should preach the abandoning of Iahveh, must be put to death.* More terrible still is the case of a city from which comes one who attempts to seduce people from the worship of Iahveh. The inquiry having been made, and the accusation found to be true, " thou shalt surely smite the inhabitants of that city with the edge of the sword, destroying it utterly, and all that is therein."†

One shudders at the thought that, in inquiries of this kind, all that was required was the denunciation of two or three witnesses, with the somewhat shadowy security that these witnesses would cast the first stone.‡ Two persons who had come to an understanding might destroy a man without appeal. In the seventh century B.C. it is probable that these texts did not lead to any one's death; they were Utopian ideas, presupposing a good deal of simple-minded impudence in those who invented them; they were not real laws, regularly applied. It is bad enough that there should have existed fanatics capable of conceiving such bad ideas. Two thousand years later these mischief-making texts were destined to bear fruit, and they sent to the stake, more especially, a host of unhappy Israelites. Our Western world, with its clumsy good nature, could not understand that, by simple figure of

* Deuteronomy, ch. xiii. v. 1 and following.
† Deuteronomy, ch. xiii. v. 15-16.
‡ Deuteronomy, ch. xvii. v. 6-7.

speech and by hyperbole, such horrors could have been put to paper, with the *arrière-pensée* that there would be none to apply them, or to take them seriously. The terrible *Directorium Inquisitorum* of Nicholas Eymeric follows Deuteronomy word for word, and this time thousands of unhappy beings were victims of the culpable levity of this dreamer.

The judicial institutions were, moreover, the most defective part of these ancient codes. The ordeal which was the base of the book of the Alliance is not commanded in the new legislation; but in cases of difficulty, it was enjoined to go to Jerusalem and lay the matter before the Levites and "the judge that shall be in those days," and whoso did not obey should be put to death.* Other texts prove, moreover, that the ordeal, especially that of the bitter waters for the woman accused of adultery, continued in use.†

The conception of the royalty is just such as would be formed by an *anav*, by an *ébion*, opposed to display and pomp. The king will be selected by Iahveh from among his brethren in Israel.‡ The luxury of horses is pointed out as a danger; if the king gave himself over to it, he would be capable, in order to procure them, to take the people back

* Deuteronomy, ch. xvii. v. 8-12. This is intentionally left doubtful, and seems worded purposely to increase the royal power and create a jurisdiction for the sovereign.

† Numbers, ch. v. v. 11 and following, an ancient law.

‡ Deuteronomy, ch. xvii. v. 14-20.

into Egypt, and that is a road which must not be travelled over again.* The king must not keep up a large harem. He must not possess too much gold or silver. He must avoid pride and not despise his brethren if he would enjoy a long reign. He must procure a copy of this law, the text of which he will get from the Levite priests. He must have it ever before his eyes, and read it so that he may observe it in every particular. The spirit which the law breathes is an anti-military one. The pietist desires to have a king after his own image. But this is very inconsistent on his part. The king is especially instituted in the event of war.† Now war is an affair of race. The military temperament is a matter of hereditary affinities and of education. A military caste is not going to let itself be lectured by saints; a king cannot take the programme of his house either from democrats or bigots.

All the religious innovations of Josiah are to be found in the code which was the work of his advisers. The improbability and the lack of local colouring would have been too glaring if Moses, before the crossing of the Jordan, had designated Jerusalem as the only place of worship. Upon the other hand, the singular invention by which an attempt was made to render the unity of the place

---

* An allusion to the attempts at an Egyptian alliance, which was the predominating idea during the reign of Josiah, and to which Jeremiah was always opposed.

† 1 Samuel, ch. viii. v. 20.

of worship, the fiction of the tabernacle, conceivable from the Mosaic epoch was not yet devised. The author of the Deuteronomical code makes use of a vague expression: "Unto the place which the Lord your God shall choose out of all your tribes to put His name there, even unto His habitation."* This place will be the only one where the Israelite may make his burnt offerings, his sacrifices, his tithes, his firstfruits, his votive and spontaneous offerings, the firstborn of his flocks and herds. The three great festivals of the year are to be celebrated there by him and his family, with the Levites, before Iahveh.† As I have already said, the world to which such a code adapted itself was a very little one.

The spectacle of a whole family moving about with its offerings, its cooking utensils, its following of Levites and of poor people, must have been a very strange and touching one.‡ The festivals round about the temple, full of pious joy and of trust in Iahveh, left a precious recollection behind them. At Jerusalem the priests of the temple joined in them, and upon these occasions the Levites ate their fill, which did not often happen to them.

It is evident that such a life of constant tra-

* Deuteronomy, ch. xii. v. 5 and following.
† Deuteronomy, ch. xvi.
‡ See especially ch. xvii. Compare ch. xii. v. 12; ch. xiv. v. 29; ch. xvi. v. 11, 14.

velling could not have long been the rule of any society or agglomeration of men. We must not lose sight of the fact that these laws represent a state of things which the man of God would have liked to see established much more than a real state of things which actually lasted. We must also remember that Josiah died in 609, that his death was followed by an anti-pietist reaction, which only ended with the kingdom of Judah, so that the beautiful ideal of which the author of Deuteronomy dreamed scarcely lasted thirteen years, and assuredly more than thirteen years would have been required to put such an abnormal regime into regular working order.

The internal worship of the temple of Jerusalem does not appear to have undergone many changes. The theory of the sacrifices in Deuteronomy is of the simplest description. They are of two kinds: holocausts, in which the victim is consumed; sacrifices, in which the victim is killed, and then eaten at the family board.* It was felt desirable to lay down rules for the division of the meat between the priest and the person who offered the sacrifice, but without entering into the details which were afterwards deemed necessary.† The predominating thoughts of the author of Deuteronomy, though to

---

* Deuteronomy, ch. xii. v. 11 and following; ch. xiv. v. 22 and following; ch. xv. v. 19 and following; ch. xvi., xvii., etc.

† Leviticus, ch. i.-ix., xii., xvi., etc. Numbers, ch. xxviii., xxix., etc.

a high degree sacerdotal, are not exclusively liturgical. They are above all moral and puritanical. The diviners, the sorcerers, the false prophets, religious prostitution, the erection of the *aseroth*, the incisions on the forehead and the habit of cropping the hair, and especially the horrible practice of passing the children through the fire, these are what he abominates.* This was equivalent to taking up, but with additional severity, the programme of reform so tentatively initiated during the reign of Hezekiah.

The situation created for the Levites by the innovations of Josiah led to the most singular consequences. In the eyes of the author of the Deuteronomical code,† Levite is synonymous with priest; his favourite expression is "Levite;" he has no idea of a hierarchy among the *cohanim*. The high priest evidently had not yet come into existence.§ All the Levites, according to the present codes, officiate at the altar. The Levite who thinks

* Deuteronomy, ch. xii. v. 31; ch. xiv. v. 20 and following; ch. xvi. v. 21; ch. xviii. v. 9 and following

† Deuteronomy, ch. xvii. v. 9, 18; ch. xviii. v. 1 and following; ch. xxi. v. 5; ch. xxiv. v. 8; ch. xxvii. v. 9. Deuteronomy, ch. x. v. 6-9, appears to be an interpretation. Compare Deuteronomy, ch. xxxi. v. 25.

‡ חנהנים חלויים. See especially ch. xii. v. 10 and following; ch. xviii. v. 6 and following.

§ The compiler of the extant books of the Kings, which is posterior to the captivity, places by anticipation high priests in the earliest periods (Jehorada, Hilkiah, Seraiah).

fit to come from his village and dwell at Jerusalem takes rank at once among his brethren, serves at the altar, receives his share like the rest, independently of the price which he may have obtained from his patrimony.* These Levites thus formed a hungry sacerdotal host, congregated partly in Jerusalem, partly in the small houses outside, and living like parasites on the remainder of the nation. The author of the code of Josiah has a liking for this class of disinherited persons, and he would have the community adopt them.† The tithe and the firstfruits are to be consumed in Jerusalem. The case in which the giver may reside too far from Jerusalem is provided for; he may realise his tithe in cash, which he will then spend in Jerusalem, always bearing in mind the Levites.‡ A triennial tithe (a kind of alms) must in addition be bestowed in the villages, so that the Levites, the strangers, the orphans, and the widows may eat and be filled.§ The socialistic character of all these measures will strike the most superficial of readers at a glance. It must always be borne in mind that these measures are conceived for a State of very small size.

---

* Deuteronomy, ch. xviii. v. 6-8. The distinction referred to in 2 Kings, ch. xxiii. v. 9, was perhaps a transitory measure.
† Deuteronomy, ch. xii. v. 12 and following.
‡ Deuteronomy, ch. xiv. v. 22 and following.
§ Deuteronomy, ch. xiv. v. 26-29; ch. xxvi. v. 12.

CHAPTER XVI.

FIRST APPEARANCE OF SOCIALISM.

THE fixed opinion of the modern day being that the best religious code is liberty—inasmuch as creeds are strictly the domain of the conscience of each one of us—these ancient religious legislations of the East present themselves to our judgment under very unfavourable circumstances. The civil and political side, the moral, social, and religious side, are all mixed up. But, whether rightly or wrongly, we do not admit that the State should concern itself with moral, social, or religious questions. Charity and right appear to us as two distinct domains. Perhaps it is as well that they should now be separated, but it is assuredly good that they should formerly have been allied. Force was the sole ruler of primitive humanity. The weak did not find any advocate until much later. We now believe that the oldest advocates of the oppressed were the prophets of Israel, and that is why we accord them so eminent a place in the history of civilization.

The code conceived under Josiah, which is known as Deuteronomy, is the first of any extent in which an attempt was made to establish a system of guarantees for the weak, at the expense of the rich and of the strong. No doubt the Book of the Alliance, anterior by two centuries to Deuteronomy, contained, side by side with more or less barbarous directions, some singularly minute rules as to cleanliness, humanity, and politeness. The book of Deuteronomy goes still further in the same direction. Never was love for the humble and the neglected carried so far. We find it making provision for the poor in all the acts of religion. It shows affection for the Levite, for the Levite is a poor man. The widow, the orphan, the stranger isolated in the land, are never overlooked in its prescriptions.*

In regard to usury, Deuteronomy does not do much more than reproduce the Book of the Alliance. Usury is absolutely forbidden between Israelites; it is allowed, and even encouraged, towards the stranger. † Usury, to be exact, would have no place in a true Israelite society, for the faithful Israelite, specially protected by Iahveh,

---

* Ch. xxiv. v. 17-18. This passage is taken from the Book of the Alliance, Exodus, ch. xxii. v. 20 and following; ch. xxiii. v. 9.

† Deuteronomy, ch. xv. v. 1 and following. Compare ch. xxiii. v. 20-21.

FIRST APPEARANCE OF SOCIALISM. 187

would be secure from the greatest of all misfortunes, that of having need to borrow.*

The code as to slavery†, taken nearly entirely from the Book of the Alliance, adds to the directions of the ancient code rules equally inspired by a sentiment of humanity. The right of asylum is developed so as to create a counterpoise for the cruel law of blood for blood.‡ The fatal confidence which all the ancient forms of justice have in evidence is attenuated in a manner which is assuredly very insufficient.§ Then, again, the "Levirat," an institution of which this legislator alone gives the theory,‖ in conformity moreover with the old Semitic customs,¶ implies a regard for the rights of woman very rare in antiquity.

In a word, the code of Iahveh, discovered by Hilkiah, is one of the boldest attempts ever made to protect the weak. It is the programme of a sort of theocratic socialism, the aim of which is mutual solidarity, which ignores the individual, which reduces almost to zero civil and military order, which suppresses luxury and lucrative industry and trade. The restrictions placed upon the right of accepting pledges,** go far beyond the very

* Psalm xxxvii. v. 21. See Deuteronomy, ch. xv. v. 4-11.
† Deuteronomy, ch. xv. v. 12-18.
‡ Deuteronomy, ch. xix. v. 1-13.
§ Deuteronomy, ch. xix. v. 15-21. Compare ch. xxi. v. 1-9.
‖ Deuteronomy, ch. xxv. v. 5 and following.
¶ See the narratives relating to Onan, Thamar, and Boaz.
** Deuteronomy, ch. xxiv. v 6, 10 and following.

humane regulations to be found in the *Book of the Alliance.* The passage relating to the hired servant is an excellent one (see Deuteronomy, ch. xxiv. v. 14-15). Even as far back as this, special efficacy is attributed to the poor man's curse; and the way is paved for the admission that his prayer has a special value in the sight of God—an idea from which the Middle Ages will deduce social and economical consequences of such gravity. The injunction not to muzzle the ox while he is treading out the corn,* belongs to the same order of ideas which modern socialism has pounced upon as a weapon, only because wholesome political economy has failed to avail itself of them. The eliminations effected in the ranks by the priest before a battle,† are one of the most delightfully ingenuous incidents which it is possible to imagine. The rules of war for the besieged city showed, taking into account the cruelty of old, an advance in civilization. The rights of the beautiful woman made captive are conceived with tact.‡ The directions relative to the man who has two wives,§ to the man who has just taken a wife,|| to the rebellious son,¶ to adultery, rape, birds' nests,** certain instructions

* Deuteronomy, ch. xxiv. v. 14 and following.
† Deuteronomy, ch. xx. v. 1-9. Compare ch. xxiv. v. 5.
‡ Deuteronomy, ch. xxi. v. 10-14.
§ Deuteronomy, ch. xxi. v. 15-17.
|| Deuteronomy, ch. xxiv. v. 5.
¶ Deuteronomy, ch. xxi. v. 18-20.
** Deuteronomy, ch xxii.

FIRST APPEARANCE OF SOCIALISM.

as to cleanliness, and especially the reason which is assigned for it,* the curious directions as to virginity,† had in their time more or less good reason. The cause of manslaughter is very wisely provided for.‡ The rule as to fugitive slaves § seemed anarchical to modern states, which are supposed to be liberal. The gathering of grapes and corn would almost seem too liberal in certain countries.‖ The capital penalty is dealt out unsparingly, as in all ancient legislations, but corporal punishments are limited,¶ and the whole code testifies to an instinctive horror of the shedding of blood.

What can be more thoughtful than the counsel to leave a few sheaves when harvesting, not to strip the branches of the olive-tree quite bare, and to leave a few gleanings in the vineyard, so that the poor may have his share.** The author of this code assuredly loved Israel only; but with what deep affection he did so! He understood nothing about liberty; in his idea, the different members of a society guarantee one another mutually, and are all mutually responsible; but how fine was his conception of the happiness of brethren dwelling

* Deuteronomy, ch. xxiii. v. 10 and following.
† Deuteronomy, ch. xxii.
‡ Deuteronomy, ch. xxii. v. 8.
§ Deuteronomy, ch. xxiii. v. 16-17
‖ Deuteronomy, ch. xxiii. v. 25-26.
¶ Deuteronomy, ch. xxv. v. 1 and following.
** Leviticus, ch. xix. v. 9; ch. xxiii. v. 22 seems anterior.

together in unity, and with what heartfelt joy must the wealthy bands of peasants, bringing to the temple their fruits, have sung the Psalm cxxxiii., beginning, "Behold! How good and pleasant it is for brethren to dwell together in unity," the text of which is much altered.

In presence of so much that is good and beautiful, we forget certain blots, a tiresome and prolix tone of preaching, various cruel instructions which, let me repeat, were not applied,* and abuses of the principle of solidarity, which would spoil the book if, by a fortunate contradiction, the author himself, when he is not blinded by his Monotheistic frenzy, did not protest against this principle. The fathers will no longer be put to death because of their children, or the children because of their parents; each one will be put to death for his own sin.† This is a great advance upon the Decalogue,‡ where God visits the sins of the fathers upon the children even to the third and fourth generation. The old principle of reversibility lost ground. It must be remembered that what responds chronologically in Greece to the Deuteronomical code is the legislation of the

* The death of Jesus was not the consequence of the Deuteronomical principle, inasmuch as He was crucified, not stoned.

† Deuteronomy, ch. xxiv. v. 16. Compare Jeremiah, ch. xxxi. v. 29.

‡ Exodus, ch. xx. v. 5.

FIRST APPEARANCE OF SOCIALISM. 191

mythical Draco. The Hebrew code of the year 622 contains errors, with many fanatical pages which one would like to see effaced, but it also contains clauses which might excite the envy of modern communities. This code was in its time a law of progress.

Who was the author of a book the godfathers of which are so well known to us, and the paternity of which is, as if designedly, concealed. It is, in the critical view, a subject for great astonishment that the name of Jeremiah should not be pronounced in ch. xxii. of the Second Book of Kings in respect to the appearance of the Thora. From beginning to end, this Thora is instinct with the spirit of Jeremiah; they are his ideas, his style.* The Deuteronomical Thora is the complete realisation of the ideal preached by the prophet of Anathoth. How comes it that Jeremiah does not figure in the narrative of the discovery of the book when seven or eight other persons are mentioned? Among

---

* These analogies are too well known to need being set forth in detail. It is thought sometimes that it was Jeremiah who imitated Deuteronomy, but that is against all probability. When Jeremiah quotes a *Thora* he is in harmony with Deuteronomy; but there is always the Book of the Alliance behind. Deuteronomy was only in the eyes of Jeremiah, and is only in reality, the Book of the Alliance amplified. Compare Exodus ch. xxiv. v. 7; Deuteronomy, ch. xxviii. v. 69; Jeremiah, ch. xi. v. 1-8. Compare also Jeremiah, ch. xxxiv. v. 8-22 with Exodus, ch. xxi. v. 2-6, and Deuteronomy, ch. xv. v. 12-19, not omitting Leviticus, ch. xxv. v. 39-46. The resemblance of Jeremiah, ch. vii. v. 23, and Deuteronomy, ch. xxvi. v. 17-18, ch. xxix. v. 12, is uncertain.

them there is at least one, Ahikam, who appears elsewhere among the most intimate friends and protectors of Jeremiah.* How is it that, in order to get information as to the threats contained in the book, the prophetess Huldah is consulted instead of Jeremiah, who was so well known, who was the most active agent of the reform,† who went out each day to the gates of the city to preach, who ruled it over the king and his officers.‡ That the code which embodied his ideas should have been promulgated without being communicated to him is a most improbable occurrence. If this code was published in agreement with him, it was because he was altogether, or nearly altogether, the author of it. If no historical text were there to tell us that the Smalkalde articles are the work of Luther, we should be entitled to affirm that these articles, formally summing up the ideas of Luther, were not published without his knowledge.

The priest Hilkiah, the inventor of the new

* Jeremiah, ch. xxvi., xxxvi., xxxix.-xl. The tone of the narrative in the episode of the invention of the Thora, and in the episode of the roll of Jeremiah, burnt and written out afresh, is quite the same.

† It has been objected that Jeremiah is not named in the book, whereas Isaiah is. But it must be remembered that the last reviser of the book of Kings is the same who edited Jeremiah; he would not like there to be repetitions in the two books, and he placed all that concerned the biography of Jeremiah in the book named after him.

‡ Jeremiah, ch. xvii. v. 19 and following.

FIRST APPEARANCE OF SOCIALISM.

Thora, is, according to some, identical with the priest Hilkiah, the father of Jeremiah, who in 622 was still young. The preoccupation which the Deuteronomical code reveals with regard to the Levite priests reduced to destitution, and especially with regard to the Levites who come from the provincial sanctuaries to settle at Jerusalem,* would quite tally with a priest of Anathoth, who claimed to treat upon equal terms with the other ministers of the Temple. But Hilkiah was a very common name, and the identity of the two is not probable. We have therefore no means for tearing aside the veil with which this matter was concealed. The portion of pious fraud which it implied led to combinations which put us off the scent, and which only reveal themselves by improbabilities and lack of logic. All that we can say is that the code designated by the Alexandrian translators as Deuteronomy was composed in the time of Jeremiah, among the associates of Jeremiah and according to the ideas of Jeremiah.

Let me add that the book of Jeremiah contains a fragment † which seems to be the promulgation of the recently discovered code. As a general rule, the strophies or surates of Jeremiah appear to be either anterior to the reform of Josiah or posterior to the death of that prince. One or two fragments at the outside appear to be of between the years

* Deuteronomy, ch. xviii. v. 6-8.
† Jeremiah, ch. xi.

622 and 609,* and it is easy to conceive that during this period of full triumph the prophet should have broken off his threats, and have left the supposed revealed text to speak for itself.

The little book so cleverly put forward met with complete success. It stood out as a code by itself, complete, and embodying what had hitherto been scattered about in quite fragmentary form. The number of the copies of this Sacred History was so limited that no one raised objections, which, in a period of greater publicity, would have been crushing. To those who were familiar with the parts of the Iahveist legislation already in existence the answer was given that there were two distinct revelations made to Moses; one upon Sinai or Horeb, the other in the plain of Moab, before the going over Jordan. These ancient centuries must not be credited with our critical exigencies. Novelty was a cause of strength; a recently published book enjoyed a period of fashion during which it exercised its maximum effect. This is the explanation of all the apocryphal writers: Daniel, Baruch, Henock, etc. These books, when they appeared, gave more pleasure than the old books, for they harmonised more with the sentiments of the time. The people were constantly in need of fresh revelations, and they would not admit that the source

* For instance, that in which the prophet goes upon each Sabbath day to the gate of the children of the people and preaches to them about the Sabbath. Ch. xvii. v. 19-27

of them could be exhausted. Jeremiah, if he composed Deuteronomy, did not, after all, commit a graver offence than those which were reiterated very often after him. It is one of the laws of religious history that a revelation, a form of devotion, a book, a pilgrimage, soon grow old; piety is ever in need of something new, and this order of things, which is often represented as being immutable, is, on the contrary, subject to perpetual renewal. The eternal verities are those in respect to which our poor humanity is apt to vary the most.

CHAPTER XVII.

LITERARY WORK ABOUT THE TIME OF JOSIAH.

THE Thora, which composes nearly the whole of the section of the Hexateuch now called Deuteronomy, was not the only outcome of the great religious movement which filled the reign of Josiah. This Thora existed at first for some time as a distinct book, and then it was thought that isolated the publication would be weak, as the Thora presupposes patriarchal and Mosaic history. The effect aimed at by the sudden discovery and the separate publication of the book was secured. This law of Iahveh, the result of fraud upon the one side and of connivance upon the other, had been the instrument of the reform. The question now was how to maintain it, and, in order to effect this, it was natural to place it in the volume of sacred history, as if it were the last act in the life of Moses before his death beyond Jordan. But a grafting operation was necessary, and thus a long fragment* was pieced on at the beginning of

---

* The four first chapters up to v. 43 of the fourth, from the past of the Pentateuch which is called Deuteronomy.

the book; various additional notes were added to the end,* and so were in juxta-position to the song of Moses,† a fragment which already formed part of the Sacred History.

Who effected this peculiar operation of piecing and joining? It has sometimes been ascribed to the author of the new code; ‡ at other times there have appeared reasons for bringing these insertions down to the time of Zedekiah.§ The author of the reconstruction was, in any event, some one of the school of Jerusalem,‖ and he did not stop here. In his desire to give the closing pages of the Sacred History a thoroughly edifying character, he gravely interpolated the part relating to Josiah, inserting in it set speeches supposed to have been pronounced by Joshua upon solemn occasions, and which display piecings of unmistakable similarity with the long sermons of the code and the tirades.¶

---

* Ch. xxix., xxx., and xxxi., with the exception of a few pericopes. Perhaps also the scene on Mounts Ebal and Gerizim, ch. xxvii.

† Deuteronomy, ch. xxxii.

‡ The style is quite the same in each; but there are several difficulties of arrangement.

§ Compare Deuteronomy, ch. iv. v. 29 and following, with Jeremiah, ch. xxix. v. 12 and following, and Deuteronomy, ch. iv. v. 20, with Jeremiah, ch. xi. v. 4.

‖ Same passages.

¶ See Reuss, Introduction, pp. 214-216; de Wette, *Einl.*, § 162. Deuteronomical modifications of the same kind are to be found in the other historical books.

Thus the book of Sacred History, which was probably already begun to be called the Thora (what had hitherto been the accessory tended more and more to become the principal), grew in size from century to century, swelling as it went. This precious volume, in the state which it had attained under Josiah, or, to put the matter in another way, as it was at the time of the catastrophe which put an end to the kingdom of Judah, comprised about two-thirds of its present contents.

The patriarchal histories which fill what is called Genesis were, apart from a few explanatory notes, very much as they now read.

The history of Moses, as it is to be found in Exodus, up to ch. xxiv., and in Numbers, from ch. xx. to the end, including the two small ancient codes, the Book of the Alliance and the Decalogue, was in the main as it stands now. Nevertheless, a few legends, smacking of the prophetic agada, and in most cases duplicating the more ancient texts, were still lacking.

Deuteronomy has undergone very little change. The book of Joshua, upon the contrary, will receive considerable interpolations after the captivity; lastly, there are decisive reasons for bringing down till after the captivity what may be called the Levitical Pandects, including the latter part of Exodus, Leviticus, and the first part of Numbers, not to speak of other intercalations. Two capital institutions, of which there is no trace either in the code of the time of Josiah or in the earlier books,* characterise these Levitical additions, that is to say, the tabernacle, a singular fiction which aimed at conceiving the unity of worship before the building of the temple at Jerusalem, and the asserted institution of Levitical cities by Joshua. Not only does Deuteronomy fail to recognise these institutions, but it may be said to exclude them, inasmuch as each page of the book implies the unity of worship established upon quite different bases,† and inasmuch as the rules of charity relating to the Levites would not be at all applicable to a richly endowed clergy, such as that which would be inferred by the 21st chapter of Joshua.

It would be erroneous, nevertheless, to consider all the laws which now compose the Levitical Pandects as posterior to the code promulgated under Josiah. I have shown ‡ that there were, in connection with the temple, a body of small codes, a sort of established custom supposed to be revealed,§ which was not yet embodied in the great Thora. The author of the Deuteronomical code appears to have been familiar with and to have summarised several of these special small Thoras. It is not beyond the bounds of possibility

* It is quite impossible, upon the other hand, to admit that if these two institutions had been conceived at the time of Josiah Deuteronomy would not have contained some allusion to them.

† Deuteronomy, ch. xii. v. 8.

‡ See above, p. 53 and following, and below, p. 169.

§ Deuteronomy, ch. xxiv. v. 8.

that, in the time of Josiah, just before or just after the compilation of Deuteronomy, several of these ecclesiastical capitularies, which were to be the basis of a future canon law, were written by some one in the sacerdotal world. It is permissible to suppose that some of the fragments utilised by the code of Hilkiah had not long been written when the pious forger made use of them. Thus, for instance, the treatise upon vows (*nedarim*),* the code of the nazirs,† all that relates to the ordeal of the bitter waters,‡ an usage already so ancient, may date from this period. These small compilations would thus have been for a long time in existence in sporadic form, like so many *Extra Vagantes*, destined to be codified later on. For it is most significant that the Levitical code § has no unity, whereas Deuteronomy must have been written without any break, in the course of a few days.

All the works of this period are characterised by their exalted piety. The prophetical spirit was in the ascendant; the lay spirit underwent a temporary eclipse. It is to this period that we should be tempted to attribute the prophetical agadas, a body of compositions intended to exalt in the past the character of the prophets, to represent it in its

* Leviticus, ch. xxvii.
† Numbers, ch. vi.
‡ Numbers, ch. v. v. 11 and following.
§ Distributed through Exodus, Leviticus, Numbers, and Joshua.

wonder-working and awesome phase, and to place it in all respects far above royalty. A legend with a fixed date, for instance, is that of the prophet of Bethel, who is said to have resisted Jeroboam, to have been devoured by a lion, and whose tomb was respected by Josiah.* It was supposed that this prophet had foretold Josiah, and had announced his reforms. All this is set forth in a narrative analogous to the recitals of the time of the Judges, and showing that pietism had not extinguished the taste for that which is simple and grand.

Each prophet thus had his agadic book. These prophetic *midraschim*,† words or acts of Nathan the prophet, of Gad the seer, of Ahijah the Shilonite, of Iddo, of Shemaïah, of Jehu the son of Hanani,‡ and more generally the acts of the seers,§ were analogous with the *Kisas el-anbia*, in which the Mussulmans find so much delight, lives of the lower order of saints, dear to credulous peoples. In other words, there existed, parallel to the books of the

---

* 1 Kings, ch. xiii.; 2 Kings, ch. xxiii. v. 15 and following.

† This word became synonymous with legend. 2 Chronicles, ch. ii. xv. 22; ch. xxiv. v. 27.

‡ 1 Chronicles, ch. xxix. v. 29; 2 Chronicles, ch. ix. v. 29; ch. xii. v. 15; ch. xiii. v. 22; ch. xx. v. 34; ch. xxvi. v. 22; ch. xxxii. v. 32; ch. xxxiii. v. 19. It must not be supposed that all these *midraschim* were distinct books. They were the rubrics of a history divided by prophets instead of by kings. It is thus that we still speak of "the books of Samuel." Compare 1 Chronicles, ch. xxix. v. 29.

§ רברי החוים (2 Chronicles, ch. xxxiii. v. 18, 19); חווי is certainly meant for חיים.

Kings and in some cases tangled up with them,* books of the prophets, relating their acts and in some cases their sayings, with that indifference to chronology and disregard of the reality which has, at all times and in all countries, been characteristic of the legend. These *midraschim* were not preserved in their original form; but they possessed considerable importance, for they were afterwards introduced into the text of historiography properly so called. The compiler of the present books of the Kings, after the captivity, took these texts, devoid of all exactitude and full of exaggeration, and fused them in his narrative, thereby lowering very much the historical alloy of the annals of Israel. The result for the early history of Israel was very much as if Merovingian history written after Gregory of Tours were regarded as incomplete, and an attempt was made to complete it, without regard for contradictions, with Aimoinus and the poorest of the lives of saints. The author of the Chronicles, in the second half of the fourth century B.C., was familiar with these same prophetical agadas, and doted on them. He introduced these faulty data by the handful into the contexture of Jewish history, and this is what deprives his book of nearly all historical value.

Moses being a prophet, and the first and greatest of the prophets, had his place in these biographies, which were written especially with a view to edifi-

* Take Isaiah, ch. xxxvi to xxxix.

cation. In order to relate his life in accordance with the demands of the piety of the age, it was, of course, to the already consecrated Sacred History that the compiler went for his facts. I consider it as probable that there was a *midrasch* upon the life of Moses, in which nearly all the data of Sacred History were taken up, blunted and loaded with fabulous incidents after the captivity. The last of the compilers, carried away by the weakness which the compilers of legends have for pretending to be complete, even when their documents are mere reduplications of one another, gathered up all these narratives, and reintroduced them in their altered shape into Sacred History. He did not, after all, commit a critical offence much graver than that of the historian in our own day who completes the books of the Kings with those of the Chronicles, which are worked-up rearrangements of the former. Thus are to be explained the repetitions piled upon repetitions,* which make the life of Moses in the Hexateuch as it stands the most incoherent and badly ordered narrative it is possible to conceive.†

* See above, p. 46 and following.

† Compare, for instance, Exodus, ch. xi. v. 1-3, to Exodus, ch. iii. v. 21-22; ch. xii. v. 35-36. Exodus, ch. xxxiii. and xxxiv., are full of repetitions and obscurities, which are not to be explained by the mere combination of the Iahveist and the Elohist. The small Thora (Exodus, ch. xxxiv. v. 10-28) is an abridged and modified repetition of the Book of the Alliance (the Iahveist version), and yet (v. 28) this summary is called the "Ten Commandments" (Elohist version). Exodus, ch. xxxiii. v. 1-6, is a second instance of the same kind. All that relates to the *ohel moëd* (Exodus,

It is just the same as if any one were to embody in a book all the treatises in that volume, together with all the notes which were used in composing it. The narrative is constantly reverting to the same facts; after the relatively authentic version comes the version at second hand, although the latter, far from adding to the first, merely serves to distort it. It is like Livy completed with elements from no matter what source, even with narratives derived from Livy himself which had undergone all sorts of alterations.

In proportion as Israel inclined towards pietism the lyrical side of its genius gained more and more the ascendancy. Several psalms were doubtless composed about the time of Josiah and were the expression of that fervent piety of which Jeremiah was the inspirer. It is very difficult for us to distinguish them from the psalms of the *anavim*, in the time of Hezekiah.* I should be much inclined to date back from this time the psalms which express the happiness of Jewish life when it is conscientiously practised. Well-defined moral ideas are the principal conditions of happiness, and the Thora provided this first base of a happy life, besides promising him who observed it that he should succeed in all things. To meditate it, to endeavour to practise it in all respects, was re-

ch. xxxiii., v. 7-11) is distinct from the great invention (Exodus, ch. xxv. and following), which is posterior to the captivity, and yet neither the Iahveist or the Elohist were familiar with the *ohel moëd*.

* See above, pp. 38 and following.

garded as the most supreme of joys. The Thora is in this sense the book which has made the greatest number of people happy.*

This poesy, made up of gentle reproaches, these bitter complaints of the just always irritated by the prosperity of the wicked, and inclined to be angry with their God if He does not cause them to gain their suits, cannot but strike us as rather monotonous. The defect of the Psalms is that they express only too well one of the traits of the Jewish character, which is the tendency to complain, the everlasting lamentation, the appeal to the Eternal One against persecutions which are often imaginary. This defect dates more particularly from the times of Jeremiah and Josiah. Religious inspiration, still so lofty in this troubled age, easily becomes soured. The triumph of the *lécim* under Manasseh and Amon, their return to power under Jehoiakim, left a feeling of rancour in the consciences of the *anavim* which was never destined to be removed. The state of feeling was very analogous to that of the Catholic party in France after the failure of the attempt made on the 16th of May, 1877, by Marshal MacMahon and his advisers and after the ruin of the Union Générale. These self-made victims of a cause which had identified itself with that of God could do nothing but recriminate.

It is thus that the literature of the time of Josiah

* Psalm i. Compare verse iii, with Jeremiah, ch. xvii. v. 8.

compared with that of Hezekiah's time gives evidence of marked inferiority. The decadence of the style is very pronounced. The Hebrew of Jeremiah and of Deuteronomy is flabby, prolix, and poor, and the plastic sentiment of the ancient writers is lost. The profane part of the literature, which was still in existence during the reign of Hezekiah, had completely disappeared by the time of Josiah. Israel will produce no more works such as the ancient *Iasar*, like Solomon's Song, the Proverbs, the poems of Agur and of Lemuel, the Strong Woman, and Job, the tone of which is so free. Every work now has a tendency serving to fortify the faith or the hopes of Israel. Israel is henceforward exclusively a religious people. In the time of Josiah, Greece had not yet developed a quarter of its genius, and yet even already its triumph is certain. Though only just learning to write, her incomparable Homeric *epos* is being recited; her admirable lyric poetry is set to music and to the dance; Thales of Miletus has been born, and clear-minded men are already endeavouring to formulate a naturalist theory of the universe, Solon's aim being to found the just city upon reason alone.

Israel will never found either a State or a philosophy, will never have an exclusive profane literature, and yet its part is an immense one. Israel founded the protest of the poor, the demand for justice, equality, fraternity in the bosom of the brotherhood—the Church, in a word, which is in its way a complete society, an organisation of justice and equality. Greece had prepared the enduring framework of civilization; Israel will import an addition to it, an alteration of immense importance, care for the feeble, the unswerving demand for individual justice. Our Aryan civilizations, based upon the immortality of the soul and the sacrifice of the individual, are too cruel. Let us, at all events, acknowledge the right of the psalmist who protests and who weeps. Jeremiah is in a measure right. The remedies by which he hopes to correct the inevitable injustices of this world are chimerical; the society which he conceives would be still-born; but he adds a factor which is essential to the work of humanity. He is of all those who preceded John the Baptist the man who contributed most to the foundation of Christianity; he must be regarded, despite the interval of centuries which separated them, among the immediate precursors of Jesus.

There was one point, moreover, in which the philosophical situation of these ancient Jews resembled our own. They set themselves to justify the temporal government of Iahveh without giving themselves the facilities which the hypothesis of life beyond the tomb offers in the way of compensation. We, too, are obliged to explain life, to give it an aim and to render it endurable, without that great resource which so strongly helped the instructors of humanity in all ages. Strange to say, Judaism succeeded in obtaining prodigies of devotion without ever appealing to hopes the object of which was placed beyond this life. We are obliged to do the same. We are obliged to give men a motive for living and for living properly, without alleging anything which they could regard as a lure or a deceptive promise. Jeremiah evaded this by persuading his contemporaries that the events of the world, from rain and drought down to the revolutions of empires, were arranged for rewards or as punishments for the children of Israel. This resource is also lacking for us in the present day; but we have that of the psalmist, the secret tears, the outpouring of the heart confessing its troubles. That is why the Psalms, when all the rest disappears, remain our book of prayer, our inward song, our eternal consolation.

A birth of capital importance, as it may well be called, was that of piety, the piety which is independent of all dogma, the consolation and force of life. An exquisite expression, " to seek God,"* summed up religion in all that was most intimate and true. To express the act of prayer there were words in ancient Hebrew of extremely delicate shades,† while later on the Christian translators

---

* דרש אלהים.

חנה, to speak in a whisper to oneself; שיח. See vol. ii. p 505.

introduced distinctions even finer. The Latin version of the Psalms, thanks to a series of delicious counter-meanings,* effaced what was in places rather dead in the original Hebrew.† It idealised the heaviest of the imageries, it rendered what was unintelligible touching, what was monotonous full of charm. The Church composed the breviary, the exquisite electuary of pious sleep. A St. Bernard derived the most ethereal mysticism of hymns from a limited horizon. From the graduated uses of *meditari* in the Psalter came the orison, perhaps the most original creation of Christianity, the science of which it is the secret, the gift which belongs only to itself.

---

* These counter-meanings came in a great measure from the altered condition in which the text has come to us. The collection of the Psalms having been made very late, at an epoch when writing was very cursive and indistinct, no book of Hebraic literature contains so many mistakes.

† For instance, Psalm iv. v. 3, 9, etc.

CHAPTER XVIII.

REVOLUTIONS IN THE EAST.—DEATH OF JOSIAH.

SUCH were the strange pursuits upon which, alone of all the world, the tiny kingdom of Judah was engaged. Thirty-eight years after the reform of Josiah, the Jewish nation disappears, just as thirty-seven years after Jesus all trace of the Jewish nationality vanishes. These milk fevers of Israel, symptomatic of the great travails of humanity, were so intense that each crisis ended in an apparent death, soon to be followed by unexpected resurrections.

The movement which agitated Israel was, in fact, destined to lead up to the religion of the human race; a nationality could not emerge from it. Jerusalem received from the prophets its distinctive stamp. It will become the holy city of all religions; it will never be a city of profane culture. Jeremiah set his seal upon it, and that darksome genius will reign there perpetually; common sense will be excluded from its walls; all kinds of fanaticism will give battle there, until it reaches the state in which we find it in the present day—a madman's cell, full of peril for the reason of those who dwell there, the magnetic pole of all the insanities, a *champ clos* in which the demented of the most diverse kinds meet to dispute and to die.

The ideal which the prophets had before them was a peace amid which, all trace of a military aristocracy having disappeared, the only questions to be discussed and settled were those of social reform. But the general condition of the world lent itself less and less to these Utopian fancies. While the Thora was being founded at Jerusalem, under the double influence of Josiah and of Jeremiah, the gravest revolutions were occurring upon the Tigris and the Euphrates. Nineveh had retained its supremacy over the East during the reigns of Manasseh and of Amon. Assurbanipal succeeded Esherhaddon and represented in its plenitude the ideal of the King of Assyria, at once cruel and powerful. The Medes, although threatening, were as yet but a black spot upon the horizon. Assyrian feudalism reached the vastest extension which any agglomeration of men under a central power had hitherto been able to attain.

We have seen how, about 750, the prophet Nahum announced the downfall of Nineveh, with that hidden joy which fills the heart of a Jew when he foresees the ruin of his enemies. Moreover, one is never mistaken when one predicts of human undertakings that they will perish.

Nafela nafela Babel is a prophecy always realised. The oracle of Nahum was verified at the end of five-and-twenty years. Asshur-edil-ilani, the successor of Asshurbanipal, was the last King of Nineveh. The Assyrian empire, already weakened by the Scythians, succumbed to the Medes about 625 B.C. The city never recovered, and the population either emigrated or moved to the opposite bank of the river. Nineveh fell in a day, and Mossul was built upon the other side, leaving untouched that vast field of ruins which had such prodigious surprises in store for modern science.

The downfall of Nineveh did not involve the consequences for things in Syria which might have been anticipated.* Babylon henceforth concentrated upon herself all the forces of action appertaining to the ancient Asshur. The Medes did not exercise any appreciable influence on this side of the Euphrates, while the Scythians appear to have invaded the valleys of the Orontes and the Jordan. Babylon resumed the part which Nineveh had deprived it of for nearly a century and a half. As far back as the reign of Hezekiah, the viceroy of Babylon, Merodach Baladan, had made his appearance in the affairs of Palestine. After the disappearance of Nineveh, Nabopolassar, an As-

---

* The downfall of Nineveh, although announced by Nahum, did not leave any trace in the Hebrew writings. Jeremiah does not allude to it, and there is nothing topical in Ezekiel, ch. xxxii. v. 22-23.

syrian general, who had proclaimed himself King of Chaldea, was for fifteen years undisputed master of the East. His suzerainty was recognised by the kingdom of Judah, and Josiah evidently regarded himself as under a bond to him, for we shall see how he let himself be brought to ruin rather than desert him. The way in which Josiah acts as sovereign in the territory of the ancient kingdom of the North * goes to show, in fact, that the new Babylonian dynasty let the King of Jerusalem regard himself as sovereign of all the land of Israel.

The inevitable complications which must occur in human affairs made it impossible for so small a people as this, surrounded by others of the same race who might have been its allies, but from whom religious hatred separated it by a deep division, to remain neutral. If the Ninevite or Chaldean empire had lasted as long as the empire of the Achemenide, it is probable that the small kingdom of Judah would have resigned itself to the payment of tribute and to a subordinate military position. But the masses which hurtled round about it were too vast to admit of its enjoying a life of repose. The geographical position of Palestine was ill suited to the pacific part after which its prophets aspired. A very ancient adage is that of Psalm lxviii.†

---

* See above, p. 166.

† See verse 31. בּוֹר עַמִּים קְרָבוֹת יֶחְפָּצוּ

Egypt had, under the active impulse set by Psammeticus I., made great progress, and his son, Nechoh II., opened up trade and navigation, and undertook great enterprises which might have been of immense service to civilization. The conquest of Syria, which was always the temptation to the sovereigns of Egypt, supplanted, however, all his other ambitious aims. Nechoh had formed a very large navy, which opened up the coasts of Phœnicia for him, and he had in his pay numerous bands of Greek mercenaries, who conferred upon his Libyan and Ethiopian hordes a solidity which they had never previously possessed.* It appears that the plan was to attack Syria from its central part, and in the spring of 609 the bulk of the Egyptian army disembarked somewhere near the foot of Mount Carmel, and penetrated into the territory of the ancient kingdom of Israel without meeting with any resistance.

Josiah regarded himself as the sovereign of these countries,† and it appears that Nechoh had, before entering upon the campaign, informed him that he was not the object of the attack and had asked him not to intervene.‡ But Josiah was true to his pledge, and being a vassal of Babylon he thought

* For description of this army see Jeremiah, ch. xlvi. v. 7 and following.

† See above, pp. 166, 213.

‡ 2 Kings, ch. xxiii. v. 29; the addition of the Syriac appears to be original. Compare 2 Chronicles, ch. xxxv. v. 21.

it his duty to oppose the passage of Nechoh. The plain of Megiddo was the key of Palestine, and it was there that all the battles which decided the fate of the country were fought. Josiah marched bravely thither, was defeated, and slain in the mêlée,* being only thirty-eight years old. His servants placed him on a chariot and brought him to Jerusalem, and buried him in the garden of Uzza, in the sepulchre of Manasseh and of Amon, his predecessors.

The extreme aridity of the historical information which we possess concerning this epoch makes it impossible to offer any conjectures as to the act which put an end to the life of Josiah. The character of this sovereign, who played so prominent a part in the history of his time, is quite unknown to us. In proportion as the physiognomy of David is so clear, and as we can realise the personality of Hezekiah, in the same proportion is it impossible to give any opinion as to what Josiah was like. Docile in religious matters as he was to the counsels of the prophets, it would be rash to assert that it was in obedience to their advice that he set out upon the fatal expedition which was to cost him his life. Jeremiah appears as a rule opposed to the Egyptian alliance; †

* 2 Kings, ch. xxiii. v. 29 and following; Herodotus, ii. 159. A very doubtful allusion in Zechariah, ch. xii. v. 11.

† See above, p. 180.

nevertheless, there is a passage in Deuteronomy very favourable to Egypt.*

How comes it that the pietists, who had made such unscrupulous use of the authority of Josiah to secure the passing of their ideas of reform, had so little care for his memory, and how is it that the book of Jeremiah has preserved so few traces of him? † Above all, it would be interesting to know how the pietists explained the premature and undeserved death of this prince after Iahveh's own heart. In the view of the thorough-paced Iahveist a misfortune always was caused by a man's own fault, but it would have been hard to contend that in Josiah's case it had been caused by his impiety. "Like unto him was there nothing before him, that turned to the Lord with all his heart, and with all his soul, and with all his might, according to all the law of Moses; nor after him arose there any like him." ‡ The true culprit to whom the catastrophe of Megiddo was imputable was Manasseh. "Notwithstanding, the Lord turned not from the fierceness of his great wrath, wherewith his anger was kindled against Judah, because of all the provocations that Manasseh had provoked him withal." § Thus, in contradiction of

* Deuteronomy, ch. xxiii. v. 8-9.

† The eulogy in Jeremiah, ch. xxii. v. 15-16, is indirect. The documents referred to in 2 Chronicles, xxxv. v. 25, were certainly composed after the event and falsely attributed to Jeremiah.

‡ 2 Kings, ch. xxiii. v. 25.

§ 2 Kings, ch. xxiii. v. 26. This is the best refutation of what

REVOLUTIONS IN THE EAST. 217

the many promises of pardon made by Jeremiah, the crime of Manasseh was beyond expiation. All the systems which seek to justify the temporal government of Providence are driven to imagine the existence of an absurd, a ferocious, or a jealous God. Better, therefore, not attempt to justify Him at all.

According to the narrative of Herodotus,* the immediate consequence of the victory of Megiddo was the capture of the important city of *Cadytis*. There is an enigma here which has never been properly solved, and the least improbable hypothesis is that this name applies to Jerusalem,† designated by the epithet already given to it by the pietists of *Qedosa* or *Qedisé*, " the Holy." ‡ After the battle of Megiddo, Jerusalem was quite open to Nechoh, and if he did not enter the city it was because he did not choose to do so. Matters in any event took a very tumultuous turn. At the news of the death of Josiah the people proclaimed one of his younger sons, aged twenty-three, the offspring of

---

the book of Chronicles relates about Manasseh. What ! We are asked to believe that Manasseh was pardoned, while Josiah is punished in his stead.

* Herodotus, ii. 159.

† The passage in Herodotus, iii. 5, seems to refer rather to Gaza, but Herodotus is often a little vague. Strabo also believes that the sea is visible from Jerusalem.

‡ Jerusalem must have been called קרשתיח (*Cadustiah*). Compare Jeremiah, ch. xxv. v. 29 : ציר אשר נקרא שמי עליה. Compare Isaiah, ch, xl. v. 14 ; Epistle of James, ch. ii. v. 7.

Queen Hamutal, who appears to have been regarded as more patriotic than his elder brother Eliakim, who was twenty-five.* He called himself Shallum,† and took as his royal name that of Jehoahaz, "he whom the Lord hath chosen." We do not know for what reasons Jehoahaz was disliked by the *anavim* ;‡ but this antipathy had not time to develop itself. Events of the gravest importance were occurring in the east, and it seemed as if the axis of the world was about to be changed, and as if Egypt was about to take over the sway which Assyria had held for a century and a half.

Nechoh, after the battle of Megiddo, pursued his victorious march northward. He did not go beyond the Euphrates, and Karkemis was the furthest point reached by him in his expedition against Assyria.§

* These figures are very doubtful. Josiah is supposed to be of this age in 634 or 632, when aged at the most thirteen or fifteen.

† Jeremiah, ch. xxii. v. 11.

‡ 2 Kings, ch. xxiii. v. 31 and following. The passage of Jeremiah, ch. xxii. v. 10 and following, seems rather favourable to him than otherwise. Perhaps the author of the book of Kings has been rather too free with his ill-natured comments, after Josiah.

§ The town of Karkemis, marking the usual point at which the Euphrates was crossed at the Assyrian epoch, was formerly identified with Circesium, at the junction of the Euphrates and the Cobar. In our day, the savants guided by Assyriological and Egyptological researches make it much further north, at Mabourg, at Djerabis, or at Kalaat-Nedjm. Circesium, however, still has many partisans (see *Journal des Savants*, Nov. 1, 1873). It was not so difficult in ancient times as it is now to cross the desert by Palmyra. An army returning to Babylon from Hamath or Riblah

But in Syria the Egyptian rule was much more solidly established than it had been for a long period. Upon his return Nechoh halted at Riblah, in the land of Hamath, a central point at which all the invaders of Syria established their head-quarters.* There he received the homage of his vassals, Jehoahaz among them. Nechoh received him very unfavourably and deposed him,† putting in his stead his eldest brother, Eliakim, the son of Josiah and Zebudda, who took the name of Jehoiakim, "him whom the Lord raised." Jehoiakim appears to have been unpopular, and he was regarded as so completely the creature of Nechoh that it was said he owed his royal name as well as his throne to the Egyptian conqueror.‡ There are certain facts which go to show that Jerusalem underwent the indignity of an Egyptian occupation.§ A tribute of one hundred talents of silver and a talent of gold was imposed upon Judea. Jehoiakim obtained this money by taxing the rich in proportion to their possessions, and this was found to be a very heavy burden. Nechoh, loaded with the wealth of Syria, returned to Egypt, taking

had no need to march up to Thafsaca, much less to the passes near Aleppo. The patriarchs going from Canaan to Padan-Aram are supposed to go straight across the desert. Genesis, ch. xxix. v. 1; xxxi. v. 23; xxxii. v. 11.

* See below, pp. 284, 298.
† And not "put him in bonds," which is an error of the copyist.
‡ 2 Kings, ch. xxiii. v. 34.
§ Psalm lxxix.

with him as captive the ill-fated Jehoahaz,* who died soon after in exile.

The dominion of Nechoh over Syria lasted about three years, and Jehoiakim seems during the whole of this time to have been in complete subjection to him. A considerable proportion of opinion in Jerusalem seems to have been favourable to Egypt, which was the country where articles of luxury were chiefly manufactured, its carriages and carved furniture being especially prized. Jehoiakim and the nobility of Jerusalem thought above all of procuring for themselves these things, and such worldly tendencies of course enraged the austere school of the prophets, who made Egypt more and more the object of their hatred and their curses.

* An allusion in Ezekiel, ch. xix. v. 4.

CHAPTER XIX.

JEHOIAKIM—THE PIETISTS IN DISGRACE.

THE sentiment which had led Josiah to show favour for the reforms preached by Jeremiah was so purely a personal feeling that three of his sons and one of his grandsons, who reigned after him, are marked with the same stigma as the worst of the kings. But we must not be led astray by these declamations, for extreme bigots are never content. What may be done for them is only their due; what is not done is a crime. It is evident that Jehoahaz, Jehoiakim, Jehoiachin, and Zedekiah were by no means princes after the *anavim's* heart. But to imagine that they put down the worship of Iahveh, of which Josiah had been the promoter, would be to form a very false conception, and that is the capital error of the books of Kings. It might be thought, in reading this very inferior work, that the kings of Judah succeeded one another like white and black, like the friends and the foes of Iahveism. If things had happened in as decisive a fashion as this, we should find a reflection of it in the book of Jeremiah. The tone of the book of Jeremiah is one of sustained anger, not an alternation of satisfaction and wrath. The truth is that the kings of Judah all admired Iahveh as the national god, their names alone sufficing to prove this. There were no impious sovereigns in those days. To deny the national god would have been to repudiate themselves; the only difference being that there were degrees in their zeal. In the eyes of some among them the worship of Iahveh was what that of Chemosh was for Mesa, what the worship of Salm was for Salmsezab. In the eyes of others, disciples of the prophets, the worship of Iahveh was big with social and political consequences; it involved a morality, a reprobation of public usages, and a contempt for military preparation which no serious patriot could approve.

The reaction which followed the death of Josiah was therefore very similar to that which followed the death of Hezekiah. The pietist sect, master of the king's conscience, had excited grave discontent among the worldly people. The king had irritated his wives and sons by his bigotry, and people had got sick of official hypocrisy. The situation was very similar to what it was in France at the end of Charles the Tenth's reign, and the condition of the religious party, after the battle of Megiddo, was the same as that in which

JEHOIAKIM—THE PIETISTS IN DISGRACE. 223

the clerical coterie found itself after 1830. Jehoiakim, who appears to have been a liberal and a moderate prince, was regarded very much in the same light as Louis Philippe is in our day by the Catholic school; he was set down as impious, though he had done no more than safeguard the most elementary rights of the Crown.

What makes it clear that the anavite movement was not persecuted, but simply that it no longer enjoyed the favour of the Court, is that this movement was not to any appreciable extent interfered with by the ill-humour of the sons and grandsons of Josiah any more than the Catholic movement was arrested by the Revolution of 1830. The twenty years which elapsed between the death of Josiah and the fall of Jerusalem were as fruitful for the development of Judaism as the preceding years. Religious reform was so sure of triumph that the good or ill will of the rulers was of mere secondary importance. The code discovered or rather put together under Josiah, although not applied in civil life, continued to exercise influence. Jeremiah's part becomes a more prominent one than ever, and around him is formed a group destined to carry with it into exile the anavite train of thought. Habakkuk, Uriah, and other prophets still keep the fire ablaze and feed the furnace. Hanan, son of Igdaliah, called "a man of God," * gathered around him numerous

* Jeremiah, ch. xxxv. v. 4.

sons in one of the *liska* or chambers of the temple, in the first floor above that of Maaseiah, son of Shallum,* the keeper of the door (that is to say, near the entrance of the grand courtyard). The uncompromising declaration that Iahveh always gave his servants, and all the more so when they disregard all human precautions, what is called Mussulman fatalism, but what is in reality Jewish fatalism, became an absolute dogma, a thorough craze.

The dynasty, with the military and patriotic party, seemed like isolated fortresses in the midst of the nation, carried off in a contrary direction by a set of zealots. With its credit and forces exhausted by pietism, despised by the saintly, the Court had come to be no more than a mere aristocracy, with no hold upon what really appealed to the soul of the people.

They were not, to all appearance, devoid of good qualities, these last princes of Judah, who courageously struggled against national disorganisation. But it is dangerous for a nation to have a religion to incubate. Nebuchadnezzar and Titus were in reality the instruments, if not of God, at all events of a divine law. The nation which labours for humanity is always a victim to the universal work which it accomplishes. In any case the existence of a lay power at Jerusalem had become an impossibility. At the first glance we find, in the history

* We may assume that he was born about 620 B.C.

of the Jewish race two elements which present a strange contrast: upon the one hand brilliant heroes after the fashion of the old Arab horsemen, the Gideons, the Sauls and the Davids; upon the other hand, the saints; morose, sordid, and monkish in their aspect. One of these elements destroyed the other. The struggle which finally eliminated from Israel manly and warlike traditions took place after the death of Josiah during the years of crisis which I still have to describe.

We have seen how Jehoahaz, during his very brief reign, excited the strong antipathies of those who had been his father's friends, while the hatred of Jeremiah and his adepts for Jehoiakim was still deeper. A religious party which has been in power and has fallen becomes furious with those who are reluctant to submit to its behests. Jehoiakim was no doubt wrong in not assuming the outward air of hopeless sorrow which the circumstances rendered advisable, but there are cases in which it is courageous to react against the general despondency. Jehoiakim was accused of building palaces in the midst of all this public distress by means of forced labour. In the very beginning of his reign, a manifesto was issued by Jeremiah in which all the regrets for the past, all the rancour against the present, are expressed in tones of concentrated bitterness.*

* Jeremiah, ch. xxii. v. 1 and following. The allusion in verse 10 to "the dead" is to Josiah, and the allusion in the same verse "him that goeth away" is to Jehoahaz.

If this speech was really made at the gate of Jehoiakim's palace, that king must be credited with the possession of at least one virtue, and that is patience. "Be just to the weak, and the dynasty will endure. If not, the city will be destroyed." This appears very moral, but poor Josiah had carried it out, and that did not prevent him from dying at eight-and-thirty. To argue, upon the morrow of Megiddo, that Josiah had been duly rewarded was to go rather too far in the way of paradox. It does not do, through excess of zeal for justice, to give to the world too defective reasons for doing what is right. The virulent hatred of luxury,* the insults levelled at Jerusalem because its houses are handsome,† the dogged determination to prevent all profane development and more especially the formation of a wealthy military class, were much more deleterious than a few fine open windows and a suite of spacious apartments in a palace. Of course, if Jehoiakim did not pay his workmen, he was wrong; but since we have lived to see how fond democratic opinion is of denouncing as robbers those who find work for the people, we have become chary of believing such allegations.

A still more violent scene occurred in the temple.‡ Shortly after the delivery of this furious

---

* Compare Jeremiah, ch. xxii. v. 13-14.

† Jeremiah, ch. xxii. v. 23.

‡ Jeremiah, ch. xxvi.

invective Jeremiah, moved by the spirit, took up a position in the sacred courtyard to address the pilgrims of Judah who had come to worship there. His tones were haughty and threatening. If the people did not observe the law which Iahveh had given them, if they did not hearken to the prophets, the temple of Jerusalem will be as Shiloh, and the city will be destroyed. At these words, the priests, the prophets, and the people rose in anger and threatened to kill him. He owed his life to the princes and officers of the palace, who set a fine example upon that occasion, by protecting the lives of their adversaries. They recalled how, in the time of Hezekiah, Micah had spoken as strongly, but had not on that account been put to death. Upon the contrary, his words were taken to heart; God was appeased, and God "repented Him of the evil." Jeremiah's strongest protector was Ahikam, the son of Shaphan, the same who, as seen above, was concerned in the episode of the discovery of the Thora.† This universally respected man threw his protection over the daring agitator, and prevented him being handed over to the people to be put to death. As a general rule, the Government displayed extreme patience towards Jeremiah, doubtless out of recollection of his connection with Josiah and of the attention which had been showered upon him.

* See above, pp. 171, 173, 192. He was the father of Godolias, see below, p. 301.

The furious utterances of Jeremiah were of almost daily occurrence. A drought, a year less favourable than the preceding one, became arguments in his hands.* The sins of the people were the cause of this, and arguments such as would be used by a man profoundly ignorant and obstinate were put in the mouth of Iahveh. He would have done with His people, and would have no more vows or burnt offerings.†

This system of terrorising, organised by an individual outside of the State, was subversive of all public order, and when Jeremiah tells us that the false prophets were hostile to the alarmists,‡ we are inclined to think that the rôles were reversed. From the earliest years of Jehoiakim Jeremiah announced the fall of Jerusalem.§ Doubtless, in his eyes, the instrument of divine punishment was not to be Egypt. The standard of Chaldæan power had not yet been raised, but Jeremiah had the conviction that the devastating force would come, as it had so often done before, from the east and from the north. The imagery derived from the battle of Megiddo abounds in his mind.‖ He declared that the future would see still worse things, and he was right; but how sad

---

* Jeremiah, ch. xiv. and beginning of ch. xv.
† Jeremiah, ch. xv. v. 1-4.
‡ Jeremiah, ch. xiv. v. 13 and following.
§ Jeremiah, ch. xiv.
‖ Jeremiah, ch. xv. v. 4-9.

it is to be right in opposition to the illusions of one's country!

Jeremiah had imitators, who, not being protected by the same respect and the same recollections, found that the authorities were much more severe, or, it may rather be said, not so lenient for their extravagant language. Jerusalem had a handful of these "tonguesters," who can only be compared to the radical journalists of our own day, and who rendered all government impossible. One, Urijah, the son of Shemaiah of Kirgath-jearim,* poured forth the most awful threats against the city and against the land. Such determined discouraging of the nation at so critical a moment was more than the king, his captains, his princes, and the whole of the military and patriotic party could bear. It is always painful for a soldier to hear it declared that his efforts are unavailing. The soldier stands in need of being encouraged, and the man who says to him, even with the best of reasons, "You are sure of defeat," is certain to exasperate him. The officers and princes resolved to kill Urijah, who fled into Egypt. Jehoiakim sent Elnathan, the son of Achbor, and several others after him, and when they had brought him back Jehoiakim "slew him with the sword, and cast his body into the graves of the common people."

An understanding, it will be seen, was impossible

* Jeremiah, ch. xxvi. v. 20, and following.

between the fanatics, who preferred seeing their country annihilated to its being less saintly than they would have it, and between soldiers, who were in no wise impious, but who were incapable of conceiving the higher phases of religion. The patriarchal simplicity which was at the bottom of the prophetic spirit did not permit of the formation of a real army. The patriarchal spirit presupposes that the tribe will not be in contact with any powerful State. The prophets were bent upon maintaining these puerile ideas at a time when a State much better organised than that was an urgent necessity. The anger therefore which they excited among sensible laymen is easy to be understood. A certain air of external swagger is the more or less necessary accompaniment of a soldier, while the royalty, upon the other hand, presupposes a palace decorated with some little style, a certain amount of pomp and show. The prophet, regarding all that as so many crimes against Iahveh, was in reality the destroyer of the State, the enemy of his country, just like the extreme democrat of our day, who will not hear of the derogations from the principle of equality which are necessary in order to have an army. A society which is too kindly in disposition is weak; the world is not made up of perfect people; there are certain abuses which are necessary and inevitable. Buddhism, which at a later date realised the moral programme of the prophets, has rendered all the populations which have given themselves up to it incapable of all political and national life.

Amid so many contradictions, leaving only the choice between errors, who can pretend to be without offence? He who is afraid of being mistaken and does not denounce any one as blind; he who does not quite know what may be the goal of humanity, but who loves it all the same, it and its work; he who seeks after the truth with hesitation, and who says to his adversary, "Perhaps you see better than I do;" he, in short, who leaves others in possession of the full liberty which he assumes for himself—that man may sleep in peace, and await with assurance the judgment of the world, whatever it may be.

CHAPTER XX.

NEBUCHADNEZZAR AND JEREMIAH.—THE SCOURGES OF GOD.

An important event took place in the fourth year of Jehoiakim's reign (605), which produced a permanent change in the political state of the East. A warrior, who seems to have been of the first order, appeared upon the world's arena, in the person of Nabokodrassar, or, according to the usual form, Nebuchadnezzar,* son of Nabopolassar, who, for nearly half a century, reproduced at Babylon the wonderful success in war which the Shalmanesers and Assurbanipals had attained in Nineveh. The scourge of God was ready. Iahveh loves war; the days of battle are his festivals. Has not the God of Israel always some dispute to settle with the nations?

Nabopolassar, hampered by the great struggles that he maintained in order to found his empire, had been forced to endure the supremacy of Necho at Carchemish. In 606, the youthful

---

* The Hebrew texts contain sometimes *Nbukdnasr* or *Nbukdrasr*, through a phonetic not graphic variation. The second form is the best.

Nebuchadnezzar attacked the Egyptian army and completely defeated it. This time, as usual, the fate of Syria hung upon a single battle !* The retreat of the remnant of the Egyptian army towards the south was a prolonged rout.†

The tidings of the battle of Carchemish produced a great impression at Jerusalem. The Iaheveists, as a rule, were more favourably disposed towards Assyria than towards Egypt. Jeremiah was beside himself. He followed the usual custom of the prophets in being always on the watch for news, and now composed a *sir* upon this subject, in imitation of the ancients,‡ in which he seems to follow the course of the battle. The events taking place by the Euphrates, the multitude of the fallen appear to him a great sacrifice § in honour of Iahveh, Lord of Hosts. A few days later Jeremiah composed a new piece, that he might have the pleasure of announcing to Egypt the impending visit of the conqueror.‖ His mockery is atrocious. Egypt is a fair heifer; a gadfly from the north will come to madden her. Her mercenaries are there, in the lower lands of the Nile, like fattened oxen. Woe to them!

From this time the gloomy giant of Jerusalem has found his man. In his eyes, Nebuchadnezzar is a servant of God,¶ a minister of God, executing

* 2 Kings, ch. xxiv. v. 7.   † Jeremiah, ch. xlvi.
‡ Jeremiah, ch. xlvi. v. 1-12.   § וכח.
‖ Ch. xlvi. v. 13 and following.
¶ Jeremiah, ch. xxv. v. 9; ch. xxvii. v. 6; ch. xliii. v. 11.

his decrees. He always alludes to him with a kind of religious awe. The theory of the scourges of God, so dear to the fathers of the Church, now commences. God strikes the nations with terrible instruments, which he destroys after he has used them. He punishes through men whom he afterwards punishes in their turn. This philosophy of history, which became the tenet of Bossuet and of modern Catholicism, is due to Jeremiah. In the surates of Jeremiah, previous to the ruin of Jerusalem, the reverse action of the scourge, broken in its turn,* is not clearly expressed, but after the captivity his disciples completed the theory by slight interpolations.†

According to the vision of the furious zealot the earth becomes a field of carnage. Corpses cover the land like a dunghill. This time Iahveh triumphs in the wickedness of men! ‡ This delicious vista entrances the sinister visionary. "Terror on every side" § is his watchword. All the enemies of Iahveh

* The idea of the punishment of the scourge is clearly found in Habbakuk. See below, p. 242.

† Chapter xxv. of Jeremiah has unquestionably received some interpolations after the captivity. This is proved by comparing the Hebrew with the Greek text. Notice v. 18 particularly. Verses 11-14 and the four last words of v. 26 are written by a disciple of Jeremiah, but they are quite in the spirit of the master. It is possible that the whole chapter may be from the disciple, who added ch. l., li. Verse 7 of ch. xxvii. also appears to be an interpolation; it is missing from the Greek.

‡ Jeremiah, ch. xxv. v. 32 and following.

§ Jeremiah, ch. xlix. v. 29 : מגור מסביב.

will be exterminated. We have explained elsewhere*
that the worshipper of Iahveh is always in some
degree the worshipper of force. At this time the
god of Jeremiah was really the sword of Nebuchadnezzar, which he looked upon as the sword of
Iahveh.† He apostrophises it as though he disposed of it.

This cruel survey, this geography of massacre
and hatred, called *Onera* ‡ in the Middle Ages,
which so strongly affected the Joachimite imagination in the thirteenth century,§ resembles the
howling of a wild beast at the smell of blood.
Philistines,‖ Tyrians, Sidonians, Cyprians, Egyptians, Medes, Elamites, Moabites,¶ Ammonites,**
Edomites,†† Hamath, Arpad, Damascus,‡‡ are all
doomed to destruction. The Kedarites and other
Arab tribes can only hide themselves in holes,
Nebuchadnezzar the king of Babylon had decreed
their ruin.§§

* Vol. ii. p. 394, 395 and following.

† Ch. xlvii. v. 6-7 : חרב יחוח, *mucro Domini*.

‡ Ch. xlvi., xlvii., xlviii., xlix. Compare the enumeration,
ch. xxv. v. 18 and following.

§ See *Nouvelles études d'hist. relig.*, p. 237.

‖ Ch. xlvi. The title placed at the head of this chapter by the
scholiasts is erroneous; it is not found in the manuscript used by
the Alexandrine translators.

¶ Ch. xlviii., partly taken from Jonah the son of Amittai,
already copied by Isaiah (ch. xv., xvi.), and partly from the
canticle upon the taking of Heshbon (Numbers, ch. xxi.).

** Ch. xlix. v. 1-6.   †† Ch. xlix. v. 7-22.

‡‡ Ch. xlix. v. 23-27.   §§ Ch. xlix. v. 28- 3.

The terrible joy displayed by the Jewish prophet at the extermination which is to befall these peaceful tribes, quietly living upon the fruits of their labour,* is something horrible, and the sympathy expressed by the man of god for the Tamerlane who is to destroy them is even more so. The devastating Iahveh, to whom Attila is a perfect servant, represents Jeremiah's ideal. The spectacle of this destruction enchants him; he applauds it and delights in it. The frightful descriptions which fill the *Onera* are perhaps the chapters in which Jeremiah has shown the most talent. He revels in them like a mist of blood. The idea that force represents the will of Iahveh, the dreadful expression of "god of armies," † the idea that the supreme justice is executed through battles, scenes from which God is far absent, all this is truly the nocturnal side of Jeremiah. He approves of Nebuchadnezzar because Nebuchadnezzar crushes all civil and industrial civilisations, which his patriarchal instinct leads him to detest. To him destruction represents strength, and therefore it must be a proof of Iahveh's approbation. At a later period Christian teaching abused these ideas in a deplor-

* Compare Judges, ch. xviii. v. 7.

† We allude to the idea only; for the expression of *Sabaoth* retains, in Jeremiah and the most modern Hebrew writers, the same meaning that it had with the most ancient prophets. The translation κύριος τῶν δυνάμεων comes from the Alexandrine translators, who, themselves, in many cases put Σαβαώθ or παντοκράτωρ. The Oriental translations have never admitted the sense of armies.

able manner. The hideous laudations of successful massacre which have so often sullied Catholic documents are derived from the book of Jeremiah, one of the most dangerous portions of the biblical canon. No, the *mucro Domini* is not in any man's hands, nor does it work for any one. Attila is not the minister of God in any sense. He personates evil, the negative of God.

From Carchemis, Nebuchadnezzar advanced towards Egypt by the traditional route through Cœle-Syria, adopted by the Assyrian expeditions. He marched slowly, subduing the populations as he passed through them.* Jeremiah's enthusiasm for the invader redoubled as he drew nearer to Judea. He probably believed that Nebuchadnezzar would depose Jehoiakim, and that the crisis would lead to the massacre of those who had compromised themselves in the Egyptian occupation. As the latter were also his personal opponents, he hoped in this way to witness the end of the enemies of Iahveh.

* A curious monument of the passage of Nebuchadnezzar existed at Wadi Brissa, near Riblah, at the foot of Djebel-Akkar; but unfortunately it was nearly destroyed a few years ago. See Pognon, *les Inscr. babyl. du Wadi Brissa* (Paris, 1887). The inscription of Wadi Brissa, like all the inscriptions of Nabuchadnezzar, related chiefly to the buildings he had made at Babylon and at Borsippa; however this one appears to have been more topical (See Pognon, p. 21-22). Another inscription of Nabuchadnezzar is to be seen at the mouth of the Dog River, near Beyrout. Sayce, in the *Proceedings of the Soc. of Bibl. Arch.*, November, 1881, pp. 9 and following; Schrader, p. 364. This stele is nearly illegible.

In his exaggerated language, Jeremiah seems unable to weigh his words. He acted like a French journalist who, in 1870, might, in all good faith, have called the Prussians the ministers of God, have applauded the defeats caused by our errors, and have predicted worse disasters in the future if the people did not reform. The ferocious joy which the prophet affected was only counterfeit, a figure of rhetoric. But what a defiance to public opinion such an attitude became at that time! Jeremiah appears to have chosen the most critical moment in Jehoiakim's reign to carry out one of his boldest projects, for impressing the people and imposing his ideas of reform upon the obdurate.

As yet, Jeremiah had not written his prophecies,* but he now thought that, united in one volume and adapted to the terrors of the Chaldean invasion, the predictions relating to Judah added to those referring to the other nations, would produce a great effect.† He therefore took a roll and dictated all his former prophecies to one of his disciples, Baruch, son of Neriah, brother to Seraiah,‡ an important personage at the court. Soon afterwards a great assemblage of people from all the country took place at Jerusalem to celebrate a fast (December, 605). The courts of the temple were crowded, and Jeremiah

* Vol. ii. pp. 355 and following.
† Jeremiah, ch. xxxvi.
‡ Jeremiah, li. 59.

announced his intention of going there, but at the last moment he feigned that something prevented him from carrying out this arrangement, and sent Baruch instead, commanding him to read the volume which had been dictated to him aloud to the people. The courts of the temple were surrounded by *liskoth* or *cellæ* which, lighted by the doors only, resembled the *qobbé* of the Mahomedan mosques, so that any one, standing on the threshold, could address all present. Baruch chose the *cella* of Gemariah, the son of Shaphan the scribe, in the upper court at the entry of the new gate of the temple, and installed himself there. An immense effect was produced by the contents of the volume, and Micaiah, the son of Gemariah, seeing the people's emotion, at once went down to the scribes' chamber in the royal palace.

All the ministers, Elishama the sofer, Delaiah the son of Shemaiah, Elnathan the son of Achbor, Gemariah the son of Shaphan, and Zedekiah the son of Hananiah happened at the moment to be assembled there. Micaiah related to them the substance of Baruch's communication to the people, and they sent a messenger to the temple to fetch the imprudent reader, in order that he might re-read the manuscript before them. The terrible words raised great alarm in all present, for, though the harshness of Jeremiah's denunciations was well known, this collection of his gloomy predictions produced an impression which made them seem quite new. It was said that the splenetic prophet had purposely condensed in these pages all the evil which Iahveh designed to bring upon his people. The ministers questioned Baruch upon the manner in which the roll had been dictated, and advised him and Jeremiah to conceal themselves immediately. They then went to the king, told him what had occurred, and, at his command, showed him the book which had caused so much excitement.

A council was held in the king's chamber in the winter palace. A lighted brazier stood in front of the king's seat, because of the severity of the season; and the ministers all stood beside him. Scarcely three or four chapters had been read when the king's anger broke forth. The words contained in the volume, "The king of Babylon will destroy the land, and will exterminate both man and beast," shocked him, not unreasonably. He took the roll in one hand, the scribe's penknife in the other, and commenced cutting the manuscript into pieces, throwing them into the fire until the roll was all burnt.

The princes standing round did not share the king's assurance. Some of them hearing these atrocious threats, wished to rend their clothes, as Josiah had done under similar circumstances. Elnathan, Delaiah, and Gemariah implored the king not to burn the roll which contained the words of Iahveh, but Jehoiakim was inflexible. He would not leave one fragment of the roll unburnt, and ordered Jerahmeel, the qualified *ben ham melek*, Seraiah the son of Azriel, and Shelemiah the son of Abdeel, to arrest Jeremiah and Baruch.

According to the words of the enthusiastic Jeremaist, who has transmitted this record to us, "Iahveh hid them." The royal precautions were useless. Jeremiah once more dictated to Baruch the words which Jehoiakim believed effectually suppressed, adding to them new and more terrible threats. The heavenly voice again repeated that Jehoiakim should have no successor, that his body should be cast outside the city, exposed to the heat and cold, that Jerusalem and Judah should be totally destroyed. Nothing could soften the furious prophet. Less implacable than his master, Baruch found it hard to write down such terrible words against his native land.* The dreadful predictions which he copied into the roll troubled his mind, and he complained bitterly to Iahveh of the uncongenial task which he had imposed upon him. Iahveh deigned to speak to him, to revive his courage, but his words appear to us more forcible than consoling. In a catastrophe which will overwhelm the whole human race it is scarcely worth while asking to be excepted. Baruch's life shall be safe wherever he may be, let him be content with that assurance.

The apparition of this great military power which appeared to be the grinding stone of Iahveh, ex-

* Jeremiah, ch. xlv.

cited the popular imagination to the highest degree. About the same time, the inspired Habakkuk * issued amongst the pietists some prophecies strongly resembling those of Jeremiah, yet superior, through the literary talent displayed in them.

Habakkuk, less unjust than Jeremiah, expresses pity for the victims and anger against the invaders.† God will punish them in their turn, for, after all, they are more guilty than those whom they punish.

We are not accustomed to such protestations against triumphant violence from Jeremiah. Habakkuk further consoles us by assuring us that the fortresses built with the sweat of the nations will not stand.

Habakkuk was a patriot, Jeremiah a fanatic. But historical fame is reserved for the man who exaggerated. The sensible writer is almost forgotten; but the furious declaimer, who never sacrificed one grain of personal enmity to the good of his country, has become one of the corner stones in the religious edifice of humanity.

* Hab. ch. i. v. 5 and following. See above, p. 143.
† Hab. ch. ii.

CHAPTER XXI.

THE FIRST CAPTIVITY.

JEREMIAH's antipatriotic hopes were disappointed. Nebuchadnezzar went to Jerusalem, but he committed no hostile action there, and Jehoiakim retained his throne upon the condition of recognising the sovereignty of Babylon.[*] No doubt, Jehoahaz, who had encouraged the Assyrian alliance and had fallen victim to it, was dead in Egypt or he would probably have been recalled. It appears, however, that Nebuchadnezzar never crossed the frontier of Egypt.[†] He retraced his steps and hastened back to Babylon; it is believed that tidings of the death of his father, Nabopolassar, hastened his return.[‡]

By this death Nebuchadnezzar officially received the title of *King of Babylon* (604),[§] which had been erroneously given to him in Syria for some years;[||]

---

[*] 2 Kings, ch. xxiv. v. 1.
[†] Maspero, pp. 540-541.
[‡] Berose, in Jos., *Ant.*, X. xi. 1.
[§] Jeremiah, ch. xxv. v. 1.
[||] Jeremiah, ch. xlvi. v. 2, 26, and ch. xxxvi. v. 29.

his father had reigned twenty years; and he occupied the throne of Babylon for forty-three years.

This state of peace in subjection lasted three or four years in Judea. During this time the prophetic agitation redoubled. The king and the party of the *anavim* were always on bad terms.* The latter continued to assert that all military preparations were an insult to God, that fasting was better, and that the prayers of holy men were the best weapons of war. This pious enthusiasm increased in proportion to the diminution of the material forces of the land. What circumstances induced Jehoiakim to abandon his policy of resignation and madly rebel against Babylon (601)? We have only suppositions upon this point. The origin of this error, which led to such terrible consequences, seems to have laid in the hostile relations of the kingdom of Judah with the Arameans of Damascus, the Ammonites, and Moabites. One of the bad sides of the character of Israel is seen in the fact that, as a rule, the nation was unpopular with its neighbours, and usually lived on bad terms with them. In Deuteronomy this ill-feeling towards the Ammonites and Moabites is given as a precept.† During the last years of Jehoiakim the kingdom of Judah was continually invaded by bands of Arameans, Ammonites, and Moabites, who, no doubt, acted under orders from Nebuchad-

---

* 2 Kings. ch. xxiii. v. 37.
† Deuteronomy, ch. xxiii. v. 4 and following.

nezzar; and, in fact, companies of Chaldeans were found amongst the invaders.*

These frightful ravages have left their traces in the writings of Jeremiah.† The land of Iahveh is devastated by all the beasts of creation. Brigands devour it. The labourer sows but does not reap. The sword of Iahveh is drawn. Israel is punished by its unbelieving neighbours, who have taught it to swear by Baal. But if, later on, the latter wish to adopt the laws of Israel and to swear by Iahveh, he will receive them. They shall be incorporated with the Israelitish nation. Otherwise they shall be exterminated. The disturbed state of Syria raised the most singular hopes in vivid imaginations, side by side with the most gloomy prospects.

Jehoiakim appears to have coped bravely with this desperate situation, which probably lasted two or three years. Behind the brigandage of the nomads loomed the Chaldean power with its train of horrors. Egypt was reduced to impotence. Since the battle of Carchemish it had never recrossed the torrent of el-Arisch;‡ yet it considerably forced the policy of Jerusalem. It would certainly have been wiser to submit to the will of Iahveh, manifested to Jeremiah by the sword of Nebuchadnezzar. We know too little about the political history of this period to be able to form a single conjecture

---

* 2 Kings, ch. xxiv. v. 2.
† Jeremiah, ch. xii. v. 7-17.
‡ 2 Kings, ch. xxiv. v. 7. Compare Jeremiah, ch. xxii. v. 20.

upon what the unfortunate princes, upon whom the sad fate of governing a dying nation devolved, might or might not have done. We do not even know how Jehoiakim ended his life. But it appears most pro' 'ble that he died at Jerusalem, and was buried with Manasseh, Amon, and Josiah in the cave of the garden of Uzza.* But, just then, the political horizon was extremely gloomy; the great Assyrian expedition destined to crush the rebellion of Jehoiakim was probably already advancing. It may be, even, that Jehoiakim was killed in some fight on the outposts. Jeremiah† had prophesied during the king's life that his body should not be buried, but cast forth beyond the gates of the city. But Jeremiah had also said that he should have no successor, and this prediction was certainly not fulfilled.‡

Jehoiakim was only thirty-six when he died (598). His son Jeconiah or Coniah, aged eighteen, was then proclaimed king. At this epoch it was customary for the monarch to change his name upon ascending the throne, and Coniah therefore

---

* 2 Kings, ch. xxiv. v. 6; the Greek text of 2 Chronicles, ch. xxxvi. v. 8 (cf. Thenius, p. 446). The received version of the Chronicles was written with the object of vindicating Jeremiah.

† Jeremiah, ch. xxii. v. 19; ch. xxxvi. v. 30. See above, p. 143.

‡ Jeremiah himself recognised that Jeconiah really occupied the throne of David, ch. xiii. v. 13. The editor of Jeremiah, after the captivity, evidently paid little attention to some of the unfulfilled rophecies

THE FIRST CAPTIVITY.

called himself Jehoiachin,* which has the same meaning. His mother was Nehusta, the daughter of Elnathan of Jerusalem, probably the same person as Elnathan, son of Achbor, whom we have more than once seen fulfilling the duties of the king's minister † in his struggle against the prophets.

Nehusta occupied the position of Sultane Validé ‡ with the powers of Regent.§ Like her father Elnathan she believed in the necessity of restraining the intemperate language of the prophets. The young king soon possessed a large harem,‖ and Jeremiah pursued the unfortunate young prince and his mother with the same hatred that he had displayed towards Jehoiakim.

But events were hastening forward. If the Chaldean army had not reached the borders of Judea when Jehoiakim died, it appeared there a few days after his death. First came Nebuchadnezzar's generals with bands of Chaldeans and Arameans.¶ They commenced by seizing the cities in the south of Judah, which offered the least resistance.** As the cities were taken, the trans-

* Jeremiah always calls him Jeconiah. The prophet had the habit of using the original name. For instance, he calls Jehoahaz by his first name Shallum.

† Jeremiah, ch. xxvi. v. 22 ; ch. xxxvi. v. 12, 25.

‡ חגבירה. Jeremiah, ch. xiii. v. 18.

§ Jeremiah, ch. xiii. v. 18.

‖ 2 Kings, ch. xxiv. v. 15.

¶ Jeremiah, ch. xxxv. v. 11.

** Jeremiah, ch. xiii. v. 19, and the incident of the Rechabites (Kenites), who sought refuge in Jerusalem.

portation of the people was carried out upon a large scale. Jerusalem was crowded with fugitives. One would have thought that the approach of so great a danger would have caused all party hatred to disappear. But it had no effect. Two manifestoes from Jeremiah appeared at the very moment that the siege was about to commence. They are two diatribes against Jehoiachin and his mother. The prophet was furious because they did not ask for counsel from Iahveh, that is, from himself. Israel had been spoilt by strangers. It was a marred garment, because it had been plunged in strange waters. Iahveh would therefore show no mercy. "Humble yourselves, sit ye down low," he cries to the young king and to the queen-mother, "Jerusalem shall endure the greatest insults. Iahveh himself shall discover her skirts before her face, and her shame shall appear." Her prostitution has been seen even upon the hills in the field.*

Chapters xxii. and xxiii. of Jeremiah† are still more personal against Jehoiachin and his mother Nehusta. Jerusalem the faithless spouse has fled to the mountains. Her lovers (the heathen allies upon whom she depended in her struggle against Babylon‡) are in captivity. During that time she dwelt in cedar.§

* Jeremiah, ch. xiii.
† Jeremiah, ch. xxii. v. 20 and following, unto v. 8 of ch. xxiii.
‡ 2 Kings, ch. xxiv. v. 7.
§ Allusion to Jehoiachin's palaces. Jeremiah, ch. xxii. v. 7 and following.

Thus the house of David is repudiated. The faithful people shall have no more kings. It is no longer question of a kingdom, but of gathering together the scattered Israelites, of making a fold where holy men could multiply and become a new stem. A mysterious scion of the house of David (in a symbolical sense) would preside over this new state of Israel, and would be the centre of the perfect world of the future. This theocratic king is described by Jeremiah from the model of Josiah. He is less a king than a shepherd; the people whom he governs is no longer a nation, but a flock. We see that Christianity is only the realisation of these dreams. Jeremiah is the most radical destroyer that any royal house ever found opposed to it; he is also one of the most powerful creators in the religious world. Let us forget the odious side of such a position. The interests of the political and spiritual cities are always conflicting. Glory to those prophets of Israel who with great ability commenced a struggle which has filled the centuries, and is not yet ended. But we must pity Israel, who in this terrible conflict has lost its terrestrial existence, its native land!

The storm drew nearer each day. Those who were rich enough to make the journey took refuge in Egypt.* Fugitives from the open country crowded into Jerusalem. The *liskoth* of the temple were

---

* Jeremiah, ch. xxiv. v. 8.

filled with people. Amongst these refugees was one interesting group, the Rechabites.* These ascetics were of Kenite origin, bound by a kind of vow to the ancient patriarchal life, which displayed some analogy to the schools of the prophets, and they received many marks of esteem from the pietists. Their family, however, was quite distinct from the Beni-Israel,† and it is doubtful whether they accepted the Thora and the revelations which the prophets endeavoured to impose upon Judah. Their admission into Jerusalem was therefore preceded by some hesitation. Jeremiah decided the question; he insisted that the Rechabites should be fully received into the Church of Israel. They were lodged in the *liska* of the temple conceded to the school of Hanan, the son of Igdaliah, who led a similar life. This apartment was near to the *lisku* of the *sarim*, above that of Maaseiah, the son of Shallum, the keeper of the door. The chief of the Rechabites, Jaazaniah, the son of Jeremiah, the son of Habazziniah, impressed every one by his devout life. Jeremiah made it the subject of an exhortation to the Jews to be as faithful as these Kenites to the covenant made by their fathers.

The preparations for besieging Jerusalem were commenced before the arrival of Nebuchadnezzar. All the machinery for conducting a siege revealed

* Jeremiah, ch. xxxv.

† The names of *Jonadab, Juazaniah, Jeremiah*, and even *Habazziniah* are Iahveist.

THE FIRST CAPTIVITY. 251

to us by the Assyrian bas-reliefs was brought against the city. All the members of the religious party were inside the town, Jeremiah, Habakkuk, Hanan son of Igdaliah, the Rechabites, and Ezekiel, no doubt expecting one of those miraculous interventions which were reported in the time of Hezekiah. Habakkuk, to encourage his fellow-citizens during the siege, composed a psalm* in imitation of the ancient canticles, opening as they did† by a brilliant picture of the theophany of Sinai. No doubt the image of the impending apparition of Iahveh for his great day was prefigured in this theophany. Iahveh, still a god of thunder, will come from the south to the assistance of his anointed,‡ that is, of his chosen people, whose distress has now reached a climax.

The young king and his *sarim* bravely defended themselves until the approach of Nebuchadnezzar in person was announced. At that epoch a siege lasted a long time. The Jews may have hoped that within a certain time Nebuchadnezzar might die, or be diverted by other objects from an enterprise which could be only secondary in his eyes. But when tidings arrived that the all-powerful king was coming himself to superintend the military operations, the regent's councillors decided that

---

* Notice the technical words: סלה, בנגינות, למנצח, תפלה, על שגיונו.

† See vol. i. p. 165 and following.

‡ Verse xiii. משיחך in parallelism with עמך.

the city must surrender. When Nebuchadnezzar approached, no doubt from the north, Jehoiachin marched out of the city, with the regent, his mother, Nehusta, all his household, his officers, ministers, and eunuchs, and surrendered themselves to the King of Babylon. They seem to have been received very harshly. Jehoiachin was deposed, and his extreme youth did not save him from being carried into captivity, from which he was not freed until thirty-six years later. In all he had reigned only three months.*

Nebuchadnezzar neither destroyed the city nor massacred the population. He carried out in Jerusalem the system of transportation which Shalmaneser had adopted in Samaria and the kingdom of the North, but on a smaller scale. The king, the queen-mother, the king's wives, his eunuchs, all his household, officers, ministers, officials, the well-to-do people, and every man who could carry arms, were transported to Babylon or to Mesopotamia.† According to an apparently ancient and authentic estimate,‡ three thousand and twenty-three people were carried away: about one-sixth of the population of Jerusalem. But it comprised the whole civil and military aristocracy. The conquerors

* 2 Kings, ch. xxiv. v. 10 and following; Ezekiel, ch. xvii. v. 11 and following.

† Jeremiah, ch. xxix. v. 1 and following.

‡ Jeremiah, ch. lii. v. 28. The account in 2 Kings, ch. xxiv. v. 16 is exaggerated and contradictory.

were under a common delusion that in removing the head of the nation they effectually crippled it. They did not realise that an intense vitality diffused through a large body reasserts itself, even when the vital parts have been amputated. A garden is destroyed by cutting off the flowers, but the growth of a meadow is increased by mowing. The system of class division in Israel was not strong enough for the transportation of the important men to arrest the movement of the nation. Another circumstance rendered the arrangement made by Nebuchadnezzar, in order to crush the hierosolymite opposition, almost useless in attaining the end he had in view.

In the long list of those carried into captivity, given in the book of Kings, there is no mention of priests, Levites, or prophets.* They all remained in Jerusalem, surrounding the temple, despoiled, it is true, of its most valuable treasures, but doubly venerated on that account. Now, the spirit of the nation was in a great measure embodied in the Levitical and prophetic party. Jeremiah was not transported. Did the Assyrians realise that this rough opponent had been their most powerful auxiliary? This is not probable. They did not enter into these questions of sects, and neither Hanan, the son of Igdaliah, nor Habakkuk, appear

* The book of Jeremiah, ch. xix. v. 1-2, mentions priests and prophets at Babylon (towards 592), but too casually for us to draw any conclusion from the words.

to have been disturbed. There were many exceptions to this rule, since Ezekiel, who formed part of the first list of captives, was a *cohen*. But if a great number of the *cohanim* had formed part of this first transportation, the author of the book of Kings would certainly have mentioned it; as to the Levites, doubtless in his eyes they formed part of the *dallat am ha-arec*, the inferior mass of the people, who were not worth the trouble of transportation.

Nebuchadnezzar therefore pursued a very superficial policy at Jerusalem. He acted like a power that, seeking to destroy the ascendency of Paris, drove out of it all the rich and important men, leaving all the people, the journalists, and political writers. It was easy to foresee that the incendiary elements which remained in the city would again take fire. The rough Chaldeans only recognised material strength, and apparently the military power of Judah was annihilated. The poverty must have been overwhelming, the country was devastated, and the agricultural population had almost disappeared.

Everything valuable, according to the ideas of the time, became the prey of the conqueror.* The treasures of the temple and of the royal palace were carried away by the Chaldeans. The golden vessels of the temple were broken in pieces and removed. The brazen vessels of the temple and of the wealthy

* 2 Kings, ch. xxiv. v. 13 and following.

houses of Jerusalem were left.* Those portions of the temple that were of brass, particularly the two pillars, the great sea, and the bases, were equally respected.† The religious services were probably continued even during the last fatal days of the siege, for no doubt the Levites and *anavim* found excellent reasons that confirmed them in their faith at that disastrous time. These misfortunes had all overtaken the city in order that a prophecy of Isaiah should be accomplished,‡ which punished the vanity displayed by Hezekiah in showing his treasures to the messengers of Merodach-Baladan.

The blow dealt at Jerusalem by Nebuchadnezzar's expedition was not therefore so serious as might be supposed.§ Jehoiachin's uncle, Mattaniah, son of Josiah and Hamutal, who was then thirty-one years of age, was placed upon the throne by the King of Babylon, instead of the deposed king.∥ His royal name was Sidqiahou, which the Greek and Latin versions have changed into Zedekiah.

---

* Jeremiah. ch. 27, v. 19 and following.

† Jeremiah, *l. c.*

‡ 2 Kings, ch. xx. v. 12 and following. (Is. ch. xxxix.) See above, p. 100.

§ There is scarcely any trace of it in Jeremiah.

∥ According to Kings, 2 ch. xxiv. v. 18, he was only twenty-one. He would then have been born thirteen years after his uterine brother Jehoahaz. This is contrary to all the customs of the East, where the women usually have their children in rapid succession at about eighteen or twenty years of age. Besides, the passage in Jeremiah, ch. lii. v. 10, infers that his children were adults in 588.

CHAPTER XXII.

THE REIGN OF ZEDEKIAH.

ZEDEKIAH, like his brother Jehoahaz, had imbibed from his mother, Hamutal, a strong prejudice against the pietists, who had directed the national policy during the later years of his father's reign. Jeremiah and the prophets were almost as hostile to him as to Jehoahaz, Jehoiakim, or Jehoiachin, solely because he was tolerant; and the tolerance of the sovereigns opened the door to a religious eclecticism, insufferable to the fanatics.* It appears that this eclecticism permitted idols to be installed even in the temple itself.† In any case the practice of burning incense on many of the roofs in honour of Baal ‡ had recommenced, heathen rites were secretly practised,§ and cases of Molochism had

* See below, pp. 267-268, the description of the customs o. Jerusalem given by Ezekiel.
† Jeremiah, ch. xxxii. p. 34.
‡ Jeremiah, ch. xxxii. p. 34. See above, p. 149.
§ Ezekiel, ch. xxiii. v. 11 and following.

THE REIGN OF ZEDEKIAH.

again occurred in Ben-Hinnom.* Jeremiah, therefore, never for one day during the whole reign of eleven years, ceased uttering the most violent denunciations against the official world. Sometimes he is animated by a real feeling of justice.† But, as a rule, this furious soul is less filled with melancholy than with anger. On the whole, circumstances had verified his prophecies; but this only rendered him more imperious and more exacting. Far from becoming reconciled to the conditions of social life in the city, he plunged deeper into contumacy in his foolish admiration for the Rechabites and his indifference to profane civilisation.

Zedekiah appears to have tried every means of saving the remnant of his lost nation. The journey apparently made to Babylon in the fourth year of his reign‡ was intended to deceive his suzerain. During this time he negotiated and armed. A dynasty, even in decadence, is always a centre of the national spirit.§ Towards the year 595, the kings of Edom, Moab, Ammon, Tyre, and Sidon, held a sort of congress through their ambassadors at Jerusalem, no doubt in order to form an alliance against the

---

* Jeremiah, ch. xxxii. v. 35 (cf. ch. vii. v. 30 and following); Ezekiel, ch. xvi. v. 20-21; ch. xxiii. v. 37; perhaps ch. xliii. v. 7.

† Jeremiah, ch. xxi. v. 11-12.

‡ Jeremiah, ch. li. v. 59.

§ Jeremiah, ch. xxvii. and xxviii. The first verse of ch. xxvii. contains one evident mistake of the copyist, *Jehoiakim* for *Zedekiah*. The verses 7 and 19-22 of ch. xxvii., which are missing in the Greek, are suspected of at least partial interpolation.

common enemy. Hope reawakened on every side. Several prophets arose, especially one Hananiah, the son of Azzur of Gibeon, and in the name of Iahveh announced that the rule of Babylon would soon come to an end. Hananiah went to and fro in the city, repeating the words: "I have broken the yoke of the king of Babylon! I will break the yoke of the king of Babylon!" The relief was to come in two years. A great number of the people believed in these promises, which flattered their hopes and their passions.

Jeremiah felt that these dangerous illusions could only be counteracted by methods of extreme violence. To render his belief in the certainty of the future captivity more visible, he went through the streets and public places for several consecutive days, wearing pieces of wood bound with cords upon his neck, in imitation of the yoke worn by oxen at the plough. He also pretended to have received a command to send similar yokes to the five kings, with the following message, supposed to be dictated by Iahveh: "I have made the earth, the man and the beast that are upon the face of the earth, by my great power and by my outstretched arm; and I give it unto whom it seemeth right unto me. And now have I given all these lands into the hand of Nebuchadnezzar, the King of Babylon, my servant; and the beasts of the field also have I given to serve him. And it shall come to pass, that the nation and the kingdom which will not serve the same Nebuchadnezzar, King of Babylon, and that will not put their neck under the yoke of the King of Babylon, that nation will I punish, saith Iahveh, with the sword, and with the famine, and with the pestilence, until I have consumed them by his hand." The horrible doctrine, that a man is guilty of sin if he do not submit to the tyranny of the day, because it is supposed to have received a commission from God, was preached by Jeremiah in every key. A stranger, an infidel, shall enjoy the rights of legitimacy, solely because he is a great destroyer, impudently asserting himself. Iahveh is on the side of Nebuchadnezzar; therefore, whoever resists Nebuchadnezzar resists Iahveh. The less pessimist and more patriotic prophets, who announced that the enterprise would succeed, were liars. "They prophesy a lie unto you, to remove you far from your land; and that I should drive you out and that ye should perish. But the nation that shall bring their neck under the yoke of the King of Babylon, and serve him, that nation will I let remain in their own land, and they shall till it and dwell therein." "Bend your neck," said Jeremiah to Zedekiah, "that ye may live." Iahveh hath decreed that all who will not serve the King of Babylon shall perish. Iahveh hath commanded the false prophets to prophesy falsely; so that he may have a reason for dispersing the rebels and causing them to perish. One of the promises most frequently repeated by the prophets who opposed Jeremiah, particularly by Hananiah, was that one of the first fruits of the victory of the allied kingdoms of the region of the Jordan, besides the return of Jehoiakim and his fellow captives, would be the restitution to Jerusalem of the golden vases belonging to the temple, which Nebuchadnezzar had carried away. This spoliation had reduced the temple to a state of poverty that weighed painfully upon every Irsaelitish heart. The possibility of contradiction upon such an important point irritated Jeremiah considerably. He cared little for the temple or for the vessels used in the ritual. The desolation of the sacred building was rather a confirmation of his threats. His reply to the hopes awakened by Hananiah is curious.* The duty of the true prophets is to predict evil. When they prophesy good things, there is only the event to prove their mission; the presumption, according to the prophetic history of the past, being always in favour of the dismal hypothesis.

The people were evidently predisposed towards Hananiah. One day, when Jeremiah, wearing the yoke upon his neck, was seated in the court of the temple, in the presence of the priests and people, Hananiah, emboldened by the unpopularity of the fanatic, who frequented all the public places, defy-

* Jeremiah, ch. xxvii. v. 16 and following. The account is confused. There are two texts superposed. The second text, 21-22, has been substituted *post eventum*.

ing the hopes of the patriots, gave vent to his anger. He took the yoke from the neck of the prophet of evil and broke it, uttering these solemn words: "Thus saith Iahveh, Even so have I broken the yoke of the King of Babylon. Within two full years will I break the yoke of Nebuchadnezzar, the King of Babylon, from off the neck of all the nations." No doubt his words were vigorously applauded, for Jeremiah retired in confusion. In a few days he regained his ascendency: "Thou hast broken the bars of wood; but thou shalt make in their stead bars of iron;" thus indicating that the revolt, for which they were preparing, would cause a state of tolerable subjection to be replaced by a state of unendurable slavery. Alas! he was right. It is a terrible fact that, at certain times, there is no medium between unpalatable wisdom and the wilful blindness demanded by patriotism.

Hananiah died two months later. It was asserted that Jeremiah had foretold his approaching death as a punishment for the false mission he had assumed.

The correspondence between Jerusalem and the captives in Babylon was very active; and it contributed in no small measure to fan the fire on both sides. Overflowing piety impregnated all the messages that came from the banks of the Euphrates. Imagine, in the years that followed 1871, the letters that might have passed between the exiles of Noumea and the communists left in Paris, they would give some idea of the mutual excitement which this correspondence must have maintained in the two fractions of the Jewish family. The letter written in the style of a sermon, the epistle (*iggeret*), became the usual type of the sacred literature of the Jews, and replaced the prophetic surate, which was intended for recitation.

One of Jeremiah's prophetic visions relates to this period, and clearly expresses the opposition which existed between the two divisions of Judah.* In it we plainly see the little value which the prophet placed upon the small kingdom which still survived, and the frankness with which he proclaimed it, at the risk of discouraging those who had endeavoured to save something from the recent shipwreck of their native land. Two baskets of figs were placed before the temple, the one full of good figs, the other of bad ones. The first represented the captives in Chaldea; the second, those who had remained in Jerusalem, particularly Zedekiah, his officers, and the Jews who had settled in Egypt. Repentance, according to the Iahveist ideas, was a purifying sentiment. The exiles had expiated their faults; Iahveh had touched and purified them; Iahveh would replant and restore them. On the other hand, Jerusalem did not reform, but refused to

* Ch. xxiv., partly repeated in ch. xxix. v. 16-26, a transposed passage. We must remember that these surates were only written during the captivity, and therefore several points may have been forced in them.

listen to the true prophets. Zedekiah and his court would be exterminated; the house of David was nearly ended.

In fact, from this time, the idea became established that the band carried into captivity by the Chaldeans, and to which ten years later a large number was added, was the true Israel. Jeremiah reserved all his sympathy for these unfortunates.* The exiles of the Euphrates contributed by their letters to the inculcation of the same feeling. They looked upon themselves as victims already forgiven, whilst Jerusalem continued to irritate Iahveh. A group of Hierosolymites had been sent in cantonments to a place called Tel-Abib, upon the borders of the Chebar, a tributary of the Euphrates which descended from the mountains in the interior of Mesopotamia. Amongst them was the young priest from Jerusalem, Ezekiel, the son of Buzi, whom we saw carried away by the conquerors in 598. He was the centre of a pious group which met in his house and listened to him as an oracle.† Five years after his transportation the Spirit of God came upon him and showed him strange visions. The turn of the prophetic imagination had changed. Their conceptions of the glory of Iahveh had become more complicated.

* Certain passages in Ezekiel (ch. xiv. v. 1 and following), however show that idolatry was not completely extirpated from amongst the exiled community.

† Ezekiel, ch. viii. v. 1 ; ch. xiv. v. 1; ch. xx. v. 1, 4.

Iahveh is no longer found in the roaring tempest, the bursting storm, the burning fire, the passing wind. He now dwells in an azure heaven, an empyrean of light, he is surrounded by supernatural monsters, living machines, wheels within wheels, a vast system of the transmission of force, which only differs from our idea of transcendent machinery by the consciousness and the individual wills with which this great organisation is endowed. This was the beginning of the style in which the Apocalypses were written, and which was so much appreciated during the epoch of the Maccabees, and afterwards by the Christians. Above all, it was the commencement of the Kabbala, which developed itself later on, during the decadence of Israel.

The mysterious chariot, the holy *merkaba* of Ezekiel,[*] bore with it the germ of many aberrations. The cherubim and the symbols of the sanctuary suggested the chief elements of this style. It is also possible that the symbolic bulls of Assyria, which Ezekiel might have seen, had some influence over his conceptions. In any case, it is certain that at this epoch, new monsters appeared to disturb the imagination of Israel, which, until then, had been so eurythmic and so pure. The limits which the prophets of Hezekiah's century imposed upon themselves, even in their moments of wildest inspiration, had almost disappeared. A kind of romanticism

---

[*] Compare the money alluded to, vol. i. p. 160, note 2.

manifests itself, which is quite opposed to the good taste, classic in its way, displayed in the ancient literature. The style of Ezekiel is inferior in every way to that of the writers of the eighth and seventh centuries. The image is frequently eccentric and misses its aim. Sometimes, however, it is wonderfully forcible.* Many of those striking expressions called "Biblical" are taken from Ezekiel. The Apocalypse of Patmos is only an elaborate copy of the great apparitions of the river Chebar. Christianity owes more to Ezekiel than to any other prophet, perhaps excepting the second Isaiah.

Ezekiel's ideas are almost identical with those of Jeremiah. There is no trace of rational philosophy in them. Sometimes an instinct of some depth leads him to represent Iahveh as the supreme force, the central organism of the universe; but this central motor intervenes in the most minute way in human affairs. The Providence of Ezekiel is perhaps less capricious, less personal than that of the ancient prophets; still Iahveh follows a very decided policy, of which Israel is always the centre. According to Ezekiel and all the prophets, Iahveh is a God jealous of mankind; any superiority is an insult to Him. He lowers the mighty, exalts the humble; dries up the green tree and makes the dry tree flourish.† When He wishes to punish His ways

* Notice particularly the fine succession of images, ch. xxi.
† Ezekiel, ch. xvii. v. 24.

are really curious. He commands evil in order to avenge himself; and punishes a nation by prescribing detestable rites, such as the sacrifice of children. Wishing to inflict the most cruel chastisement upon a people in the loss of its firstborn, he leads it to kill them itself by prescribing "Molochism."* This enormity is not greater than when Iahveh misleads the nations, hardens Pharaoh's heart, or inspires false *nabi*, to the undoing of those who listen to them.

It is, however, remarkable that in Ezekiel the justice of Iahveh is less summary than in the other Hebrew writings. Sincere conversion is followed by the obliteration of the past; a man is not responsible for the crimes of his ancestors. Each individual is punished for his own faults only. He who repents is saved, but he does not save others.† One would think that the author wishes to protest against the idea cherished by the school of Jeremiah that the piety of later generations cannot efface the crimes of their fathers. The despairing people of Judah had but one explanation of the misfortunes which overwhelmed them in spite of their piety, namely, the inexpiable crimes of Manasseh. Ezekiel seemed to fear that this principle might be applied to his fellow captives, and that Iahveh would render them responsible for the misdeeds of the Hierosoly-

* Ezekiel, ch. xx. v. 25-26.

† Ezekiel, ch. xiv. v. 14 and following; ch. xviii. v. 1 and following.

mites. A guilty town might contain three men like Noah, Daniel, and Job. These three men should be saved by their piety, but they should not save any one with them.* A pious man surrounded by evil need not be discouraged, the chastisement which would fall upon the sinful would not touch him.

Nearly every year, from 595 until the last investment of Jerusalem (590), Ezekiel sent his prophetic visions to his brethren in Judah.† We should expect to find a tone of consolation in these messages, but it does not exist, they contain nothing but threats and bitter reproaches.‡ The author is singularly well informed as to all that is taking place in Jerusalem. He knows the leaders of each party and all the influential men by name.§ Jehoiachin's misfortunes have not improved them. Some impious men even assert that this catastrophe is a proof that Iahveh has abandoned the land, that He no longer cares for the title of God of Judah.‖ The Hierosolymites are worse than the heathen.¶ The most serious men practised idolatry and worshipped the rising sun. Idols were seen on all sides; on the banks of the river the women performed the pathetic rites of the Adonis.** There were Levites

* Ezekiel, ch. xiv. v. 19-23.
† Ezekiel, from ch. i. to ch. xxiii. inclusively.
‡ Ezekiel, ch. xx., xxi., etc.
§ Ezekiel, ch. viii. v. 11; ch. xi. v. 1.
‖ Ezekiel, ch. viii. v. 12, and ch. ix. v. 9.
¶ Ezekiel, ch. 5.
** Ezekiel, ch. viii. v. 14.

who officiated in the foreign ritual of the uncircumcised aliens who celebrated the worship of Iahveh.*
These abominations took place at the door of the temple, only separated from the sanctuary itself by a single wall. The king presided over them and sanctioned the monstrous cruelties of the worship of Moloch.† The temple itself was sullied by them, and the most abominable practices defiled the sacred inclosure.‡

The prophet particularly delighted in the allegory of the two sisters, Oholah and Oholibah, signifying Samaria and Jerusalem courting aliens from their earliest youth, doting upon them from the portraits that they saw drawn in vermilion upon the walls, abandoning themselves to every crime with them, to find at last ignominy and death in their infamous caresses.§

It is true that all these writings are extremely exaggerated. In this picture, strangely painted in the blackest tints, the personal antipathies of the cleric, the information which he daily received, are too strongly felt. We realise the pious coterie with its gossip and petty tattle. In the eyes of the exiled prophet the elders connected with the sanctuary are the most guilty; ‖ false prophets and a low class of

---

* Ezekiel, ch. xliv. v. 5 and following.
† Ezekiel, ch. xliii. v. 7 and following. Cf. xxxiii. v. 39.
‡ Ezekiel, ch. viii.
§ Ezekiel, ch. xxiii.
‖ Ezekiel, ch. ix. v. 6.

female sorcerers swarm on every side.* And, still more singular, there are people who do not believe in prophecies.† The saints form a select party in the city, lamenting the crimes committed around them. Innocent blood flows in the streets.‡ The messengers of the celestial vengeance mark the elect by tracing the sign *thav* (a cross, the ancient *thav* formed this sign) upon their foreheads; the remainder of the people is doomed to death; the massacre would commence in the temple and its neighbourhood.§

There is no difference between the policy of Ezekiel and that of Jeremiah.∥ Ezekiel apostrophises the king in the roughest manner.¶ Nebuchadnezzar performs a providential mission; he is the agent of Iahveh and must be respected. Zedekiah is guilty. He had sworn to Nebuchadnezzar that he would not arm, that he would be humble and weak; now he is perpetually seeking war chariots and soldiers from Egypt. By this he insults Iahveh, who has given the power to Nebuchadnezzar.** He shall be punished for his perjury and carried to Babylon, where he will expiate his

---

* Ezekiel, ch. xiii. and xxii., the whole chapters.

† Ezekiel, ch. xii. v. 23-28.

‡ Ezekiel, ch. xxii. v. 3, 6; ch. xxiv. v. 6, 8, 9, and the surplus of the Greek after v. 14.

§ Ezekiel, ch. ix.

∥ See particularly ch. xvii., xix., xxi.

¶ Ezekiel, ch. xxi. v. 30.

** Ezekiel, ch. xvii. v. 11 and following.

crime.* His army will be destroyed, the remnant of the nation will be dispersed.† Then Iahveh will gather his people together from out of the countries where he has scattered them. All Israel will be reunited and restored in one centre, Jerusalem.‡ Jerusalem and Samaria will meet with the same fate; § but the ulterior future will belong to Jerusalem only.

To the captives in Mesopotamia, Ezekiel can only advise patience. Absolutely hostile to any idea of revolt against a power which appears to him the expression of fatality or rather of the will of Iahveh, he counsels them to wait patiently for the end. Not all the prophets of the captivity are equally resigned. Exiles usually create illusions for themselves, and many of the captives in Babylon believed themselves on the eve of returning.‖ Prophets arose amongst them who foretold their speedy deliverance. The unfortunate colonists, deceived by these promises, made no stable settlement in the land of their exile. Instead of cultivating the land which had been given to them they considered themselves but temporary captives, who might be restored to their homes from one day to another. Ahab, the son of Kolaiah, and Zedekiah, the son of Maaseiah,

---

* Ezekiel, ch. xii., xxi., etc.
† Ezekiel, ch. xv., etc.
‡ Ezekiel, ch. xx. v. 40.
§ Ezekiel, ch. xxiii.
‖ Jeremiah, ch. xxix. (towards 592).

THE REIGN OF ZEDEKIAH.

are particularly quoted, for it seems that they incited the Jews to rebellion. Movements like those of Hananiah of Gibeon, in Judea, must surely have contributed to these dreams of self-blinding patriotism.

Jeremiah once more resumed his self-imposed mission of discouraging the national hopes. He took advantage of an embassy, composed of Elasah, the son of Shaphan, and Gemariah, the son of Hilkiah, sent by Zedekiah to Nebuchadnezzar to transmit a letter to the exiles.* This message contains some wise counsels, which during many centuries have formed the rules of the dispersed Jews.† On the other hand, if Jeremiah wished to serve the ends of the Babylonian government he could not have expressed himself better. We know that, in great national misfortunes, a man, by too much sincerity, easily acquires the similitude of a traitor, an enemy to his country.

The prophet is never tolerant towards his fellows. If we had all the private correspondence of the saints we should find several pages amongst them like the one in Jeremiah xxix.‡

---

* Jeremiah, ch. xxix.

† שלום דרשו את שלום הציר אשר הגליתי אתכם שמה ... כי בשלומה יהיה לכם. This renders a Jew's advice almost invariably useful in all matters relating to the internal affairs of a country. But it is clear, on the other hand, that it makes them good municipal councillors, but not true patriots.

‡ Jeremiah, ch. xxix. v. 15-23, suppressing 16-20, which are missing in the Greek, and are only an equivalent of ch. xxiv.

Jeremiah's letter produced a very bad effect in Babylon. One of the exiled prophets, Shemaiah the Nehelamite, wrote to the keeper of the temple, Zephaniah, the son of Maaseiah, asking why he had not rebuked Jeremiah for making himself a prophet ? *

Zephaniah read the letter to Jeremiah, who replied by a cruel prophecy against Shemaiah.

Here is the sore of Hebrew prophetism, of Mussulman Madhism, and of Semitic inspiration in general. The greatest sin, according to believers, is refusing to listen when God speaks through his true prophets.† But who is the true prophet? By what sign can he be recognised? Really there is but his own assertion, which always leaves a loophole for adverse statements. The prophet has neither strength nor reason behind him; he rarely appeals to miracles. *Quod gratis asseritur gratis negatur.* A frightful dilemma, which, combined with the dogma of the identification of God with his prophet, cannot fail to engender terrible fanaticism and to provoke atrocious injustice! Jeremiah horrifies us when we see him revelling in the prospect of a rival prophet being slowly roasted to death by Nebuchadnezzar; Jeremiah considered it perfectly natural. The unfortunate man, in ex-

---

* The successor to Pashour. See above, p. 138.

† Jeremiah, ch. xxxvii. v. 2.

pressing an opinion that differed from his own, had inculcated rebellion against Iahveh.

Still, in all this book, we must make allowance for the colossal exaggeration which every thought received from Oriental rhetoric. And we must also remember that had the people listened to Jeremiah's odious declamations frightful massacres would have been averted. In critical moments the patriot who tries to make the vanquished realise the power of the conqueror is always taken for an ally of the foreigner. "Submit yourselves to the King of Babylon that ye may live." These were hard words for the listeners. Imagine, in the month of July, 1870, a journalist marching through the boulevards of Paris, a horse's collar round his neck, predicting the victory of the Prussians; every one would certainly have considered the action of the enthusiast highly reprehensible. In these circumstances no one can be excused for seeing clearly until after events have spoken for themselves. Jeremiah's conduct cannot therefore be entirely condemned. Events soon proved that if he were greatly mistaken in the style of his prophecies, he was perfectly right in the substance of his words.

CHAPTER XXIII.

PIOUS DREAMS.

THE idealism of Israel never appeared more triumphant than in this terrible moment when the future seemed closed to it. Precisely at this time, the race, that was always protesting against fate, founded the religion of faith and hope. Jeremiah's melancholy nature did not tend towards such dreams, but certain facts prove that the Jewish imagination was able to create a paradise for itself, even in those years, when the sword of Nebuchadnezzar was apparently sole monarch of the world. The greatest contrasts were evolved by this wonderful genius, endowed with such extraordinary religious virtuality, yet often seeming to delight in its own negation, and to take pleasure in mocking itself.

We readily attribute to this period a prophet, in some respects opposed to Jeremiah, whose writings have been unaccountably preserved to us.*

---

* Zechariah, ch. xii.-xiv. See vol. ii. p. 391-392. This fragment, save for the interpolations which may be found in it, is anterior to

He was certainly one of the most sensible men of his time. A strong partisan of the house of David, he still appears to mourn for the death of Josiah and the defeat of Megiddo.* In the ideal picture of the future, he classes together the end of idolatry and the end of prophetism; the latter institution had become so much depreciated. In fact the abuse of prophetism had produced a reaction. Many sensible people had taken an aversion to this strange profession, which frequently covered a great deal of charlatanism and dishonesty.† The most varied schools at last proclaimed that prophecy would soon be the common gift of all the community and not the privilege of a few of its members.‡

So that wise parents seeing their son inclining towards the trade of a prophet would put him to death, or thrash him, to prevent him from becoming an ill-omened being. The prophets themselves would be ashamed of their chimeræ; they would prefer labouring in the fields to prophetism. The reform predicted by this visionary, himself inimical to visions, consists in the spirit of prayer and

---

the Captivity, and posterior to the battle of Megiddo. Zechariah, ch. xiv. v. 9, is an allusion to Deuteronomy, ch. vi. 4. Zechariah, ch. xiii. v. 3, also appears to be an allusion to the laws of Deuteronomy against false prophets.

* Zechariah, ch. xii. v. 11.

† The book of Jonah relates to the same class of ideas; but we believe it to bep osterior to the Captivity. See below, p. 416, and following.

‡ Zechariah, xiii. 2 and following,

purity. The day of Iahveh would see a complete transformation of all things. Judea, now so barren, would become the source of the irrigation of the world.* Living waters issuing from Jerusalem would flow on one side to the Mediterranean, on the other to the Dead Sea, and they would be as abundant in summer as in winter. The enemies of Judah should be punished; but they should afterwards be converted and assemble yearly, to celebrate the feast of tabernacles at Jerusalem. The nations that did not come should have no more rain. Everything should bear the mark of IAHVEH, everything should become sacred. Horses, previously devoted to the use of luxury and war, and as such excluded from Jerusalem,† should now belong to Iahveh. Sacrifices to Iahveh might be offered in any vessel, so that merchants should no longer be seen in the temple asking money for the hire of basins and trafficking in holy things.‡

The author of these strange pages, who might easily be called the Great Idealist of Israel,§ was a prophet or perhaps a priest. Those who are familiar with religious history will not be more surprised to find the words against prophetism

* Compare Joel, ch. iv. v. 18, and Ezekiel, ch. xlvii. v. 1-12.
† Zechariah, ch ix. v. 10; ch. x. v. 5.
‡ Zechariah, ch. xiv. v. 20-21.
§ It is remarkable that the writer, who maintained the same spirit during the Captivity, the so-called second Isaiah, has also remained anonymous, or rather his work has also been handed down to us under the name of another prophet.

PIOUS DREAMS.

issuing from the mouth of a prophet, than to see the protestations against the clericalism of the Middle Ages emanating from priests and monks. How many priests have been seen in our own century, fretting against the cassock, and proclaiming that one day a peasant's smock will be preferred to it! The cry of reform against the abuses of the sanctuary always starts from the sanctuary itself. It was natural that satirical attacks upon the prophets should come from one who wore "the hairy mantle."*

From all sides Israel was thus approaching idealism, the conception of a new religion (a new covenant), which should replace the ancient alliance, and in which all the world should be priests—of a law written in the conscience of each man, which he need not learn from any one else,† which he would find in the inspirations of his own heart.‡ The extraordinary liberality of Jewish ideas upon individual inspiration left the path open to every change, to any religious progress. The covenant of Sinai did not prevent the Jews from dreaming of a more refined compact. They did not imagine that this idea could be any insult to Moses. If Christianity,

* See below, p. 417 and following, referring to Jonah.

† Compare Deutero-Isaiah, ch. liv. v. 13.

‡ Jeremiah, ch. xxxi. v. 33-35. It is possible that the disciples of Jeremiah, who edited his book during the Captivity, have added something here to their master's thought; but that could only make a difference of a few years. See below, p. 330, and following, p. 363 and following.

in proving that it had fulfilled the ancient prophecies, had confined itself to quoting these verses,* it would have avoided a good many tricks of futile exegesis. Christianity soon forgot the programme, which its founder had borrowed from the prophets, and became like other religions, a religion of priests and sacrifices, of observances and superstitions. But the germ planted in religious tradition by the inspired writings of Israel could not perish. All who seek a God without priests, a revelation without prophets, a covenant written in the heart, are in many respects disciples of these ancient visionaries.

The ritual was always the great source of embarrassment to the religious zealots of Israel. Carried to their logical consequences, the arguments of the pious men of that date would have led to the suppression of all sacrifices. The puritan Iahveists, like the Essenes of a later date, loudly asserted that praise (*toda*) and prayer are the only sacrifice acceptable to God.† And yet the temple, at first little appreciated by the pietists,‡ had for the last century become the centre of Iahveism, as much from the idealistic and reforming point of view as from the materialistic and popular aspect.

---

* Compare 2 Corinthians, ch. iii. v. 3 and following; Hebrews, ch. viii. v. 8 and following. The expression $\kappa\alpha\iota\nu\acute{\eta}\ \delta\iota\alpha\theta\acute{\eta}\kappa\eta$ of the early Christians refers to the fine passage quoted above from Jeremiah. It seems that Jesus also used this passage. Mark, ch. xiv. v. 24; Matthew, ch. xxvi. v. 28.

† See particularly Psalm l.

‡ See vol. ii. p. 120 and following.

The anonymous writer of whom we have been speaking is much attached to it.* Not one of the prophets hints at the possibility of suppressing it, and we shall soon see that after its total destruction in 588, the sole thought of the *anavim* was how to rebuild it. It thus happened that the school which in principle was most hostile to the temple became the fanatical supporter of the temple; that the idea of a pure worship, in which God has no visible dwelling place, spread by the side of the house of stone built by Solomon. As we have already said, the temple in the course of time had become a mosque—a centre of religious agitation. The courts and the smaller buildings which surrounded it had been enormously enlarged. It had become the subject of many prophecies, and the new Levitism which had developed since the reign of Josiah was an inflammable material, already carefully prepared for the reception of the *anavite* ideas. In truth during these critical years there was not much distinction between the two groups of Levites and prophets.

All this little world grouped itself round the temple, and lived in a moral activity that certainly no other temple of antiquity ever excited. The Levites all became saints, full of love for Iahveh. The same jealousies arose between them and the priests that are seen between servants courting the same master. These pious sacristans envied the

* Zechariah, ch. xiv. v. 20-21.

haughty priesthood, which had an exclusive right to approach the altar. They consoled themselves with the reflection, that soon the most humble vessels used in the ritual would be held in equal honour with the vessels of gold handled only by the priests.* The Psalms continued their rich and powerful development. It is a pity that the sixteenth Psalm has been so much altered; it is perhaps one of the finest Levitical elegies.†

All the melancholy of clerical life, all the tender recollections of devout observances practised with others, all the alternations of bitterness and hope felt by a pious heart in its struggle against the evidences of a sad reality, are admirably expressed in a Psalm,‡ which, unfortunately, is rendered obscure to us by numerous errors and many allusions difficult to understand. The author seems to have been thrown by the troubles of the time into the region of Hermon of the Upper Jordan, towards Banias.

The temple in its last days therefore sheltered some pious souls, who in the midst of the storms in the outer world found perfect happiness beneath its roof. Men with upright hearts who know Iahveh have nothing to fear.

The image, most reassuring to the devout per-

---

* Zechariah, ch. xiv. v. 20.

† Psalm x. appears to belong to the same time; it is also much altered. We may say the same of Psalm iv.

‡ Psalm xlii. and xliii. united. Compare Psalm lxiii.

sonages who lovingly clustered round the sacred walls, was of the large wings widely spread, sheltering under their protection the *gerim* or neighbours of Iahveh.* Was it not evident that Iahveh, for the sake of his own honour, would defend his house, his inheritance, his servants, against all the dangers which threatened them? †

* Psalm xvii. v. 8; xxxvi. v. 8; lvii. v. 2; lxi. v. 5; lxiii. v. 8. Cf. vol. ii. p. 44.
† Psalm cxviii. v. 6, etc.

CHAPTER XXIV.

DESTRUCTION OF JERUSALEM.—THE SECOND TRANSPORTATION.

THE situation of the unfortunate Zedekiah, between those who wished to debar him from every hope of revenge and the legitimate aspirations of the patriots who surrounded him, was no longer tenable.* Jeremiah, foaming with rage, daily sounded his frightful alarm-bell. On the other hand, Egypt was rising. The Egyptian alliance always gleamed before the eyes of the Judaites; fate had decreed that they should be drawn into it.† It was an error, but one of those errors which it is impossible to avoid. The accession of Hophra (Apries), King of Egypt, inaugurating an energetic and brilliant reign,‡ appears to have been the decisive cause of

---

* Account of these events in 2 Kings, ch. xxiv. v. 18 and following, reproduced in Jeremiah, ch. lii. and ch. xxxix. Compare 2 Chronicles xxxvi. v. 11 and following.

† Ezekiel, ch. xvii. v. 17; ch. xxix. v. 3 7, 16; Jeremiah, ch. xxxvii. v. 5; ch. xliv. v. 30.

‡ Maspero. pp. 547 and following.

an event which might be considered virtually accomplished some time before. Tyre and the other cities of Phœnicia entered the league. But apparently the Ammonites, Moabites, Edomites, and Philistines remained faithful to the King of Babylon. Ezekiel, on the banks of the Euphrates, soon heard of the intended movement. One of his finest visions * was that in which he saw the Chaldean sword afar off, hesitating which road it should take. The sword of Iahveh was ready to be drawn from its sheath to strike Israel, "good and evil." But once unsheathed it would not return into its scabbard; the whole world would be smitten. "A sword, a sword, it is sharpened, and also furbished: it is sharpened that it may make a slaughter; it is furbished that it may be as lightning to give it into the hand of the slayer. Cry and howl, son of man; for it is upon my people! . . . . " In fact, the seer was commanded to describe a kind of map, in which we see two roads starting from Babylon, with sign posts, upon which a hand was engraved, showing that one led to Jerusalem, the other to Rabbath-Ammon. The King of Babylon stood at the junction of the two roads consulting the oracles, to see which he should take. Jerusalem fell to the first lot, the turn of Rabbath-Ammon would follow later.

In 590 the rebellion broke out. Nebuchadnezzar

* Ezekiel, ch. xxi.

was then at the climax of his power. He could concentrate his whole strength upon Syria. The conqueror dragged a whole world, peoples, and nations after him.* The head-quarters were established at Riblah, near the sources of the Orontes. From there the army proceeded to the coast, probably through the present Wadi Brissa.† Sidon appears to have surrendered without a struggle. Strong in its insular position, Tyre resisted. The efforts of the assailants were confined to preventing the Tyrians from communicating with the main land, and, above all, from replenishing their water supply. Whilst the blockade continued, Nebuchadnezzar attacked Judea. Zedekiah shut himself up in Jerusalem, abandoning the provincial cities to the enemy. The siege of Jerusalem commenced. The city, protected on three sides by steep declivities, was pregnable only on the north. The besiegers encamped on the plateau now occupied by the Russian establishments.‡ Then the siege towers were erected, and the lines of circumvallation traced out, according to the slow but infallible methods of Assyrian warfare. The siege of Samaria had lasted three years; that of Jerusalem lasted two. During this time the religious excitement was extreme.

---

* Jeremiah, xxxiv. v. 1.

† Inscriptions at Wadi Brissa and Nahr el-Kelb, both at important passages in the road. See above, p. 237, note.

‡ See above, p. 89, 90.

In the sixth century, under the pressure of Nebuchadnezzar, we see the same phenomena that, sixty years later, were produced during the attack under Titus. It is, in fact, a general rule that in besieged capitals—particularly if these capitals have a religious and humanitarian character like Jerusalem and Paris—factions become exasperated and, almost inevitably, end in excess. Zedekiah and his officers wished for war to the death. Jeremiah, assured of the fatal termination of the siege, wished them to surrender to the Chaldeans immediately. According to the very just expression of the officers,* "he weakened the hands of the men of war who remained in the city." In reality the old prophet was right. But in some cases true wisdom consists in letting fools alone. Moreover, the violence of his language exceeded all bounds. We cannot reiterate too often, that in modern days the true analogy of the prophets are the journalists of the most immoderate style. Jeremiah resembled many personages we have known; he was a compound of a Felix Pyat and an implacable Jesuit. He was even miserly of his prayers. At the approach of Nebuchadnezzar, Zedekiah sent Jehucal, son of Shelemiah, and Zephaniah the priest, son of Maaseiah, to Jeremiah, saying, "Inquire, I pray thee, of Iahveh for us; peradventure Iahveh will deal with us according to all his wondrous works, that he (the enemy) may go up from

---

* Jeremiah, ch. xxxviii. v. 4.

us."* Jeremiah's reply was hopeless: the judgment of Iahveh is irrevocable; every one will be slain; no mercy will be shown. Another time,† the gloomy seer urges those who wish to save their lives to give themselves up to the Chaldeans; those who resist will have no choice between the sword, famine, or pestilence. In his interviews with Zedekiah,‡ he offered the king the prospect of life, of favour even, or of honourable burial, if he would submit to the Chaldeans. Here we already see the dawn of a kind of monachal spirit, a stranger to all ideas of military honour, and regarding a struggle against fatality as pride. Valour had not much sense in the eyes of people who thought that death was the supreme evil, the proof of Iahveh's desertion. We feel above all that the prophets—partisans of Nebuchadnezzar—were very glad to see the rebellious Jerusalem destroyed, to make way for a pious Jerusalem which would be entirely in their own hands.

Ezekiel affected more reserve; but, as a fact, his previsions were equally gloomy. One of his surates is supposed to have been written on the very day of the investment of Jerusalem.§ It consists of a series of reproaches and threats. Two parables

---

* Jeremiah, ch. xxi. v. 1-7, and ch. xxxvii. v. 3 and following. Here there is some confusion of persons. *Pashour* is an error; שלמיה = מלכיה. Compare ch. xxxviii. v. 1.

† Jeremiah, xxi. v. 8-10 and 13-14.

‡ Jeremiah, xxxiv. init. and xxxviii. v. 17 and following.

§ Ezekiel, ch. xxiv. the whole chapter.

were shown to him. He first sees a cauldron in which the flesh and the bones will seethe together (this is the besieged city), without the cauldron losing any of the rust formed by stains of blood upon it, so that it must be burnt in the fire. Then his wife, the delight of his eyes, "died, and he is forbidden to mourn for her." In presence of so much crime* mourning would be out of place. Soon a fugitive from Jerusalem will arrive with the tidings that all is over. The prophet may then speak again. Until that time he will be dumb.

One thing, however, consoled Ezekiel for the dangers encountered by Jerusalem, this was the confidence with which he believed in the destruction of the cities of Phœnicia.† This industrial, wealthy, mercantile civilisation, appeared to him the climax of abomination. When Sidon shall be ravaged by pestilence, when her streets shall flow with blood and be strewn with the dead, then men shall know what it costs to mock at the presumption of Israel. Then the national vanity of Israel shall be no more tormented by "a pricking briar, nor a grieving thorn of any that are round about them, that did despite unto them." To despise

* Ezekiel, ch. xxiv. v. 23.

† Ch. xxvi., xxvii., xxviii. The dates of the prophecies relating to Tyre and Egypt appear to have been partly altered by the copyists. They are irreconcilable together. Moreover, Ezekiel does not seem to have dated these chapters until after the event. There is another erroneous date in ch. xxxiii. v. 21.

Israel is to despise Iahveh, and this offence can be only expiated by blood.*

In the eyes of Ezekiel, Tyre is also a personal enemy of Iahveh. All the nations are exhorted to join together against her. She shall be totally destroyed. Fishermen shall dry their nets where she once stood. Sneers, irony, and concentrated rage, combined with the great beauty of the images and the originality of the expressions, render these chapters masterpieces of literature. Still we feel shocked at the coarse insults lavished by such powerless rage. And there is something ludicrous in the position of a fanatic leaping for joy over disasters which have not taken place. In fact, Nebuchadnezzar could not take the inland city,† he was obliged to content himself with ravaging the continental city (Paletyr).

Ezekiel's fury against Egypt is equally eloquent and equally puerile.‡ Adopting a proverbial image,§ suggested by the fragility of the papyrus, he announced that Egypt should once more prove a reed, which pierced the hand of the man who leant upon it. The prosperity of Egypt was considered

---

* Ezekiel, ch. xxviii. v. 20-26.

† Ezekiel himself infers this, ch. xxix. v. 17 and following. See *Miss. de Phen.*, p. 526-527, note. For the authorities quoted by Josephus (*Contre Apion*, i. 21; *Ant.* X. xi. 1) with the intention of confirming the misinterpretaion of Jeremiah and Ezekiel, see vol. p. 438, note 1. Besides Josephus only says ἐπολιόρκη.

‡ Ezekiel, xxix. v. 1 and following.

§ 2 Kings, xviii. v. 21; Isaiah, ch. xxxvi. v. 6.

DESTRUCTION OF JERUSALEM.

a sign of pride by the fanatics, in whom it roused serious displeasure.

Egypt should be re-established after forty years; but henceforth she should be the weakest of nations, "so that she should no longer inspire any confidence in Israel," nor lead it to commit the worst of crimes, to trust in anything but Iahveh.

The siege of Jerusalem advanced in a kind of fatalistic way. Famine became imminent. The cities of Judah fell one after the other; Lachish and Azekah were alone in their successful resistance; all the country of Benjamin was completely devastated.* The government of Jerusalem displayed both energy and activity; either to procure men capable of bearing arms, or, to please the pietists, by observing a law of Deuteronomy, which had never been obeyed, the king proclaimed the emancipation of all the Hebrew slaves.† This act, in which the king joined, was celebrated by a solemn covenant ratified in the temple. A calf was cut in two, and, according to custom, every one who made the promise passed between the two halves of the victim.‡

No doubt this was a concession to Jeremiah and the partisans of the Thora. And, for one moment, it seemed that this act of humanity had brought good fortune to Judah.

---

* Jeremiah, ch. xxxii.

† Jeremiah, ch. xxxiv. v. 7 and following. Compare Deuteronomy, chap. xv. v. 14.

‡ Compare Genesis, ch. xv. v. 10.

Up to that time no active assistance had been received from Egypt. Hophra had left all his allies to be crushed separately and they were almost despairing, when tidings were brought that an Egyptian army had been seen on the frontier.* Nebuchadnezzar hastily raised the sieges of Tyre and Jerusalem and marched towards the south. The general opinion of the prophets was that the Egyptians would be defeated and Egypt invaded. Ezekial uttered cries of joy. The great day of Iahveh, the judgments upon the heathen nations would now commence.† To the prophets, Egypt essentially represented the idolatrous world. All more or less devoted to Nebuchadnezzar, in whom they saw the agent of God, they cherished unlimited hatred towards Egypt, and regarded its annihilation as the commencement of the salvation of Israel.‡ Moreover, Ezekiel justified the devolution of Egypt to Nebuchadnezzar by reasons of high theology. Iahveh owed the man who served as an instrument in the execution of his decrees some recompense for the useless trouble that he had taken against Tyre.§ Pillage is the pay of the scourge of God. Tyre has not been pillaged, so that Iahveh is in arrears with Nebuchadnezzar for work done and still unpaid.

* Jeremiah, ch. xxxvii. v. 5 and following. Cf. ch. xxxiv. v. 7 and following.

† Ezekiel, ch. xxx. v. 3.

‡ Ezekiel, ch. xxix. v. 21.

§ Ezekiel, ch. xxix. v. 17-21.

DESTRUCTION OF JERUSALEM.

The lyrical spirit of Ezekiel never lost an opportunity of using a poetic subject that suited his taste. He declaimed upon conjectures, wrote odes and elegies upon events that had not happened, and that never did happen. The destruction of Egypt and Ethiopia by Nebuchadnezzar provided him with five declamations,* which may be reckoned amongst the most valuable specimens of ancient literature. They resemble the *Chatiments* of Victor Hugo, who also felt for Ezekiel's eccentric genius an admiration which explains a great many analogies. Egypt consoled by Asshur, the descent of the King of Egypt to Sheol, and the reception which he meets with from the princes of Asshur, of Elam, Meshech-Tubal, and Sidon,† the picture of the great armies of the epoch resting in Sheol, each hero with his sword beneath his head, are poems of marvellous effect, which our century admires, perhaps because they have precisely our own literary defects. But the fact that not one of the predictions contained in them was fulfilled, rather spoils them in the eyes of a man of good taste. They may be compared to poems, written by a romantic poet during the siege of Paris, upon the impending extermination of the Prussians and the tragic death of the Emperor William.

We do not know what took place between the

* Ch. xxx., xxxi., xxxii.
† Read צירון instead of צפון.

Chaldean and Egyptian armies.* But it is certain that Egypt was not invaded, and that its population was not transported as Ezekiel had foolishly dreamed. Perhaps the two powerful sovereigns made peace together at the expense of their weaker allies. Nebuchadnezzar promptly returned to the north. At Jerusalem, no advantage had been taken of the armistice. The little depth of the moral sense in the masses was sadly manifested. The former owners of the liberated slaves, believing that the Chaldean army was retreating, claimed their property and again reduced the unfortunate men to servitude. This time Jeremiah was justly exasperated. Iahveh announced by his mouth that he meant to bring back the Chaldean army to destroy Jerusalem and the cities of Judah; and, in fact, Nebuchadnezzar resumed the siege of the city and continued it without truce or mercy.

Jeremiah had never believed that the retreat of the Chaldeans was permanent.† It was natural that he should be suspected of wishing for their return. As he possessed land at Anathoth, and frequently went there, he was often seen in the neighbourhood of Benjamin's Gate, very near to the camp which the besiegers had occupied, and where they now retook up their position. He was thus noticed in the vicinity of the said gate on a day, which coincided but too well with the return

* Jeremiah, ch. xxxvii., particularly v. 7.
† Ch. xxxvii.

of the Chaldeans. It was asserted that he intended
to pass over to the enemy's camp. The captain of
the ward, Ierijah, son of Shemeliah, arrested him
and led him to the *sarim*, or ministers of national
defence, who caused him to be beaten with rods
and imprisoned in the house of the sofer Jonathan,
which had been converted into a prison.* He was
placed in the secret dungeons, and in a great
measure deprived of food.† King Zedekiah, who
secretly believed in him, sent for him privately,
and asked him if he had received any message from
Iahveh. Jeremiah referred him to his prophets,
who had announced that the Chaldeans would not
return. He complained of the treatment he received in the house of Jonathan, declaring that he
should die if it continued. The king dared not
liberate him, because of the animosity of the *sarim*
against him. So he gave orders that Jeremiah
should be transferred to the prison in the royal
palace, a great open court, where the prisoners,
their feet made fast in stocks attached to the wall,
were able to communicate with the public. One
loaf a day was assigned to him from the bakers'
bazaar, and this ration was served out to him until
there was no more bread in the city.

* We have two accounts of Jeremiah's prison, ch. xx. (cf. ch.
xxxii. v. 1 and following) and ch. xxxvii. This one is written by
Jeremiah himself; although a little pregnant with marginal additions, it should be preferred.

† Ch. xxxvii. v. 15, obscure; this may be through the variations
in the margin.

From his prison * Jeremiah continued to utter his sinister predictions, and to incite the people to surrender to the Chaldeans and thus save their lives. The ministers pointed out to the king the discouragement which the prophet's words produced in the men of war still left in the city. The disciples of Jeremiah, from whom we have received these accounts, pretend that the king was no longer a real power, that he was bound hand and foot to the military party. Zedekiah must have yielded in spite of himself. The ministers then seized Jeremiah and lowered him by cords into an empty cistern with a bottom of mud, in which his body was half buried. This summary deed was reported to the king, who had gone down to the Gate of Benjamin at the time, by an eunuch of the palace, Ebed-Melech the Ethiopian. The king gave orders that the prophet should be removed from the horrible place. Ebed-Melech, aided by the servants of the palace, lowered bundles of old rags to Jeremiah, who placed them beneath his armpits, and by this means he was raised without being wounded. He was again confined in the court of the prison adjoining the palace. His audacity increased. The immediate future always appeared to him under the most gloomy colours; but, beyond the desponding sadness of the present, the pessimist old man foresaw a better time, when Israel would have but

* Ch. xxxviii. v. 1 and following, a contradictory and pregnant account.

one heart and one path, when a perfect religion would exist. The city was half destroyed by the siege machines used by the Chaldeans; the royal palace, which contained the prison, was shattered; yet Jeremiah repeated his predictions of the future prosperity of Judah and Benjamin, then so deeply humiliated.* According to one version, he must have even promised the eternal duration of the Levitical priesthood and of the race of David, the latter providing princes of the royal house to Jacob for ever; † but all this passage is suspected of interpolation, or, at least, the prophet's disciples appear to have forced the colours after the event. Elsewhere Jeremiah represents that the race of David had ended its destinies and had been rejected for ever.

The king once more consulted the man of God, but he could obtain but one answer from him: "Surrender, and you shall live; without that death and fire"—as though honour were not worth saving too. Zedekiah feared the deserters, who had already gone over to the Chaldeans, and who, upon their arrival in the enemies' camp, might do him a bad turn. Jeremiah reassured him, and vividly described the reproaches which his wives, if taken

* Ch. xxxiii.

† C. xxxiii. v. 14-26, is not found in the Greek. This piece is composed of three pericopes much resembling each other and unique in their style. It might be supposed that they have been interpolated in order to favour the pretensions of Zerubbabel.

prisoners, would one day pour upon him for listening to the counsels of his attendants.* The unfortunate Zedekiah, convinced by the words of the prophet, had apparently but one wish, to obey Iahveh and surrender, but, afraid of the party which advocated war to the death, he begged Jeremiah not to let any one know of the interview which they had had. The ministers went to Jeremiah, but he was impenetrable, and maintained that he had sought the king, only to petition that he should not be sent back to the house of Jonathan, where he should surely die. He was then remanded to the prison attached to the palace, where he remained until the entry of the Chaldeans.

The end, moreover, drew nearer every hour. A breach was made in the north wall. The town could no longer defend itself. One night the men of war, dragging the king with them, made a great sortie by way of the gate between the two walls opposite the king's palace, that is by the gate near the fish ponds of Shiloh. They broke through the Chaldeans and fled through the valley towards the desert. But the Chaldeans pursued them and overtook them in the plains of Jericho. The troop dispersed. The king was seized, and his captors led him to the Assyrian head-quarters at Riblah. There he was tried as a rebel vassal; his sons were murdered in his presence; Nebuchadnezzar him-

* Jeremiah, ch. xxxviii. v. 22.

DESTRUCTION OF JERUSALEM.

self put out his eyes;* and he was bound with two chains of brass. In this state he was led tc Babylon (588), where he remained a prisoner until his death.†

After Zedekiah's futile sortie the Chaldeans entered Jerusalem. They waited for instructions from Riblah before acting further. After a delay of four weeks, Nebuzaradan, captain of Nebuchadnezzar's guard, reached the city with orders to destroy it. He burnt the temple, the royal palace, all the strong and well-built houses. The Chaldean army were employed to demolish the walls. The precious metals in the temple were all carried away. There was a great quantity of brass, the columns and all that remained of Solomon's great works being broken in pieces, placed in sacks, and carried to Babylon.‡ Only the great walls which supported the ornamentation were left, and even these were disjointed. This destruction explains the archæological poverty of Jerusalem. All the delicate work, the ornaments in sculptured wood and metal, perished. The great stones rolled to the bottom of the valley of Cedron, then much steeper than it now is.§

---

* Notice עוּר, confirmed by Botta, *Monum. de Nin.*, pl. 118. See Thenius, p. 458.

† 2 Kings, ch. xxv. v. 7; Jeremiah, ch. xxxiv. v. 3 and following; ch. xxxix. v. 7; ch. lii. v. 11.

‡ See above, p. 255.

§ Joseph., *Ant.*, XV. xi. 5; Warren, *Palestine Exploration Fund*, Excav. pl. 26.

Nabuzaradan commanded that all whom he found in the city should be transported, even those who had gone over to the Chaldeans. There were eight hundred and thirty-two persons.* He only spared a few people of the lowest class to tend the vines and cultivate the land.† The Assyrians, like the Redskins, had the odious custom of choosing the chief men of the vanquished nations and scalping them in the king's presence.‡ Nebuzaradan selected for this purpose Seraiah, the high priest, Zephaniah, the second priest, and the three keepers of the door from the officials of the temple; from amongst the civil functionaries, one *saris*, who had been set over the men of war, five § of those who held positions in the court and saw the king's face, the scribe of the *sar-saba* who enrolled the people, and sixty private individuals who were found in the city. They were all led to Riblah where the king still remained. They were then tortured in his presence.

* Jeremiah, ch. lii. v. 29. The only way of solving the difficulties of this passage is, in my opinion, to read שתים וצשרים instead of צשרה שמונה, a correction which paleographically is very admissible. The two last transportations thus took place with only a year's interval between them, the first was of the Hierosolymites, the second of Judeans.

† 2 Kings, ch. xxv. v. 12, 22; Jeremiah, ch. xl. v. 7 and following. For the restrictions, see below, p. 364.

‡ Bas-reliefs in the British Museum.

§ Or *seven*, according to the text inserted in Jeremiah.

CHAPTER XXV.

THE LAST CONVULSIONS OF JUDAH.

THE position of Judah after the siege of Jerusalem resembled, in many respects, that of Israel after the destruction of Samaria. One circumstance, however, established a notable difference between the two situations, which was greatly to the advantage of Judah. After the capture of Samaria and the transportation of the ten tribes, the Ninevite government no longer troubled about the Israelites, of whom, no doubt, a great number remained in the country. It introduced foreign colonists, who but feebly perpetuated the Israelitish religion. It was not the same in Judah. Nebuchadnezzar left a Chaldean governor in his place, who occupied himself very seriously with the affairs of the country, and soon confided them to a native official. Moreover, the Babylonian government did not introduce foreign colonists into Judea; so that conquered Judea passed through the convulsions of a dying person, whilst conquered Israel was, in a measure, decapitated at one blow.

New difficulties daily confronted Nabuzaradan. The country of Judah was filled with bodies of free lances, chiefly composed of men who had sallied out with Zedekiah. The pietists, opposed to everything military, appear to have been very severe towards them. Ezekiel hears of their evil deeds, of their disobedience to the Thora, "which will prevent them from ever possessing the land." * In fact, these men found great difficulty in procuring food; so they tortured the peasants to make them reveal the silos, which contained their hidden provisions. Nabuzaradan pursued them, and captured seven hundred and forty-five persons, who were transported in their turn.†

It was not customary for the Assyrian and Chaldean conquerors to leave garrisons in the vanquished countries. The portions of the army which had carried on the siege were recalled or forced to leave. Nabuzaradan therefore resorted to an expedient dictated by the policy of his country. Very different from the Romans, who rarely delegated their authority to natives, the Chaldeans, after the transportations, liked to form a kind of provisional government with the remnant of the power they had suppressed.

Nabuzaradan found the chief he was seeking in

* Ezekiel, ch. xxxiii. v. 6 and following.
† Jeremiah, ch. lii. v. 29. See below, p. 306.

THE LAST CONVULSIONS OF JUDAH.

Gedaliah, the son of Ahikam, the son of Shaphan, who belonged to one of the first families of the kingdom, perhaps to the royal house.* He was a moderate man, who had adopted a middle course between the patriots and the prophets; perhaps one of those who had followed Jeremiah's advice, and gone over to the Chaldeans. Nabuzaradan confided to him the daughters of Zedekiah, and several important charges. He was also overseer to the commissariat, and entrusted with all the arrangements for the retreating Chaldean army. Gedaliah, or, as he is sometimes called, Godolias, established the centre of his authority at Mispah, near Jerusalem. He endeavoured to soothe his fellow countrymen by gentleness; but, as a rule, he only exasperated them and passed for a traitor amongst those who could not forgive him for being less foolish than themselves. However, a good many Jews who had taken refuge in Moab, Ammon, and Edom before the siege, hearing of this restoration, poor as it was, came back, and, grouping themselves round Gedaliah at Mispah, began to cultivate the soil. Jeremiah soon joined this feeble germ of renewed life, and his connection with it added considerably to its strength.

Two different accounts, even in the school of the prophets, were given of the manner in which Jeremiah was saved from exile. According to one of

* It is supposed that Gedaliah is the prince of David upon whom, at times, Jeremiah appeared to rely.

them,[*] immediately the city was taken, Nebuchadnezzar remembered the man who had served him so well, and he commanded Nabuzaradan and his officers to take care of the prophet, who had devoted himself to the support of the Chaldeans. He was released from prison and placed in Gedaliah's charge, so that he might protect him. According to another version,[†] the old prophet was loaded with chains and carried away with the crowd of captives. At Ramah, Nabuzaradan recognised him and sent him back to Gedaliah, at Mispah, with every mark of consideration. We see that the two versions agree on this last point. Jeremiah certainly aided Gedaliah in his attempt at restoration, and exercised at that time a kind of sovereignty over the people. The Ethiopian, Ebed-Melech, who had saved the prophet's life, also reaped the benefit of Iahveh's protection,[‡] and appears to have used his influence for the support of the little centre of government at Mispah.

But anarchy was too strong in the land for the project, sensible enough in itself, to succeed. The group of Mispah, which might have become a leaven for future resuscitations, never assumed any great proportions. Armed bands still held the country districts. The leaders of these troops went to Gedaliah at Mispah; Ishmael, the son of Ne-

[*] Jeremiah, ch. xxxix. v. 11-14.
[†] Jeremiah, ch. xl., xliii.
[‡] Jeremiah, ch. xxxix. v. 15-18.

thaniah, Johanan, the son of Kareah, and others. Gedaliah endeavoured to soothe them, to induce them to remain in the land, to work, and to recognise the supremacy of the King of Babylon. Ishmael was far the most dangerous man of the party; he belonged to the royal race and had formed part of Zedekiah's court.

Most of the chiefs listened favourably to Gedaliah's conciliating words. But brigandage was the order of the day. The Edomites had seized one portion of the territory* of Judah. Baalis, King of the Ammonites, had entered into an alliance with the assassins, particularly with Ishmael, the son of Nathaniah. The captains warned Gedaliah that Ishmael intended to murder him, and proposed that they should take the initiative and kill Ishmael. Gedaliah refused, but he was ill-rewarded for his loyalty; for, shortly afterwards, Ishmael went to Mispah with ten men. He killed Gedaliah, all his Jewish associates, and the Chaldeans who were with him. Gedaliah had only occupied the difficult position entrusted to him for about two months. With him perished the last hope of Jewish society being reconstituted upon its ancient foundations. From this moment Ishmael became a merciless brigand. He seized everything that Mispah contained; the king's daughters, all who had mustered

* Ezekiel, ch. xxv. v. 12; xxxv. v. 5, 10; ch. xxxvi. v. 1 and following; Psalm cxxxvii. v. 7; Isaiah, lxiii. v. 18 (correction by Grætz); 3 Esdras, ch. iv. v. 50.

round Gedaliah, and all that Nabuzaradan had confided to him. A band of eighty pilgrims from Samaria, Shechem, and Shiloh, who came in mourning, with their faces cut and their beards shaved, to bring offerings and incense to the ruined temple, were murdered in the most cruel way. Ishmael was preparing to pass over to the Ammonites with his booty, when Johanan, son of Kareah, and the other chiefs, surprised him near Gibeon. His prisoners immediately deserted him and joined Johanan. Ishmael escaped with eight men and succeeded in reaching the land of Ammon.

Johanan thus found himself, near Gideon, at the head of a considerable troop, composed of warriors, women, children, and eunuchs. Jeremiah and Baruch were with them.* The fugitives passed round Jerusalem and encamped at the khan of Chimham (Geruth Chimham), near Bethlehem, on the road towards Egypt. The murder of Gedaliah had spread terror throughout the country. The people dreaded the reprisals which the Chaldeans were sure to take for the death of their prefect. Moreover, Egypt at that moment appeared to be the only country where the misery of war was not felt, and where food was plentiful.

The resolution made by Johanan and the other

* The extreme detail with which these episodes are related (Jeremiah, ch. xl. and following) are no doubt due to Jeremiah's account of them.

military leaders was final. However, as a matter of form, they consulted Jeremiah, who, after ten days, announced that he had received an answer from Iahveh. Jeremiah was strongly averse to the flight into Egypt. He promised to obtain pardon from the Chaldeans for those who remained in the country. Johanan and the other chiefs were greatly displeased with this oracle. They pretended that their annoyance was due to the influence of Baruch, and persisted in leading the whole caravan into Egypt. They carried Jeremiah and Baruch with them, and thus reached Daphnæ,* near Pelusium, where they apparently settled.

The evil genius of Jeremiah still haunted him in this quiet country, where he might have died in peace. Nebuchadnezzar was always the minister of God in his eyes, the representative of Iahveh, the instrument for the execution of His will. He had scarcely entered Egypt, when, as usual, full of his predominant idea, the conquest of the world by the Chaldeans, he predicted, against all probabilities, no doubt because he wished for it, the ruin of the country which sheltered him, for the benefit of the destroyer of his native land.† The magnificent temples of Egypt, particularly the Temple of the Sun at Heliopolis, filled him with rage. He foresees

* See the results of the recent English excavations, *Egypt Exploration Fund*, No. iv.
† Jeremiah, ch. xliii.

Nebuchadnezzar breaking, burning, massacring, transporting, torturing, and he triumphs in the spectacle. The darker side of Israelitish fanaticism was never seen in a more striking example. And besides, this time Jeremiah's prophecies of impending calamities were quite needless. Nebuchadnezzar never conquered Egypt, and the reign of Hophra was an epoch of great prosperity.*

The small Jewish colony of Daphnæ spread over the neighbourhood to Migdol and Memphis, in Upper Egypt. Idolatrous customs soon resumed their sway over these scattered people, deprived of priests and shepherds. The worship of Astarte, the Queen of Heaven, had its centre in one quarter of Memphis,† and exercised a great attraction over all the Semites residing in Egypt. This provoked a manifesto from Jeremiah,‡ written with more violence than any of his former ones. Those who worshipped the Queen of Heaven, or allowed their wives to do so, are represented as the scourge of their co-religionists. Through their sin, the refugees in Egypt will meet with the same fate as the inhabitants of Jerusalem.

The colony of Daphnæ does not appear to have

* Herodotus, ii. 161; Maspero, p. 554 and following. Josephus, *Ant.*, X. xi., only draws inferences from Jeremiah.

† Herodotus, ii. 112; Brugsch, in the *Zeitschrift für ægypt. Sprache*, June 1863, p. 9; information given by M. Maspero.

‡ Jeremiah, ch. xliv.

THE LAST CONVULSIONS OF JUDAH. 307

been very docile to the prophet. Pure Iahveism had few adherents amongst the emigrants whom chance had thrown together; for they impertinently replied that they would fulfil their vows to the Queen of Heaven, as they were accustomed to do, they, their fathers, their kings, and their leaders in the cities of Judah and the streets of Jerusalem, in the happy days when they were prosperous; for since they had ceased to offer incense and libations to the Queen of Heaven, they lacked everything. It was not easy to escape logically from this syllogistic circle. Iahveism was taken in its own arguments. Jeremiah gave the incredulous a sign by which they would be convinced; that Hophra should be delivered up to his enemies, as Zedekiah had been delivered up to Nebuchadnezzar.[*] He dared not repeat his former prediction, that Hophra should be delivered up to Nebuchadnezzar, for Nebuchadnezzar had passed out of sight. He contented himself with a vague formula, which, considering the revolutions continually occurring at that time, could not fail to be realised sooner or later.[†]

Judaism was thus totally destroyed in Palestine; Jerusalem was a heap of ruins; the country districts had retained the majority of their inhabitants; but

---

[*] Jeremiah, ch. xliv. v. 30.

[†] The tragic death of Hophra, in 569, through the revolt of Amasis, leads one to believe in a *prophetia post eventum*, proceeding from Jeremiah's disciples.

these villages, disturbed by the reforms of Josiah, had no organised worship. Iahveism was entirely transplanted; it now centred in Mesopotamia and Chaldea. The Israelitish conscience was suppressed in Judea; but, on the other hand, it increased with great vitality in Babylon.

BOOK VI.
THE BABYLONIAN CAPTIVITY.

CHAPTER I.

THE FIRST YEARS OF EXILE.

The frightful spectacle which the traveller in Africa frequently met upon his road, in the days of the slave trade, the lines of unfortunate men chained together, driven along by the whip of the slave merchant, was continually witnessed by the Asiatic world at the time when Nineveh and Babylon were at the climax of their power. The Assyrian bas-reliefs, [*] show us, with startling realism, the long files of captives, their arms bound behind their backs, in a position which in itself must have caused frightful torture, walking bowed and humiliated beneath the whip, for the greater glory of their conqueror. It was in this posture

[*] Layard, *Monum. of Nineveh*, second series, pl. xviii. and following unto L.

that the leading men of Judah accomplished the long and cruel journey from Jerusalem to Riblah (more than eighty leagues). No doubt the exiled crowd was led first to Riblah, and from there conducted across the desert of Palmyra to the confluent of the Euphrates and the Chebar.* It was then, that the natives as they passed must have often asked, "Where is their God?" and the pious Israelite murmured in his heart, "My God, my God, why hast thou forsaken me?"

If we except the men of war, who were nearly all killed or fugitives in Egypt, and the men of the lowest classes, who had remained in Judea, the Jewish nation (we mean all that really makes a nation, *i.e.*, the head) thus found itself transported, almost in its entirety, to the banks of the Euphrates towards the year 585 B.C. The essential organ of the nation was with them, I mean the ancient Scriptures, which already formed a very considerable volume. The exiles must have had some luggage carried upon asses or camels. The fate of humanity depended for some days upon the surefootedness of the animal which carried the sacred book of the future. Yet was not some volume of the Scriptures left in Judea, in the hands of the poor people whom the conqueror considered too insignificant for him to trouble about them? No

* The return journey is mentioned in Isaiah, ch. xxxv. (written at the end of the exile), and appears to have been made across the desert. The second Isaiah alludes to it in the same manner.

one can say.* But it is certain, that the literary tradition was the work of the families carried into the East.

Most of the captives were confined in Babylon; others were scattered throughout the cities and villages built on the canals† of Lower Chaldea. Babylon was a province rather than a city.‡ Numerous centres of population separated from each other by orchards, meadows, and willows§ were sown, as it were, over an enormous space enclosed by walls. The Constantinopolitan agglomeration of our own time must recall this arrangement. The most varied races brought together by captivity met each other in this enclosure.‖ The intellectual and moral contact between them was slight; conquest alone had united them, and their sole desire was to part again. The bridge which joined the two parts of the city was raised every evening, to prevent the different populations from throwing themselves upon each other and pillaging.¶ Israel, at least, never borrowed anything from its conquerors. On the contrary, burying

---

* See below, p. 364.

† נהרות ככל. Psalm, cxxxvii. v. 1.

‡ At the present time the enclosure of Babylon contains nearly twenty-five thousand inhabitants. Hillah is the most important of the groups of houses scattered over it.

§ Psalms cxxxvii. v. 2.

‖ *Hist. des langues semit.*, I. ii. 3; Quatremère, *Mem. géogr, sur la Babylonie*, p. 21.

¶ Herodotus, i. p. 186. Compare the chains of Stamboul.

itself with a sort of frenzy in its own ideas, it would not listen to anything that had no reference to its past, nor dream of any thing but its future.*

Babylon, at the time when the Jews were transported there, was reviving brilliantly under Nebuchadnezzar after a long period of degradation. The buildings and restorations completed by this king have placed him amongst the greatest sovereign builders that ever existed.† He restored the tower of Bel to its original state.‡ His last years, especially, appear to have been spent in carrying out the gigantic works required for the preservation of water, in a country which resembles Egypt in many respects.§ There is no proof that the captive Jews were employed in this way. Their occupations appear to have been more agricultural. They are found in the villages of Tell-Melah, Tel-Harsha, and Cheroub-Addan, apparently in the vicinity of Babylon.‖ The commerce and industry of Babylon were immense. They roused great anger in the prophets;¶ but it is very possible that the Jewish

---

* The hypothesis that the Jews borrowed considerably from the East, during the captivity, is founded upon a thoroughly erroneous conception of the Jews' state of mind, and of their international relations during this time.

† Nearly all Nebuchadnezzar's inscriptions relate to these constructions.

‡ Oppert, *Miss. de Mésopotamie*, i. p. 202 and following. Schrader, p. 122.

§ Maspero, pp. 557-558.

‖ Ezra, ch. ii. v. 59.

¶ Ezekiel, ch. xvii. v. 4.

laity was less hostile to them and even took an active part in them. Association with the lower classes of the population, who spoke Aramean, caused the emigrants to adopt this language, which at that epoch was generally prevalent in the basin of the Euphrates and the Tigris. Every one learnt it, but no one on that account ceased using his national idiom. The *soferim* continued to write in the old Hebrew dialect. But even those who habitually spoke and wrote in Hebrew lapsed into numerous aramaïsms from this time. Proper names, especially, became impregnated with Aramean roots.*

From a material point of view, the situation of the exiled Jews was not that of slaves; but rather of exiles or prisoners, free in all respects, except in the choice of their dwelling. The laws of the Chaldean empire, with regard to individuals, differed little from those of the Ottoman empire. The position of the Jews on the Euphrates must have resembled that of the Syrian *métualis* of our own time. The *métualis* are descended from Persians or Kurdes, who, through various adventures, were carried into Syria during the Crusades. They have lost their own language (the language in the East always resists less than the religion); but they cling obstinately to their Persian sympathies and Schiite worship, showing towards them an attachment which is quite invincible. Their condition is not servile but subor-

* משיזבאל, etc.

dinate. The land which they occupy forms part of the *Miri;* it has been conceded to them upon terms that, in certain cases, ultimately constitute a quasi-ownership.

We must consider the position of the Hebrews in Babylon as very similar to the above, except that, the Chaldean empire being free from all religious fanaticism, the situation of the Hebrews must have been less painful than that of the *métualis*, who are always exposed to affronts from the Sunnites. A great many Jews adopted professions or positions which soon placed them in comfort.* Most of them received grants of land, which enabled them to build houses and plant gardens. Their communications with each other were perfectly free, like those of the various communities of the rayahs in the Ottoman empire.† A large majority were well content to find themselves sheltered from the miseries of war; but the pietists clung to Zion with intense sentimental longing, and thought of nothing but their return. They remained poor, and resented the conduct of those who acquired riches, too frequently by pandering to the vices or luxury of the conquerors. These became a species of deserter in their eyes, who would be punished by the perfect David when he should one day govern in the name of Iahveh.‡

---

* Jeremiah, ch. xxix. v. 5 and following, and the whole chapter.
† Jeremiah, ch. xxix; Ezekiel, ch. xiv. v. 1; chap. xxxiii. v. 31.
‡ Ezekiel, ch. xxxiv. v. 20 and following.

THE FIRST YEARS OF EXILE.

It would be an error to suppose that misfortune had established equality and peace amongst the exiles. The wealthy possessed slaves and treated them with much severity.* The sacerdotal and patrician families had retained all their former haughtiness;† they had some jurisdiction over the lower classes, and annoyed them in the name of the Chaldeans.‡ The equipment for the return journey was that of a rich caravan, from which neither male nor female singers were lacking.§ Now all this wealth had been acquired in Babylon, and the little eagerness shown by the majority of the laity for their return surely arose from that prosperity, which must have been enjoyed from the earliest years of their exile. On the other hand, a great many of the poor were obliged to sell themselves as slaves in order to live. The pious considered it a duty to subscribe together for their redemption.‖

There was scarcely any association between the Israelites and the upper classes of Babylon. A great many Jews became servants in the households of the Chaldean nobility, and adopted Chaldean names, without troubling themselves about the paganism implied by these names.¶ It did not entail any

* Ezra, ch. ii.; Ezekiel, ch. xxxiv.
† Isaiah, ch. lix.
‡ The *roim* of Ezekiel, ch. xxxiv.
§ Ezra, ch. i., ch. ii. v. 65
‖ Nehemiah, ch. v. v. 8.
¶ Shesh-bazzar; Sharezer and Regem-Melech, Zechariah, ch. vii. v. 1 and following. See Daniel, ch. i. v. 7, taking this work as a legend written four hundred years later.

apostasy, and was not more shocking than when the Jews of the Roman epoch called themselves Appollonius or Hermes. So far as we can picture to ourselves a period far distant from us and still little known, we see two upper classes at Babylon, both equally unsuited to exercise any durable influence over Israel: first a warrior class, harsh and cruel, a sort of Redskins, haughty and malicious; then a learned caste, already rationalist, naturalist, atheist, from which Greece was then learning her first lessons. These two aristocracies were the direct negation of the God of Israel. Eight or nine centuries earlier, Israel, in all the flexibility of a young tribe, might have listened with avidity to the grand accounts of the old mythology of Ur-Casdim;* but a nation fanaticised by men like Jeremiah and Ezekiel was unable to comprehend a civilisation, which had learned through philosophy to deny both the gods and Providence. As to military, conquering Assyria, with almost no religion, it could inspire the finely-developed moral sense of the true Hebrews with horror only. To them Babylon was evil, nothing more.† Our opinion is that the pious Jews who were captive in Babylon wilfully closed their eyes to all that surrounded them. Their attitude was that of Bretons transplanted to Paris, who will not look at anything and depreciate all that passes

---

* See vol. i. p. 54 and following.
† Zechariah, ch. v. v. 5-11.

THE FIRST YEARS OF EXILE.

under their eyes, maintaining that the quiet life of their own village, full of affection and cordiality, is worth much more. And, therefore, the effect of this exile, which did not last more than fifty years, was to strengthen the spirit of Israel in its own ideas, to exaggerate its qualities and defects, and to confine it with more ardour than ever to its idea of a perfect law, which, if perfectly observed, would secure the happiness of the whole community.

The Levites, so numerous since Josiah, whose fate had so constantly preoccupied both the author of Deuteronomy and Jeremiah, were in a state of mendicity amongst the emigrants.* They made common cause with the *anavim*, and considerably increased the crowd of God's poor, who expected their food and their safety to be provided by the hand of Iahveh. The priests must also have suffered great distress; the reform of Josiah having rendered all worship illegal if performed outside the temple of Jerusalem, no sacrifices could be offered. The priests and Levites, who lived from the sacrifices, were without any resources. It was probably amongst this class, the spirit of which is so well represented by Ezekiel, that the ideas of return and restoration were most strongly cherished.

This accounts for the difference between the procedure of the exiles of Samaria and of those transported from Jerusalem, one hundred and thirty-three years

---

* See Ezra, ch. ii. v. 40 and following, 70, and the parallel lists.

later. The Iahveism of the captives from Samaria was not yet formed. It speedily dissolved; the ten tribes disappeared; their name retained merely a hieratic value. Judah, on the contrary, was like a metal bar during the captivity. This was owing to the influence of Jeremiah, Josiah, and Deuteronomy. The law existed; it was the great solder which held together the pieces of the little world which the conquest had broken up. As the worship of Iahveh could no longer be celebrated except at Jerusalem, it was necessary to rebuild Jerusalem at any price. Iahveh could be worshipped in any place by the ten tribes, so that as Samaria never became a holy city, there was no reason to rebuild it.

It does not appear that the captive Judaites came in contact with any considerable number of the Israelitish exiles.* No doubt the latter had already half lost their ritual or offered sacrifices to Iahveh, which in the eyes of the Judaites, were merely sacrileges. When the prophets speak to us of their hopes of seeing the restoration of Jerusalem as the capital of all the branches of the family of Israel, it is only in a geographical sense. Already, under Josiah, this hope had been realised to a certain extent by the species of suzerainty, which

* Jeremiah, ch. l. v. 4 and following is only a prophetic reservation often repeated. Passages like Ezekiel, ch. xxxvii. v. 15 and following, seem, however, to infer that there were some of the Israelites transported by Shalmaneser in Babylon, who still celebrated the worship of Iahveh in their own way.

Jerusalem had acquired over the northern provinces. The resumption of this ascendency was always an integral part of the Jewish programme; it was accomplished under the Asmonæans.

It was therefore the captivity of Babylon which definitely converted Israel into a holy people. The court and the military classes, always opposed to the prophets, no longer existed. The Levites, who were numerous amongst the exiles, retained their attachment to religious things. The lukewarm and indifferent soon resigned themselves to their fate and settled in the East, where lucrative employments were easily obtained. The pietists formed a group and fanned each other's zeal by frequent association. Disciples, as a rule, of Jeremiah, they persistently asserted the future prosperity of Israel and the righteous providence of Iahveh. This was the decisive moment. The crisis which does not destroy a budding creed strengthens it. Henceforth Judaism resembled a sheaf girdled with iron. From the first years of the captivity, the group of saints scattered over the banks of the Euphrates had reconstituted a burning centre of life, as intense as that which consumed the Jewish blood in the most feverish days of Jerusalem.

And, in fact, one of the most extraordinary points in the moral attitude of the Jewish people at this period of their history is their inflexibility, their persistence in believing and hoping, in spite of appearances. It would be an exaggeration if we were to attribute these sentiments to the whole nation. The enthusiasts were always in a small minority; but they alone wrote; they alone bequeathed their dominant thought to future generations. Their slackness was extreme on some points. The Chaldean art of divination attracted them powerfully, and they believed that they could devote themselves to it without disloyalty to Iahveh!* The rules about clean and unclean things were very minute, and were often broken.† Thousands of peaceful individuals resigned themselves to the necessities of the time, and contented themselves with a moderate Iahveism which admitted a large dose of idolatry!‡ They are not even remembered, but the protestation of the fanatics has come down to us clear and resonant as the sound of a trumpet. In all these ardent pages, there is not one expression of despair, not one trace of discouragement.§ Hence the strange fact, that the Babylonian captivity scarcely constitutes an era in the religious and literary history of Israel. The movement commenced under Josiah was continued after the ruin of Jerusalem as though nothing had happened. Only its progress was much accelerated. The lukewarm no longer counted; there were no moderate men

---

* Isaiah, ch. lxv. init.
† Isaiah, ch. lxv. v. 4; ch. lxvi. v. 17.
‡ Second Isaiah, especially ch. lxiv. v. 4, and the whole of ch. lxv.
§ The *Lamentations* would be an exception, but that it should be regarded as a work of artificial rhetoric of much later date.

left. The idealist without a country always becomes a dangerous person; the world is right to beware of him.

Henceforth the *anavim* were alone, and without counterpoise in Israel. Nebuchadnezzar had really worked for them, as Titus worked for the Christians. Jeremiah found that he was right. His disciples triumphed; their real enemies, the worldly and military circles of Jerusalem, those who dreamed of a secular policy and of free association with foreigners, had disappeared. One of the conflicting elements had strangled the other. The *anavim*, hitherto a persecuted minority, were henceforth the whole of Israel. Amongst peoples devoted to an idea, the law, as we have said twenty times, is made by the minority. The French Revolution was due to the persistency of a small number of demoniacs, who succeeded in imposing the belief that they led the nation. We hear only of the few; the flock of sheep merely serve to make up the number. History interests itself in the ambitious and passionate only.

Everything succeeds with those who have to fulfil a divine mission. The men who were most gloomy during the siege, became admirable as soon as they had no more politics to manage. Through successive eliminations, Israel became a group of the righteous, who never troubled themselves about war or politics, but accepted the suzerainty of Babylon, secretly cherishing the consoling thought that Babylon would soon be destroyed in its turn. The profane classes were mortally stricken, but on the other hand, the prophetic school had more vitality than ever. Jeremiah dragged out the last years of his life in obscurity in Egypt.* But Baruch, his disciple, and all his school, carried on the old spirit, which dated from Josiah. The national sorrows inspired them with canticles of purer harmony than ever.

* It is supposed that the second Isaiah, ch. liii., contains some allusions to the sad end of Jeremiah and to the wrongs which he endured. See below, p. 397.

CHAPTER II.

CONSOLATIONS OF THE PEOPLE.

EZEKIEL was the great consolation of the exiles in Babylon. During more than twenty years, this extraordinary man was the centre of the fiery preaching which saved the conscience of Israel from a storm, in which any other national conscience would have perished. As long as Jerusalem existed, he was in correspondence with the brethren in Judea; when Jerusalem and the temple disappeared, he was the obstinate champion of Iahveism, as the prophets understood it. Without any official title, and in spite of the opposition of rival prophets,* he acquired extraordinary authority, and traced the path of the future. We may conclude that at this period of his life Ezekiel was dwelling in Babylon. His house served as a meeting place for the elders and pious men; those even who merely believed were admitted; for the prophet

* Ezekiel, ch. xiii.

complains, that sometimes, certain of the audience listened to him with more curiosity than true piety and wish to reform.* It was a kind of synagogue, and, we may say, the first synagogue that ever existed. Since the destruction of the temple, some new institution had become necessary; a place where the Jews could assemble on certain days to strengthen each other in the national spirit, and to provide against foreign influences. The place which served for these pious meetings was first the house of some venerated chief of a respected family, just as later on the first churches were all attached to some household.† No doubt the Sabbath was soon chosen for these assemblies. The cycle of Jewish life, without temple or priests, was already commencing to define itself. The Jewish quarter in each city would contain, not a chapel to Iahveh, but an assembly room, the centre of a very fruitful movement.

Ezekiel had been speedily informed of the fall of Jerusalem by a fugitive.‡ It is so difficult to distinguish fiction from fact in the curious pages which bear the name of this writer, that we cannot tell whether the assertion that about this time he lost his wife, and received a command from Iahveh

---

* Ezekiel, ch. xxxiii. v. 30 and following.

† Romans, ch. xvi. v. 5; 1 Corinthians, ch. xvi. v. 19.

‡ Ezekiel, ch. xxxiii. v. 21 and following. Compare ch. xxiv. v. 26-27. Circesium is not far from Palmyra. News could travel from Jerusalem to Palmyra in very few days.

not to wear mourning for her, should be taken literally.* Anyway, Ezekiel was kept well informed about the incidents of the war by partisans who watched the defence of the city, and were much averse to it.† In fact, as we have seen, the character of these events was little fitted to please the pietists. Moreover, the arrival of the new captives tended to heighten the tone adopted by Ezekiel.‡ The prophet felt that this increase of his religious family also added to his responsibility. He was in charge of souls.§ He is responsible for those who perish through lack of warning. The idea of an ecclesiastical ministry is almost as much developed in Ezekiel as in Saint Paul or Clement of Rome.

Ezekiel's confidence in all the promises given to the Israelites never falters. Iahveh is bound by his word, he has entered into an engagement. It is not the merits of Israel that have influenced his actions, but the intention of saving his honour. Jerusalem and the cities of Judah will be rebuilt; the two halves of the chosen race will be reunited; the unity of Israel will be completed around Judah. Iahveh will gather together all the members of his

---

* Ezekiel, ch. xxiv. v. 15 and following. See above, p. 287. According to some commentators Ezekiel intended in this way to reproach the first captives with their indifference to the miseries endured by their fellow-countrymen in Judea.
† Ezekiel, ch. xxxiii. v. 21 and following.
‡ Ezekiel, ch. xxxiii to xxxix.
§ Ezekiel, ch. xxxiii. Ingenious discussions of moral theology.

people from the countries in which they may be dispersed. Then the Jewish life will be practised in its integrity; no more idolatry; the whole Thora will be observed;* the world will be happy.

This fixed idea assumes the most varied forms in the visions of Ezekiel. Now it is a plain covered with dry bones, over which passes the breath of life, so that the bones clothe themselves with flesh, nerves, and skin;† presently it is a vision of the ideal temple of the future ‡ which unfolds itself before him; sometimes the revolutions of the world appear to him subordinate to the destinies of his people. The prophecy of the shepherds of Israel§ is already quite Christian—full of a pastoral and unctuous spirit. This is one of the chapters of Ezekiel which has passed almost intact into the Gospel, and thence into Christian instruction. Israel has had bad shepherds, who have thought only of the profits to be made out of the flock. The flocks therefore dispersed. Their former leaders were justly deprived of their charge. Iahveh declares that henceforth he will be the sole shepherd of Israel. He will gather the flock together after its dispersion, and will lead it back to its native mountains. He will protect the sheep against the rams and he-goats. He will prevent the latter from

---

* Ezekiel, ch. xxxvii., 2nd part.
† Ezekiel, ch. xxxvii., 1st part.
‡ See below, p. 336 and following.
§ Ezekiel, ch. xxxiv.

treading down the pasture and fouling the water that the sheep are to drink. More than that. He will judge between the sheep themselves, and will defend the lean sheep against the fat ones. Woe to those who have fattened themselves amidst such universal distress! Moreover, the fat sheep thrust the lean ones aside with their horns. This must not be allowed. " I will set up one shepherd over them, and he shall feed them, even my servant David.* And I, Iahveh, will be their God. And my servant David prince among them. I, Iahveh, have spoken it."

The land of Israel shall become a terrestrial paradise; savage beasts shall disappear; a shower of blessings shall descend upon the mountains. No more masters, no more violence, no more conquering nations. How different from the fate of the neighbours of Israel, who have shown bitterness towards it! Their mountains shall become a desert; their valleys shall be filled with the dead; their cities shall become a heap of ruins. They have mocked at the calamities of Israel.

At that time the majority of the smaller peoples of Syria found the same advantage from possessing less national pride than Israel, and from bending under the storm, that the same policy produced later on, during the Roman epoch. A return to the system of petty states became more and more

---

* Ezekiel, ch. xxxiv. v. 23.

impossible. A paroxysm of wild jealousy seized the violent partisans of the patriarchal state when they saw Ammon, Edom, Moab, the Philistines, Tyre, Sidon, and Egypt still flourishing after the disasters which had overwhelmed Judah. They revenged themselves by thundering curses against the nations that seemed by their prosperity to falsify the promises of Iahveh.* Ammon had clapped its hands over the ruin of Jerusalem; it should be delivered up for a spoil to the Arabs. Moab should meet with the same fate. Edom had wished to invade the territory of Judah; it should be punished after the restoration of Israel. As to the Philistines, they should be destroyed for ever.

These great proofs of the justice of Iahveh would take place on a day of darkness,† which Ezekiel, like all the prophets,‡ believed to be near at hand.§ This "day of nations" would be preceded by terrible signs, particularly by a sort of general overthrow of all the heathen world, come forth to resist theocracy. The mythical chief of this rising in arms would be Gog, the prince of the land of Meshech-Tubal,‖ who would be at the head of all the barbarism of the north, and would lead it

* Ezekiel, ch. xxv. and chap. xxxv.-xxxvi.
† Ezekiel, ch. xxx. v. 3.
‡ See vol. ii. p. 370.
§ Ezekiel, ch. xxxviii. v. 17; ch. xxxix. v. 8.
‖ Ezekiel, ch. xxxviii. and xxxix. *Ros* is not a country. Ezekiel's geography does not extend beyond the limits of the tenth chapter of Genesis.

against restored Israel, to be finally exterminated in its turn. Israel would be enriched with its spoil and poisoned by its dead.* The name of Gog is only an abridgment of the old geographical name of Magog,† probably designating the Caucasus. It seems that this is an allusion to the Scythians, who made a great expedition into Syria in the time of Josiah.‡ We shall never completely decipher the mystery of this passage, which the author himself wished to render enigmatic by giving a symbolical signification to real facts, and by predicting for the future events that had already taken place.

The school of Jeremiah contributed as much to the consolation of the exiles as the indefatigable Ezekiel. We know nothing of the ulterior destinies of the group of Jews that had taken refuge in Egypt. Jeremiah died protesting against their lukewarmness and their tendency to idolatry. It is probable that Baruch went to Babylon, where the current of ideas was more in harmony with his own.§ The remainder of the Jewish colonies, scattered at Daphnæ, Memphis, and Heliopolis, was

* Compare Herodotus, i. 105.

† Ezekiel, ch. xxxviii. v. 1. ארץ מגוג is a marginal addition which has passed into the text. If translated according to the usual way, it should be בארץ.

‡ See above, pp. 211, 212.

§ Baruch appears to have assisted in the arrangement of the book of Jeremiah, which is inseparable from the last chapters of the books of Kings. Now these arrangements appear to have been made in Babylon. See below, p. 363.

soon corrupted, abandoned itself to Semitico-Egyptian worship, and was almost lost to Israel. The first colonies had no Thora. The colony of Alexandria, fertile in a different way, was much more modern in its origin, and dates from a period when no Israelitish group ever travelled without the Thora.

A fine poem, found amongst the works of Jeremiah,[*] is a complete epitome of Jewish hopes at this solemn hour. He who scattered Israel will gather it together again. Sion and Samaria will be reconciled; Ephraim will come and worship at Jerusalem. Are not Benjamin and Joseph sons of the same mother, Rachel? At the present time, lamentations are heard issuing from the tomb of Rachel at Ramah, the voice of a mother weeping for her children, refusing to be comforted because they are not. How happy she will be when Iahveh shall say unto her, "Thy children shall come again to their own border." The way is already being prepared, the way-marks and sign-posts are being set up. Jacob, thus restored in its unity, shall have a national prince. The prophet does not say that he will be descended from David. Unclouded joy! The holy ritual shall be re-established at Sion with unequalled splendour; the priests shall be satiated

---

[*] Ch. xxx. and xxxi. It is very doubtful if this poem were really written by Jeremiah himself. It bears a great resemblance to the work of the second Isaiah.

with fatness; the people shall be satisfied with good things.

But one thought had weighed heavily upon the pious, especially of Jeremiah's school; that, as Iahveh visited the sins of the fathers upon successive generations, they would always, however righteous they might personally be, see the horrors of Hinnom, the crimes of Manasseh rising up before them. The Jeremist, agreeing with Ezekiel on this point, announces that after the restoration sin would be personal only; a man would no longer expiate the sins of his ancestors, as he then did. Forgiveness would be absolute. All men would know the law intuitively, not by instruction. God himself would write it in their hearts. It would be a new covenant, superior to the one concluded upon the departure from Egypt, which had been broken through the crimes of the ancient people.

Thus the formula of the future had been completely defined in all the families of Israel. The holy men dispersed over the banks of the Euphrates mutually participated in the obstinate dream which henceforth inspired all their actions and all their writings. Jerusalem should be re-established, the worship of Iahveh restored. An ideal David would cause justice to reign in Israel. The prediction of the ancient seers would be accomplished; the day of Iahveh would appear, and would prove a frightful reality for the heathen. Israel, on the contrary, restored to a pastoral and agricultural life, would enjoy perfect happiness upon the mountains, rejoicing once more in their ancient fertility. Messianism thus attained a new stage of definition and precision with every fresh vision.

CHAPTER III.

PLANS OF RESTORATION.—EZEKIEL.

The incredible faith which the Jewish people had in itself, is most visible in the fertility of its imagination, when dwelling upon its future resurrection at the very moment that the things of this world appeared most adverse to it. In these years Ezekiel's passionate soul attained a height in which human nature has rarely maintained itself. The reconstruction of Jerusalem was so little doubted by this imperturbable believer that all his thoughts were occupied by plans, often eccentric, for arranging the future society in harmony with the spirit of the prophets, whose work he ardently continued.

Josiah's reform had become so absolutely the law of Iahveism, that the idea of celebrating the worship of Iahveh outside Jerusalem appeared impossible. Religion, as Jeremiah understood it, was not only a purely civic ritual, but a ritual which could only be celebrated in one particular city. This city once destroyed, it must be rebuilt at any price, under penalty of seeing the truth perish. If Jewish ideas took another turn after the siege by Titus, it was because the character of the Roman power was far more immutable than the Assyrian. Moreover, the idealist conception had made so much progress in Israel, thanks in a great measure to Christianity, that Jerusalem had become less necessary to Iahveism, and the doctors of Iabne could conceive perfect observance of the law without sacerdoce or altar.

The sacerdotal and ritualistic organization were the principal subject of the dreams of the pietists. They certainly intended to revert to the past in all its essentials, but they felt that a great many material changes were necessary, and they did not scruple to introduce them. During his captivity Ezekiel employed his leisure in musing upon plans, which he perpetually rearranged. Facing the problem which the reforms of Josiah had created without solving, the hierarchy of the sacerdotal body, he endeavoured to mentally portray the city of priests which was issuing from the unconscious effort of Israel.

These ideas, which appear in Ezekiel under many varied forms, and with changes that in some measure show us the progress of his thoughts, are summed up in a series of visions dated 575 B.C.[*]
The chapters in question form a short ideal descrip-

---

[*] Ezekiel, ch. xl.-xlviii.

tion of the new organization planned by the one whom we are authorised to consider the second founder of Judaism after Jeremiah. There are no pages in the writings of the past which reveal a stranger state of mind. They resemble a dream in which the laws of reality have ceased to exist, and even figures are flexible. The geography is entirely fanciful; the topography full of contradictions. They form an ideal code, which, assuredly, the Seer himself would not willingly have seen applied without a great many modifications. The numbers especially seem almost written down by chance, and there is some *naïveté* in the effort to correct them; the author might as well have left them unwritten. Those who pretend to base any calculations or drawings upon these eccentric visions might as well try to draw out the plan of the heavenly Jerusalem of the Apocalypse. They would have to allow room in their drawings for the river issuing from the temple, increasing with every yard, flowing down to sweeten the Dead Sea.* No prophet has trifled with the impossible so much as Ezekiel. He recalls Fourier; but a Fourier who wishes to describe his phalanstery with the precision of an architect or a surveyor.

Ezekiel depicts Israel as a pure theocracy without either a civil or military government, a magistracy or politics. Like all Jews, of every epoch, he was quite satisfied to remain in a state of

* Ezekiel, ch. xlvii. init.

vassalage, in which the people of God, free from the expense of an organized State, could enjoy the promises of Iahveh in its own way. The city which Israel dreamt of has no place in this world, except as the self-governing fief of a great empire, like the communities of the rayahs of Islam. In this city there is neither king nor military service; though Ezekiel in the early years of his captivity still called his shepherd of Israel by the name of David,* without clearly stating that he would be of the race of David, he now only calls him *nasi* (prince). The *nasi* had a territorial domain, and the right of appanage for his children; he also received some revenue, from which he was bound to provide victims for the public sacrifices. He was absolutely prohibited from imposing arbitrary taxes, such as Solomon established. As to the defence of Israel against its enemies, Iahveh took that upon himself, treating the neighbouring tribes with great atrocity. The *nasi* had a place of honour in the solemn services of worship, and a door reserved for his own use. He was a state king only for show,† not in any sense a temporal prince. The high priest, who after sixty years supplanted the *nasi* as head of Israel, was far better in many respects than this sort of spurious *corregidor*,‡ a purveyor

* Ezekiel, ch. xxxiv. v. 23; ch. xxxvii. v. 24.

† Ezekiel, ch. xliv. v. 3; ch. xlv. v. 7 and following; ch. xlvi. v. 7 and following.

‡ Police officer in Spain (note by Translator).

PLANS OF RESTORATION—EZEKIEL.

of victims, a liturgical figure, whose almost only function was to preside over the worship, although the ministers were quite independent of him in every way.

The organization described by Ezekiel is so completely ideal, that he wishes the Holy Land, now recovered, of which he traces the position according to a singularly complaisant geography, to be symmetrically divided into equal parts by rectangular zones going from the Mediterranean to the Jordan, for the twelve tribes, which no longer existed.* The holy domain and the princes' estate are described as separate squares. The capital city should also have its portion of land.† It should be neutral between the twelve tribes, like a sort of Washington, organized by representatives of all the tribes who lived on the produce of the domain. Tribes that had been long incorporated with the nation, like the Rechabites, Kenites, and Calebites, would be entirely blended with it. The liberal humane spirit of Deuteronomy is found in Ezekiel whenever national anger and puritan fanaticism do not stifle it.

The temple imagined by Ezekiel bears no resemblance beyond the general arrangement to the small edifice built by Solomon. The details given *à priori* by the prophet are carried to such a point

* Ezekiel, ch. xlvii, v. 13 and following.
† Ezekiel, xlv. v, 6; ch. xlviii. v. 8 and following, 21.

that at times the temple does not seem to be at Jerusalem.* It is a colossal barracks placed in the centre of the holy domain, and intended to contain a sacerdotal army. Even the name of Jerusalem will disappear. The city will be called *Iahvé samma*, "Iahveh is (lives) there." The priests descended from Zadok (the first priest of Solomon's temple) have the exclusive right of ascending to the altar. The Levites, against whom there were serious complaints, for they had assisted at idolatrous rites, constituted an immense difficulty. We have seen Jeremiah and Deuteronomy decide the question in the most radical fashion. In their eyes every priest is a Levite, or, as they say, "the priests, the Levites." † Perfect equality apparently existed amongst these Levitical priests. This was doubtless the expression of a wish rather than the statement of a fact. The editor of the book of Kings lays some stress upon the difference of rank amongst them.‡ Ezekiel defines the theory. The Zadokite priests are, in his eyes, the only legitimate ones. The Levites, having assisted in illegal worship,§ are servants of an inferior order; they do not appear in the public sacrifices. They are to inhabit separate villages in the suburbs of

* Ezekiel, xli. v. 1 and following; ch. xlviii. v. 8 and following, 21.

† See above. p. 183, and Jeremiah, ch. xxxiii. v. 18, 21, 22.

‡ 2 Kings, ch. xxiii. v. 8 and following. See above, p. 156.

§ Ezekiel, ch. xliv. v. 10 and following; ch. xlviii. v. 11 and following.

PLANS OF RESTORATION.—EZEKIEL.

Jerusalem.* As to the Zadokite priests they were all equal. The sacrifices and festivals are more fully developed in Ezekiel than in Deuteronomy; tithes do not exist. The sustenance of the priests is provided for by the firstfruits and the dues in kind on the sacrifices.

Such is the code of the theocracy, to which succeeding legislations made scarcely any additions, but which formed, at the time it was drawn up, the most complete innovation. Until then, no absolute distinction had been made between the priests and the Levites. Ezekiel, no doubt actuated by old priestly animosities, dating from the time of his sacerdotal youth, would only recognise the descendants of the aristocratic Zadok as true priests. This was consistent. Ezekiel wished for a sacerdotal theocracy. A body of priests concentrating all the authority in its own hands cannot be large. Ezekiel did not attain (at all events before 575) the idea of the great hereditary high priest, familiar to later times; but he almost touched it. In any case Ezekiel was, unconsciously, the father of a word which filled an important rôle in history. Through him *Zadoki* became the designation of a rich haughty priest who despised the poor. From this came *Sadducean*. The concentration of the lucrative sacerdoce in a few hands must inevitably produce bad effects. A sacerdotal aristocracy soon becomes irreligious and unbelieving.

* Ezekiel, ch. xlv. v. 5, corrected according to the Greek.

The long ritual described by Ezekiel* is less the work of a prophet than of a priest. In it we realise the prepossessions of a man who has assisted at the sacrifices, has seen the abuses of the established customs, and has long ago based his programme of reform upon them. The prophet reappears in the ideal conception of the new Jerusalem, the source of life and purity for the world to come, sole origin of the waters which purify, cure, and fertilise. The description of the slopes from Jerusalem to the Dead Sea having become an immense orchard of trees, bearing fruit every month, even their leaves possessing healing qualities, suggested the finest images to the Christian seer of the time of Galba. The celestial Jerusalem of the Apocalypse, which has consoled the world for eighteen hundred years, is a slightly modified copy of the Jerusalem of Ezekiel. Thus, in this strange genius, the eschatological visions of prophetism were united, by a phenomenon, unique in Israel, to the matter-of-fact details of the Thora.

* Ezekiel, ch. xliv. and following.

CHAPTER IV.

SACERDOTAL AND LEVITICAL THORA.

Was Ezekiel alone in thus constructing Utopias for a restoration, generally believed to be impending? Certainly not. Everything proves that in the thirty or forty years after the siege of Jerusalem there was a period when the new Deuteronomy, the code of the future, was elaborated. All pious men admitted that Israel should have a new law after the restoration.* The prophetic spirit was considered a permanent inspiration, adequate to complete and alter the Thora. The work was therefore commenced, not with the precision natural when it is a question of drawing up measures soon to be applied, but with the ambiguity suitable to rather indefinite aspirations. And, in fact, the laws added to the Mosaic code at this epoch are distinguished by their speculative, chimerical character. They are not the expedients of practical

---

* See above, pp. 277, 278.

people fighting with necessity, and doing their best to cope with the requirements of a situation which forces them to take decided measures; but they are rather general indications, which become puerile when any attempt is made to bring them into a practical form, plans resembling those that friends of the Count de Chambord might elaborate around him, or that might be discussed in socialist clubs. The code of the restoration was thus sketched out fifty years in advance. These pages were not written at the time of the reconstruction of the temple, but at an epoch when the hopes of the nation were only dreams and the country lay before them like a white paper, to which they could commit the boldest solutions of the situation without any fear of having to control their realisation.

In any case, the close connection which exists between the nine last chapters of Ezekiel and the sacerdotal and Levitical portions of the Thora is very striking. Just as Deuteronomy rises, in some degree spontaneously, by the side of Jeremiah, as the codified form of his ideas, so by the side of Ezekiel appears the sacerdotal Thora, which we should call Leviticus, if its scattered members were not equally found in Exodus, Numbers, and Joshua. The procedure of this ideal construction, if we may so express it, is always the same. The tabernacle and the Israelitish camp in the desert are drawn on a kind of square lined paper, which renders them quite analogous to the temple of Ezekiel and to his map of

Palestine, in which all the lines are straight. The stiffness, the arrangement à *priori*, the impossibility, are the same in both cases. In many places, especially in certain portions of Leviticus, the style bears a strong resemblance to that of the prophet. Change the turn of the instructions that God is supposed to have given to Ezekiel in the visions of the year 575, let them be produced as though dictated by God to Moses on Mount Sinai, any one reading these visions would believe that he was studying some chapters of Leviticus.

The Book of the Covenant, the Decalogue, and Deuteronomy remained at the base of the religious institutions of the nation; but some new and very important ideas tended to become established. The position of the Levites was always an open wound, and after the return no amelioration seemed possible for them. Following the theory of Ezekiel, the aim was rather to increase the separation between the priests and the Levites. In his opinion the priests only could serve Iahveh; the Levites waited upon the priests;* their duties were those of the hierodules occupied in the lower services of the temple. Since all modern institutions must have their root in Mosaical times, the Life of Moses was enriched by legends intended to prove that any attempt on the part of the Levites to usurp the sacerdotal functions was a crime worthy of death. The

---

* Numbers, ch. iii., iv., xviii., etc.

singers and musicians appear to have occupied a kind of honourable rank amongst the Levites. These functions were reported to have been in the hands of a Levitical family called the Beni-Korah or sons of Korah.* They were supposed—perhaps they imagined it themselves—to be descended from a Levite of their own name, who lived in the time of Moses. A terrible legend had gathered round this Korah. He aspired to sacerdotal powers equalling those of Aaron. A kind of judgment by God was commanded. The Aaronites on one side, the Korahites on the other, drew near to the temple with their censers. Fire from heaven devoured Korah, his band, and their censers.† Neither Ezekiel, Jeremiah, Deuteronomy, or the ancient prophets ever allude to Aaron as the stem of the true sacerdoce. The old histories mention Aaron but simply as the brother and prophet of Moses. On the other hand, the idea of Aaron as high priest is predominant in the later sacerdotal code. In it the priests are all sons of Aaron. Aaron is at their head like a natural president. The presbyterial rôle of Aaron and the idea of the high priest were therefore originated at the same time. There was no high priest in the old times, even in those of

* 1 Chronicles, ch. vi. v. 33 and following; ch. ix. v. 19; ch. xxvi. v. 1; 2 Chronicles, ch. xx. v. 19; the titles of eleven Psalms.

† Numbers, ch. xvi., in which we clearly see the confusion of the old Iahveist account of Dathan and Abiram with the modern legends so hostile to the Korahites.

Ezekiel.* The commencement of this office was first seen under Josiah; the army of priests grouped round the temple required a head. Yet, in 575, Ezekiel, as we have seen, avoids in his new programme placing any one priest higher than the others. It is quite possible that in his later meditations he realised the necessity for doing so, or that his disciples became convinced of it. However that may be, the myth of Aaron and the official establishment of a chief *cohen* were two proximate ideas, but two steps from those of Ezekiel. We are persuaded that they closely followed the programme of 575.† The rite of unction‡ was the sign of pre-eminence by election. The high priest is described as anointed, solemnly installed, clothed in state vestments, and forced to obey an etiquette so strict, that he is forbidden to wear mourning even for his father and mother.§

One idea still more analogous to that of Ezekiel was the invention of the *ohel moëd* or tabernacle, a kind of portable temple which Moses was reported to have had made in the desert, that could

* The history of Joash, full of improbabilities, had been retouched after the Captivity in a sacerdotal spirit. The Chronicles have rendered it quite Levitical.

† The list of high priests (1 Chronicles, v. 30 and following, Ezra. ch. vii. v. 1 and following) is full of insolvable difficulties.

‡ See *Lex. Hebr.* at the words נסיך and מ ח.

§ Leviticus, ch. xxi v. 10 and following. *Cf.* Leviticus, ch. iv. v. 2 and following; ch. vi. v. 15; ch. viii. v. 12 and following, 30; Numbers, ch. xxxv. v. 25, 28; Joshua, ch. xx. v. 6.

be folded up in some way and re-erected at every encampment.* This is really a puerile invention, and upon this point Voltaire's derision was fully justified. Nothing can more closely resemble the liturgical visions of Ezekiel, characterised as they are by improbability and an absolute contempt for reality. But, from another side, the conception of such a fable contained something very logical.† Since the reign of Josiah, unity of the place of worship had become the fundamental dogma of Israel. It was advisable that this dogma should be traceable to Moses. Through lack of criticism to raise any objection, it was easy to report that such a state of things had existed until the construction of the temple under Solomon. Before the temple, it was difficult to imagine a centralised and solemnly organized ritual. At that time little attention was paid to probabilities. A temple was invented before the temple, and no one noticed the impossibilities it involved. We do not assert that this invention was due to Ezekiel; but it must be owned that the minute descriptions we possess of this curious work are conceived in the same spirit that dictated to the prophet so many inachievable plans and chimerical combinations. The writers were evidently addressing readers who were not assiduous in their perusal of the ancient histories, for such a conception was in

* Exodus, ch. xxv. and following.
† Upon its roots in anterior texts, see vol. i. pp. 177, 178.

flagrant contradiction to the old accounts of the history of Moses. But the absence of criticism, and especially the want of any complete collection of the texts, left room for any approximate variations. What one knew the other did not know, and thus the substance of the religious writings was enlarged by additions which differed from each other and were profoundly contradictory in their statements. The arrangement of the camp of Israel in a perfect square like a chessboard is very closely allied to the conception of the *ohel moëd*.* If Ezekiel did not write this description he certainly conceived an analogous disposition. The tabernacle is in the centre; Iahveh is thus enthroned in the midst of his people. The tribe of Levi occupies the position of a guard round the ark and also provides an equipment of porters. The twelve tribes are symmetrically arranged outside them, Judah, as might be expected, occupying the place of honour. The author of Deuteronomy had imagined an analogous plan,† and had deduced from it very strict laws of cleanliness which make us smile. The editor of the Levitical code makes this a geometrical plan, absolutely resembling the map of Palestine, and the sketch of the New Jerusalem by Ezekiel. The description of the sacerdotal vestments is of the same origin as that of the

* Numbers, ch. i., ii., iii.
† Deuteronomy, ch. xxiii. v. 10-15. Perhaps there may be some Levitical interpolation.

tabernacle. They both infer great skill in the arts of needlework and decoration. Egyptian, Assyrian, and Tyrian influences are blended in them, — Egyptian features, however, keeping the upper hand, since Egyptian taste was still dominant in all works of art and industry. A sumptuous ritual and a splendid succession of festivals were a most essential feature in the thought of the religious organisers of that day.

We have seen Ezekiel* placing the Levites in a designated part of the sacred domain (evidently in the suburbs of Jerusalem) where they have special villages reserved for them to live in. This idea was afterwards developed and ended in the new Thora, in the eccentric conception of Levitical villages, another impossibility which never had any connection with the real arrangement of things.† It was supposed that after the conquest of the land of Canaan, Moses had commanded that forty-eight cities should be selected from amongst the different tribes and reserved for the Levites; it was admitted that Joshua had carried out this order. Surely this was a sacerdotal reverie of the first class, one of the most singular projects ever devised for getting rid of an intolerable social embarrassment. Far from being disinherited, the Levites, assuming such an arrangement, would have

* Ezekiel, ch. xlv. v. 5.
† Leviticus, ch. xxv. v. 32 and following; Numbers, ch. xxxv v. 1 and following; Joshua, ch. xxi.

SACERDOTAL AND LEVITICAL THORA. 349

been the richest of the Israelites. This was a much later expedient, or rather a solution upon paper, which was never executed. If an institution of this kind had existed before the Captivity, how is it possible that the author of Deuteronomy knew nothing of it? The cities which are given to the Levites in the twenty-first chapter of Joshua are alluded to in the history of Israel in the same way as any of the other cities; several of them were not even conquered in the time of Joshua. After the return of the captives, we do find the Levites lodged in the villages near Jerusalem,* but never with the regularity and legal disposition inferred by the Levitical interpolations of the books of Numbers and Joshua. It is evident that the conception in question had only one object, to solve in the direction indicated by Ezekiel this Levitical problem, which, since Josiah, proved the constant preoccupation of the religious organizers of Judah. The geometrical impossibilities of the passage, Numbers chapter xxxv., verses 4-5, forcibly recall those familiar to Ezekiel.

The jubilee year † is the boldest of the Utopias which in these later days were engendered by the strongly socialistic spirit of the prophetic school. The most ancient code of Israel contained the Sabbatical year, that is to say, the repose of

* Ezra, ch. ii. v. 70.

† Leviticus, ch. xxv. v. 8-17, 39-41, 54; ch. xxvii. v. 17 and following; Numbers, ch. xxxvi. v. 4.

every seventh year.* This was only a theoretical wish, which although repeated in Deuteronomy was never carried out. The Utopists of the fifth century took it seriously, supported it by a miracle,† and then went further still. They desired that every fiftieth year the world should return, in a sort of periodical way, to its original state, that slaves should regain their liberty, and the land be restored to its former owners. Combined with the prescription of the Sabbatical year, this law produced an economical constitution that was absolutely impracticable. No nation ever existed under such a regime,‡ and it is permissible to say that no sensible man ever took up his pen to write such things, believing that they would be applied. But none of this was written in a charter prepared for immediate use. These curious conceptions of a portable tabernacle, of the Levitical cities, and the jubilee year, absolutely distant from all applicable ideas, are visibly sisters of the chimerical Jerusalem and of the sacred topography of Ezekiel. They are not the *desiderata* of an epoch of restoration such as that of Zerubbabel and Joshua the son of Jozadak. They are the fruits of an epoch in which the

---

* See vol. ii. pp. 307, 312.

† Leviticus, ch. xxv. v. 20 and following.

‡ The Sabbatical year was practised after the exile (Nehemiah, ch. x. v. 32; 1 Macch. ch. vi. v. 49, 53; Josephus, *Ant.*, XIII. viii. 1; XIV. x. 6, 16; XV. i. 2; *B. J.*, I. ii. 4), no doubt with many attenuations; the jubilee year was never celebrated.

Israelitish Utopists, of whom Ezekiel was incomparably the greatest, worked in space, never for one moment checked by considerations of the possible. In truth, Ezekiel's scheme contains an evident allusion to the idea of the jubilee year [*] though not yet designated by the name officially given to it later on.

One hypothesis, which well reconciles all these convergent data, is the supposition that near Ezekiel and under his influence a Life of Moses was compiled from the ancient texts, with all the additions rendered necessary by the requirements of the time. The form was in some degree anecdotal. Each legal solution was brought in by some incident supposed to have presented itself to Moses or Joshua. These solutions were all conceived in a sense which favoured the pretensions of Aaron's family to the high-priesthood, and they bore a decided tinge of hatred towards the officials of the temple or Beni-Korah. In this work appeared all the recent inventions about the tabernacle, Aaron's position, the high priests, the sacerdotal vestments, and the Levitical cities. There was the story of the Levite Korah intended to show that without sacrilege the Levites could not be admitted to the privileges of the priests. The ancient narratives were repeated in it, softened and transformed into pious histories, each with a definite tendency. Thus we find in it a very

[*] Ezekiel, ch. xlvi. v. 17.

weakened version of the episodes of Balaam * and of the daughters of Zelophehad.†

Just as the author of Deuteronomy had taken nearly all the old laws from the Book of the Covenant, to revive and develop them, so the new legislator included a number of anterior prescriptions in his work, as though he supposed that the other codes were unknown or that his would suffice by itself. In view of the extremely small number of books then existing, it was desirable that each volume should contain all that referred to its subject. And, as afterwards the last arrangements of the Hexateuch were made without taking these double entries into account, strange repetitions appear in it. Nearly all the important laws were repeated three times, first in their ancient form (Book of the Alliance or Decalogue), then in the Deuteronomical form, then in the Levitical or sacerdotal form.‡ The Decalogue itself, which had been reproduced in Deuteronomy, was repeated three or four times by the sacerdotal editors.§

The moral spirit of Leviticus differs from that of Deuteronomy. The fanaticism and formalism

* Numbers, ch. xxxi. v. 8; Joshua, ch. xiii. 22.

† Numbers, ch xxvii. xxxvi.; Joshua, ch. xvii.

‡ For instance, the law upon the cities of refuge : first form, Exodus, ch. xxi. v. 13; second form, Deuteronomy, xix. (*cf.* iv. 41); third form, Numbers, ch. xxxv. and Joshua, ch. xx.

§ Exodus, ch. xxxiv., and even in the minor Leviticus (see below pp. 357, 359).

SACERDOTAL AND LEVITICAL THORA.

are identical.* The impression left by the reformers of 622 was so great that, fifty years later, their work only was repeated. Pity and humanity are carried as far as possible, always naturally, in the bosom of the Israelitish family. The poor are surrounded by so many guarantees, that one asks what, in a society based upon this model, could be the privileges of the rich. The land is not really sold;† it belongs to God only; its human owner is simply the tenant of God. If a man be forced to sell his estate, he retains so many securities upon it that we scarcely see who would be tempted to buy. The twenty-fifth chapter of Leviticus is really a document of the civil code, in which humane considerations perpetually trench upon strict law. An Israelite, impoverished or weakened by old age, was to be assisted by the community, so as to secure for him the livelihood earned by a man working for his living. Usury is forbidden between Israelites. The brother forced to sell himself must be accepted as a mercenary until the Jubilee; no Israelite could really be the slave of an Israelite. Israelitish slaves could be recruited only from amongst the neighbouring peoples and the children of aliens settled in the land. To slaves procured from these sources all the hardships of slavery are applicable; they can be transmitted as an heritage for ever, there is no

---

* Leviticus, ch. xxiv. v. 10 and following.
† Leviticus, ch. xxv.

jubilee for them. On the other hand there is a ransom and jubilee for any Israelite who had become slave to strangers dwelling in the land of Israel, and he is to be protected from harsh treatment. At the jubilee the alien loses his rights.

We see that this law is a fraternal, not a national law. It approaches the predominant ideas of certain socialistic circles. It is needless to say that no mental culture, no art, no science, no philosophy, none of those exquisite flowers which blossomed in Greece, could issue from such a *régime*. Under it everybody would have the same culture, because this culture is very mediocre. The happiness of the individual guaranteed by the social group to which he belongs is the sole object of the law.

Who will maintain this fine ideal? Who will protect these little paradises of brothers living together against the attacks of external force? The socialistic Jew feels no anxiety upon this point. The great empires founded upon the military classes are entrusted with this work. This feeling produces an attitude humble yet haughty towards these military aristocracies, which jars upon our instincts. The people of Israel always secretly consider that they have the best part, and that in spite of their subordinate position the world really exists for them alone. They are full of pity for the poor fools who pass their life in cutting each other to pieces, instead of enjoying the pleasures of a peaceful life as they do. Then when the empire, which has served to protect them, crumbles to pieces, they laugh aloud, crying that all the nations work for the fire and labour for vanity."* They forget that without the shelter of a great civil and military society their Thora would be inapplicable.

All religious orders are in the same position. The Catholic Church, disdainful of the State as it is, could not live without the State. If socialism could attain any organization, its phalansteries, groups, syndicates would exist in the State, like small egoisms caring very little about public interests. And when it is pointed out to the enthusiasts that the defenders of the State have also a right to some privileges, since they prevent the hive from being destroyed and trampled upon, they would no doubt answer, like Ezekiel, by apocalyptic predictions of the end of the nations and the future transformations of the world. They would not have the candour to admit, like Ezekiel, that they must first endure the invasions of Magog. Ideal Jerusalems bring misfortune. By stunting the development of the real Jerusalem they always lead to catastrophes, and finally to ruin and fire.

What can be said of the immense absurdity committed in transporting to the midst of the great social system a law written for a small community of brothers? It is like applying the rules of a

* Jeremiah, ch. li. v. 58.

religious order to an empire, a nation. The prohibition of usury, for instance, is thoroughly consistent in the charitable law imagined by the Hebrew utopists. It would become injurious if erected into a general rule of society. In this respect the old Hebrew laws are perfectly reasonable; the use that has been made of them in the middle ages by the Christianised world has been fatal. So true it is, that the laws of Israel are not true civil laws suitable for adoption by a State! They are dreams, often beautiful dreams, which transformed into positive legislation have not been without some danger.

On the whole, charity, kindness to the weak, owe a great deal to Israel. The law does not owe it anything. The code of Gortyna, of which we possess the original text,* is nearly contemporary with the Jewish sacerdotal code. It is superior to the latter through the clear notion of civil society, that is, of a society based upon human relationships and reason, not upon a supernatural fact, the supposed preference of a very powerful god for a certain tribe. No people except Israel ever prohibited usury amongst native subjects. The prohibition, apparently so humane, of the Jewish code has really more disadvantages than advantages. For the permission to lend upon usury to foreigners is underlined, and by a succession of curious incidents the people that has

---

* Rodolphe Dareste, *la Loi de Gortyne*, Paris, 1886.

most condemned usury has always found itself branded by the unjust epithet of usurer.* Let us add that the Jewish laws upon usury have rendered bad service to the world, for Christianity adopted them, and Christianity having become, first, a most considerable portion, and then the whole of progressive humanity, the world during some centuries submitted to a very bad law—the prohibition of loans upon interest, which considerably prolonged the middle ages and delayed civilization for one thousand years.

Without resulting in a work as clearly defined as Deuteronomy, a new code was, in fact, born in Israel. A great many hesitations were produced. The recasting of the law became the perpetual occupation of active spirits, particularly in the circle of which Ezekiel was the centre. Any endeavour to discover in detail the after-touches, amendments, caprices of penmanship admitted by the sacred scribes, would be attempting the impossible. Criticism mistakes its rôle when in these questions it insists too much upon great precision in details. The bibliography of a time when there were only one or two copies of each book could not respond to the same question as that of our own days.

What, for instance, could be more singular than

---

* It would take a long time to explain all the phases of this singular mistake. In reality, the devolution of the trade in money to the Jews dates from the middle ages, and is due to the impossibilities which the canonical law created for Christians in all money matters. It commenced in Spain, under the Visigoths.

the small code which is found embedded in the book of Leviticus from ch. xviii. to ch. xxvi. These chapters form a book complete in its unity and presenting the same characteristic expressions from one end to the other; now these expressions are exactly the ones preferred by Ezekiel, and they are scarcely found elsewhere. One is therefore led to suppose that the small book contained in ch. xviii.-xxvi. of Leviticus is only a posterior arrangement of the law by Ezekiel found in ch. xl.-xlviii. It has been thought that Ezekiel himself composed this species of fair copy, with some modifications of his original meditations, enriching it with extracts borrowed from more ancient writings.* It is perhaps wiser to believe that the small work in question was composed from the writings of Ezekiel by one of his disciples.† The institution of the high priest, the Aaronite source of the sacerdoce, the tabernacle and the Levitical cities are all mentioned in it. The document claims to be a complete summary of the laws that Iahveh revealed to Moses upon Mount Sinai. It was a new Deuteronomy adapted to the times, and implying that the code of Josiah was not much read. The closing threats (ch. xxvi.) prove that these short laws

* This was the opinion of Graf. de Kayser. What can be more striking in this respect than the passage, Ezekiel, ch. xlvi. v. 17, in which we find an allusion to the institution lengthily developed in Leviticus, ch. xxv. ?

† This is the opinion of Messrs. Reuss, Horst, Wellhausen.

newly arranged and forming complete series, were in some degree a style of literature, subject to rules and having its regular forms. Every one refashioned his own Thora, and no doubt many of these ephemeral compositions have disappeared.*

The twenty or twenty-five years which followed the transportation were thus an epoch of great creative activity. The substance of nearly all the sacerdotal and Levitical portions of the Thora appears to date from this epoch; the form was afterwards altered several times. Just as Jeremiah inspired Deuteronomy, so Ezekiel inspired Leviticus.† The three stages of religious legislation amongst the Hebrews may be thus clearly distinguished: a primary age, characterised by a grandiose genius, expressing itself in simple formulas which the whole world has been able to adopt (this is the age of the ancient prophets, of the Book of the Covenant, of the Decalogue); a second age, stamped by a severe and touching morality, marred by a very intense fanatic pietism (this is the age of Deuteronomy and Jeremiah); a third age, sacerdotal, narrow, utopic, full of chimeras and impossibilities (the age of Ezekiel and Leviticus). Like all great works, the Jewish Thora is anony-

* The fusion of these new elements of religious legislation in the already existing body of the Thora will be explained in our seventh book.

† Including under this name the Levitical portions of Exodus, Numbers, and Joshua.

mous; not entirely however, for behind the text, which has become in the highest degree sacred, it is possible to discern three or four great figures, Elijah (altogether legendary), Isaiah, Jeremiah, and Ezekiel.

CHAPTER V.

LITERARY WORK DURING THE CAPTIVITY.

SINCE the time of Hezekiah the Hebrews had been much inclined to write. Exile, by condemning them to a sedentary and retired life, increased this natural taste. A great many Hebrew pages were written by the canals of Babylon. The ancient Scriptures had been carried there in a state of some disorder. The captives occupied themselves in arranging them. We have seen that the Thora was still incomplete, no one had any idea that it was closed. Those works of the prophets which were fairly uniform in tone became mixed with deplorable facility. It is certainly possible that at this epoch a great many deficiencies and much confusion had been caused which were then clumsily repaired. Nothing, however, can be more erroneous than the rather widely diffused idea that the Hebrew literature, destroyed at the capture of Jerusalem, was in some degree rewritten from memory during, or after, the Captivity.* The transmission of the ancient texts was badly done, but it was done. No doubt Ezekiel, at the time of the first transportation, had already some books with him. Nor is it probable that the captives of 588 would neglect these treasures, which were as the food of life to them, particularly since the destruction of the temple.

The annals of the kings of Israel and Judah until the end of Jehoiakim,† still existed in a complete state. The history of the reigns of Jehoiachin and Zedekiah was preserved in the memory of Jeremiah's disciples, and was almost blended with their recollections of their master. Baruch was certainly the centre of this work. The end of the second book of Kings is thus closely connected with the book of Jeremiah.‡ The editor of Jeremiah's work would seem to have arranged the last pages of the book of Kings after Manasseh. The abridger, who, through a free use of

* Esdras is usually credited with this care, according to the Apocalypse of Esdras, written at the end of the first century of our era, (4 Esdras, ch. xiv.). Christian writers, St. Ireneus, St. Augustine, and St. Jerome, accepted this idea rather inconsiderately.

† Jehoiakim is the last king for whom the formula . . . . רברי ויתר (2 Kings, ch. xxiv. v. 5) was used.

‡ The contradictory accounts of the end of Jehoiachin (see above p. 246) should not attract too much attention. In editing the prophets the writers did not feel obliged to withdraw any unfulfilled prophecies. Apologetic scruples did not exist at that time

scissors, has placed these meagre annals in their present state, probably dates from a much later period.

The work of editing Jeremiah's writings was performed in a singularly disorderly way and with much indecision.* The copies varied in the distribution of the surates, and in several of these copies the disciples introduced ideas which the old prophet had not enunciated with equal clearness.† Later on, still larger interpolations were made in them.‡ Few books were read and commented upon with so much passion; each reader noted his reflections in the margin of his manuscripts, then afterwards, these marginal notes passed into the text. In fact, the spirit of the school was so absolute that the voice of the disciple and that of the master could sometimes blend together without any great inconvenience.

The misfortunes of the times led to the formation of a book of elegies or lamentations called *Sepher qinoth*. In it were included several already ancient poems; for instance, the elegies on the death of Josiah, which were attributed to Jeremiah.§ To these were soon added some chapters of a rather artificial rhetoric, all dwelling upon the same

* Repetitions arising from the disorder of the leaflets. Jeremiah, ch. x. v. 12 and following; ch. li. v. 15 and following.

† We have really two editions of Jeremiah, that of the actual Hebrew text and that which is represented by the Greco-Alexandrian version.

‡ See below, p. 374 and following.

§ 2 Chronicles, ch. xxxv. v. 25.

subject—the siege of Jerusalem and the Captivity. These pieces were also ascribed to Jeremiah.* They appear to have been solemnly chanted on certain occasions.† Some pathetic psalms which express repentance have, perhaps, the same origin.‡ But it is very difficult to discern accurately here, for henceforth mourning strains form the usual keynote of the hymns of Israel.

One custom established from the years which followed the ruin of Jerusalem must have greatly contributed to the development of this literature of elegiac songs. This was the practice of consecrating as fast days the anniversaries of the catastrophes the people had just witnessed, the commencement of the siege, the capture of the city, the burning of the city and temple in the months of Tammuz, Ab, and Tebeth. These fasts were accompanied by weeping, by the ordinary signs of mourning, and the cessation of every occupation, like the Sabbath day! §

It is not readily admitted that the Jews who remained in Judea displayed any literary activity during the exile of the most noble part of the nation. However, it is possible that our imagi-

* Lamentations, first verse of the Greek version, which certainly existed in the Hebrew text, used by the Alexandrine translators.

† 2 Chronicles, *loc. cit.*

‡ For instance, Psalms xiv. xxii. xxxiv. li. liii. lxix. lxxi. lxxiii. lxxvii. lxxxii. cii. xciv. cxxiii.

§ Isaiah, ch. lviii. v. 3 and following ; Zechariah, ch. vii. v. 1 and following ; ch. viii. v. 19.

nation deceives us in this respect. Certain critics attribute chapters xxiv.-xxvii of the book of Isaiah, and also chapter v. of Lamentations, to the Jews in Palestine.

We may place the death of Ezekiel towards 560. His works, consisting of written pieces, not of slowly edited recitations, were easy to collect. Ezekiel had not so compact a school as that of Jeremiah. The book containing his visions was less read and consequently less interpolated. The lofty individuality of his style was like a barrier which prevented re-touches. The book of Ezekiel is, therefore, almost the only book in the Bible which has not been altered.

The works of Isaiah were still, it would seem, in considerable disorder. We shall soon find them interpolated in the most serious fashion. Perhaps, in some of the editions then made, that inaugural scene was placed at the beginning of them,* which is analogous to those we read at the head of the books of Jeremiah and Ezekiel, in which Iahveh appears at the end of the sanctuary surrounded by seraphim,† sphinxes endowed with six wings,

---

* Now ch. vi. The date given at the head seems taken from the title, ch. i. v. 1. It was maintained that Isaiah had prophesied under Uzziah; but as that would have made his career very long, the editors confined his first prophecy to the last year of the king's reign.

† These fantastic creatures only appear here. Their origin is quite uncertain. See Dieulafoy, *l'Art antique de la Perse*, 1st part, pl. xvii.

analogous to the cherubim. Isaiah fears that he shall die, for he has seen God. His lips are impure. One of the seraphim takes a live coal from the altar of incense and touches his lips with it. Henceforth he is qualified to speak in the name of Iahveh.

We shall soon see that prophetism retained at the time of the Captivity some illustrious representatives who continued it in the purest line of the genius of Israel. They still wrote perfectly, and the ancient books were like classics, which maintained the language and which others endeavoured to imitate. The Oriental influence, which according to some authors was exercised over the transported Jews, is reduced almost to zero. Far from opening to external ideas, the Jewish spirit concentrated itself more than ever in itself, in its own traditions, its own passions, and its own animosities. It dreamed only of Jerusalem. The Jew of that date, in a foreign land, went about with his eyes shut like a Mussulman of to-day; he learnt nothing.* No scientific information penetrated those closed consciences. The idea of the Chaldean cosmogony, traces of which are found in the first page of Genesis, is derived from far more ancient sources. Babylon, in the sixth

---

* We might quote, in this respect, the example of Abdelkader, who, placed in the most favourable circumstances for self-instruction, yet confined himself to his old Arabian culture, which was singularly poor.

century B.C., was not capable of giving lessons of purified theology;* in any case, the two most eminent Jews of this epoch, the author of *Super flumina* and the author of the second portion of Isaiah, certainly owe nothing to the influence of that Babel of which they invoke or hail the ruin. The changes in the Jewish spirit attributed to the Captivity relate rather to the restoration of Zerubbabel and Joshua the son of Jozadak, and all these changes issue, by an inflexible logic, from the ancient Israelitish conception, such as the school of Elijah, the prophets of the eighth century, Isaiah, the *anavim*, Jeremiah, and Ezekiel had formulated it.

* The common errors respecting the influence of the Captivity upon the Jews arise from the erroneous ideas formerly accepted upon the antiquity of the Avesta. The Avesta is relatively modern; moreover, had it existed in the sixth century before our era, how could it have influenced Babylon before Cyrus?

CHAPTER VI.

APPROACH OF THE SIEGE OF BABYLON.

Nebuchadnezzar died towards 561, leaving the throne to his son Evil-Merodach. Jehoiachin, the last king of Judah but one, still lived in his prison at Babylon. Evil-Merodach released him, probably a measure celebrating his accession. An honourable position was assigned to him amongst the vanquished kings who filled Babylon. A sum of money was granted for his maintenance and that of his household, and it is said that he was admitted to the table of his conqueror's son.

Evil-Merodach and Neriglissar reigned but a short time; the throne was then occupied by a child, who was assassinated in 555. The house of Nebuchadnezzar ended with him. A short dynasty, like all dynasties in the East, but one which had displayed the greatest capacity and power that had yet been seen. Nabonadius, one of the conspirators, maintained the Empire of Babylon for seventeen years longer, during which period, the events which were to change the axis of the world's affairs assumed a decisive turn. The years of Babylon were numbered. To the east of the Tigris, the Aryan populations of the Medes and Persians, both terrible through their military organization, completed their definitive union under the command of one of the most powerful organizers of empires mentioned by history, Cyrus the Persian, in some respects the Charlemagne of the ancient world, and the starting point of a new order of affairs. Iran made its entrance upon the world's arena with unequalled brilliancy.

The battle of Thymbria and the fall of the half-Assyrian kingdom of Lydia (554), a war of fifteen years' duration in Bactriana and Scythia, which reunited in one great force all the healthy military populations of Iran, decided the fate of Asshur. Invincible in their day, these troops of Nineveh and Babylon, chiefly, so it would seem, recruited in the Carduchi Mountains and in Armenia, had found their masters. The chances of war, so often iniquitous, were just, at least, for this once. The old Assyrian empire, alternately Ninevite and Babylonian, did not deserve to live. The Roman empire was equally harsh; but it civilized and prepared the way for a truly humanitarian rule, the empire of the second century, which has been one of the corner stones of progress. Iran, although it did little towards civilization, was worth more than Asshur. The intellectual capacity of these feudal and warlike populations was certainly weak; but the moral faculty was vigorous amongst them. We can imagine the Persians of Cyrus resembling the Franks of Austrasia, barbarous, ignorant, naïve, honest, faithful to the oath they had taken. The system of transportation, which had justly exasperated the East, was never practised by the Persians. The numerous peoples that Assyria had oppressed commenced to breathe once more when they saw this great deliverance appearing on the horizon. The world felt relieved from the pressure of a leaden weight.

This impression was most vivid amongst the captives from Judea. The prophets had announced that Iahveh would break the rod which He had used for the chastisement of the nations. Oracles, in which the ruin of Babylon was clearly foreseen and affirmed, were circulated on all sides. When the signs that preceded the day of God's judgment drew nearer, the prophecies were multiplied and became more definite. A great many chapters, which were included in the book of Isaiah, when the volume of the prophets was compiled, date from this period. The mistake was easily made, for the Hebrew writers in Babylon often tried to imitate the style of Isaiah, or even to shelter themselves under his name. It is also possible that pieces by the ancient prophets were sometimes revived, and applied after a few alterations to actual circumstances, as Isaiah had done in his prophecy against Moab. Such is also the case with the prophecy contained in chapters xxvi.-xxvii. of the book of Isaiah, which might be taken for the style of Hosea, and which contain allusions almost certainly referring to the events of the sixth century, the destruction of Babylon, the return of the captives, and the re-establishment of Jerusalem.

We hear, in the midst of the prophetic tumult of Israel, the clear voice, the sonorous tone, the pathetic and touching accents * of one admirable poet, who wished to lose his own identity in the brightness of Isaiah. Israelitish feeling towards 550 was so unanimous, that it is difficult to decide whether in this lofty deutero-Isaiahic harmony we hear one or several voices. But it is quite certain that several songs of rare beauty have slipped in amongst the leaflets of Isaiah referring to the siege of Babylon, and sounding like the ring of poetic bugles, the flourish of trumpets, of the great

---

* The four pieces, Isaiah, ch. xiii. v. 1 to ch. xiv. v. 23; ch. xxi. v. 1-10; ch. xxxiv.; and ch. xxxv., are contemporary with the siege of Babylon. They appear to be by the same author; but it is not certain that they were written by the author of the grand poem, Isaiah, ch. xl.-lxvi., although the analogies between them are very great, and one notices some expressions borrowed from each other. Compare, for instance, Isaiah, ch. xxxv. v. 10, to Isaiah, ch. li. v. 11.

drama being played. The most striking of the prophetic utterances is a *massa* against Babylon,* in which the Medes are already indicated as the executioners of the extermination decreed by Iahveh.

The hymn which Israel shall sing on the day when her ruler falls is dictated beforehand.†

* Isaiah, ch. xiii. v. 1 to ch. xiv. v. 23.
† Isaiah, ch. xiv. .v. 4 and following.

CHAPTER VII.

CAPTURE OF BABYLON.

IN proportion as the circle closed round Babylon, so the Israelitish prophet raised his voice.* The year of revenge had come at last. The Seer considers himself as a sentinel placed by Iahveh to watch the horizon, whilst the Babylonians eat and drink.† He discovers innumerable cavalry advancing at a gallop; he joins them in imagination.

The feverish state of the Seer seems to redouble with the carnage. All the signs of the day of Iahveh reveal themselves to him.‡ And then he sees the deliverance accomplished.§ The desert which the Israelites must cross before they can

---

* Isaiah, ch. xxi. v. 1-10.

† Isaiah, ch. xxi. v. 5. From this afterwards arose the legend of Belshazzar. Compare Jeremiah, ch. li. v. 30-31.

‡ Isaiah, ch. xxxiv. Edom and Bozrah in this surate appear to personify Babylon, just as later on Edom symbolically designated Rome.

§ Isaiah, ch. xxxv. Perhaps forms one whole with xxxiv.

regain their country adorns itself with flowers in honour of such noble travellers.

It was a rule of the prophets of that time to write anonymously. Either to evade the suspicions of the Chaldean police, or because no one ventured to compare himself with Isaiah and Jeremiah, no one after Ezekiel dared to prophesy in his own name. There was a reason for the preceding verses being incorporated in the writings of Isaiah. Their author could circulate them under the name of Isaiah, or, what comes to the same thing, insert them in an edition of the ancient prophet adapted to the necessities of the times. The ideas then current upon prophecy admitted the belief that Isaiah, a hundred and fifty years before, had foreseen these events by a supernatural gift. It was acknowledged that there were passages in the prophetic treasury not yet fulfilled, but which would be accomplished as circumstances developed themselves. From this admission to fabricating these oracles was not a very long step.

Capital was made out of the name of Jeremiah as well as of Isaiah. In this case the fraud was much easier, because the school of Jeremiah still existed and continually added fresh touches to the master's work. The disciples commenced by interpolating authentic visions, for instance, that of the fourth year of Jehoiakim.* It was supposed that

---

* Jeremiah, ch. xxv. v. 12, 13, 14, 26, were added or rearranged. See above, p. 363. The permutation of the letters pre-

Jeremiah, taking advantage of Zedekiah's journey in 594, remitted to the king's chamberlain, who was Baruch's brother, a small book in which the destruction of Babylon was clearly foretold.* Later on prophecies were attributed to the prophet of Anatoth which clearly intimated the impending fall of the Chaldean empire.†

The prophet seems to believe that sheltered by the anarchy which would be produced, the Babylonian captives might then return to their own country.

It is God who excites the kings of Media; he has to avenge his temple. The world unites to crush Babylon; when the cry is heard, "Babylon is fallen," the earth trembles, echo shall tell it afar off amongst the nations. Fugitives will carry the tidings to Zion, of the vengeance of Iahveh, of the punishment of the destroyers of the temple. Then the captives will regain their liberty, the sins of those who have been thus spared will be obliterated. The hammer of the whole earth will be broken.

The gates of Babylon are broken in; the king does not yet know of it. Post after post, messenger after messenger bring him the tidings that his city is taken, the passages are occupied, the marshes on fire, and the men of war affrighted.

---

sented by the Hebrew text, Jeremiah, ch. xxv. v. 26 ; li. v. 1, 41, appears to be only tricks of the copyists.

* Jeremiah, ch. li. v. 59-64.
† Ch. l. and li.

Zion then demands her flesh and blood from the inhabitants of Babylon. Iahveh has a question of honour to settle with his rival, Bel, who has the sacred vases of Jerusalem in his temple. Iahveh will make him disgorge that which he has swallowed, then the nations will cease to flow unto the false God.

We see that already the rule of Israel is to avoid meddling in the quarrels of the powers between themselves. The people are content to take advantage of them. The disturbance produced by Chaldean vanity will cease. All the wounded upon earth will be avenged. Babylon shall never rise again. Her broad walls shall be utterly overthrown, and her high gates shall be burned with fire.

AND THE PEOPLE SHALL LABOUR FOR VANITY, AND THE NATIONS FOR THE FIRE; AND THEY SHALL BE WEARY.*

The great irony, mingled with pity, with which the thinker is inspired by that empty dream, which poor humanity, in love with its own executioners, calls glory, has never expressed itself in a more forcible touch.† Greece understood the small infantine pleasure of the interior life of cities marvellously well. The ruins of the great em-

* Jeremiah, ch. li. v. 58; Habakkuk, ch. ii. v. 13. See above, p. 242.

† It can be compared only to the final reflections of the songs of *Schahnameh*.

pires, with the rage and tears which they provoke, the loftier though profoundly sad feeling, with which the peaceful man contemplates these falls, the commiseration excited in the heart of the sage by the spectacle of the nations labouring for vanity, victims of the arrogance of the few, the vanity of all things, and fire, the last judge of human societies (which does not exclude invincible faith in an ideal future): all this Greece was unable to see, but all this has been expressed by the Jewish prophets with admirable sagacity.

וייגעו עמים ברי ריק ולאמים בדי אש ייעפן

The crisis which inspired the prophetic genius of Israel with such lofty eloquence was very long. Sagacious minds perceived that Babylon was doomed long before the Medo-Persian league had conquered it. The investment of Babylon lasted more than two years.* A blockade was impossible. The population did not believe in the danger of a

---

* The accounts formerly accepted of the siege of Babylon by Cyrus agree but moderately with the account that savants now believe can be read in the cuneiform texts (Pinches, in the *Transactions of the Society of Biblical Archæology*, v. vii. p. 139-167 ; H. Rawlinson in the *Journal of the Royal Asiatic Society*, new series v. xiii. (1889), p. 70 and following). We believe that too little attention is paid to the Greek texts, anecdotic, no doubt, in details, but fundamentally agreeing with Hebraic proclamations contemporary with the siege, which we have analysed, and which imply a much more terrible catastrophe than recent critics are inclined to think.

capture by main force. It devoted itself to its business and pleasures as though it were in times of peace.* The assailants were obliged to turn the Euphrates out of its course, or rather to drain its bed by numerous channels.† It is said that one day, when the population was entirely absorbed in one of its festivals, the Persian army entered the city by the bed of the river. In their general sense the words of the prophets were fulfilled. The power of Asshur, which had weighed upon Israel for more than two hundred years, was annihilated for ever (536 B.C.). In their turn the sons of Achæmenies were to hold the sceptre of Asia during two hundred years.

* See Isaiah, ch. xxi. v. 5
† Possibly alluded to in Isaiah, ch. l. v. 2-3.

CHAPTER VIII.

CYRUS AND THE ACHÆMENIDÆ.

ALTHOUGH a little exhausted beforehand, through the bold anticipations of the prophets, the joy felt by the dispersed Israelites when they heard the news of the fall of Babylon was a real intoxication.* The facts, however, only half fulfilled the terrible predictions uttered in the names of Isaiah and Jeremiah. Babylon was not destroyed; cities of that size have a tenacious grasp of life. It is doubtful whether the general massacre, which in prospect was used as an argument in the endeavour to induce the Jews to depart, ever took place; the city preserved its walls and its palaces.† The really mortal blow for Babylon was the siege laid to it by Darius, the son of Hystaspes, twenty years later.‡ The temple of Bel was pillaged or destroyed by Xerxes.§ Total ruin followed under the

* See the great invective, Isaiah, ch. xlvii.
† Herodotus, iii. 159.
‡ Herodotus, iii. 159; Justin, i. 10.
§ Herodotus, i. 183; Strabon, xvi. 1, 5; Arrian, *Alex.* vii. 17.

Seleucidæ. At the Roman epoch it might be said that the prophecies had been fulfilled; the space formerly occupied by ancient Babylon was a desert.*

But the decisive point was the change which took place in all the politics of the East. This was truly the victory of Iahveh. Iahveh had fought with fury and had crushed his enemies.

The Chaldean supremacy represented the reign of idolatry, force, and evil to the pious Israelite. It was, moreover, an iron rule, which never loosed one of its prisoners.† Under it, therefore, no hope could be entertained of any return home. The manners of the new dynasty were more serious, better suited to please the votaries of Iahveh. Races of relative morality were replacing the unintelligent ferocity which had been known hitherto. Without evincing any real elements of progress (Greece alone possessed them), the new empire was not violent and it allowed the movement to take place, provided its action was slow. Persia ‡ would have been fatal if it had conquered Greece, but vanquished by the latter it proved useful. It filled a great place in the world. Jewish and Christian

* Strabon, *l.c.*; Pausanias, VIII. xxxiii. 1; Dion Cassius, lxxv. 9.

† Isaiah, ch. xiv. v. 17; Jeremiah, ch. l. v. 33.

‡ The name of Persia does not appear in the Hebrew writings before *Esther* and *Daniel*. Pseudo-Isaiah and pseudo-Jeremiah only knew the name of *Medes*.

CYRUS AND THE ACHÆMENIDÆ.

progress owe it immense gratitude. Israel, who rebelled against Greece and provoked his own destruction by Rome, treated Iran as a brother, and wished him to share in Iahveh's esteem.

The Iranian religion in the sixth century B.C. was not yet separated from the Aryan trunk.* Ahura-mazda,† "the omniscient" (Ormazd), was a truly Supreme God, more abstract even than Iahveh; his rival Angra-manizu (Ahriman) was not fully developed; so that the Persian religion at that epoch was a kind of Monotheism.‡ It had no temples.§ It even reached the usual results of Monotheism, intolerance, an exaggerated horror of images.‖

This all tended to establish a great sympathy between Israel and the new conquerors. The institution of the magi, which may date back to the Media of the seventh century B.C., was not

---

* The *gathas* of the Yaçna and of the Vendidad have some analogy with the Vedas. Darmesteter, *The Zend Avesta*, v. i. p. liii.

† See the formula of the opening of the cuneiform inscriptions of the Achæmenidæ, of which the most ancient is only twenty-five years posterior to Cyrus. Compare Yaçna, init. and xxxv. 1-3.

‡ See Spiegel, *Eranische Alterthumskunde*, 2nd vol. (1873); James Darmesteter, *Ormazd et Ahriman* (Paris, 1877); *Essais orientaux* (Paris, 1883, pp. 120 and following); *Haurvatât et Ameretât* (Paris, 1875).

§ Herodotus, i. 122, 131.

‖ Herodotus, v. 102; vi. 9; vii. 8, etc.; Diodorus of Sicily, xi. 14; Polybius, v. 10. Eventually the development of Mazdeism bore still more resemblance to that of Judaism. The Parsees recall the Jews in many respects.

without some analogies to Jewish Levitism.* A very lofty morality, which has been handed down to us through the intervening centuries in the Avesta, serious manly discipline,† feudal customs of trade guilds that were very healthy for a still rough humanity, constituted amongst the Persians the ancient source of strength, which founded empires, but which prosperity quickly dissolved. If we can believe certain translations of the Assyrian texts,‡ which, perhaps, need confirmation, Cambyses, the son of Cyrus, upon taking possession of Babylon in the name of his father (for according to those new accounts Cyrus did not take the city in person), sacrificed to the gods of the country. Cyrus, when making his entry into the city three months later, addressed a pro-

* Herodotus, i. 101, 107, 111, 120, 122, 131, 138, 140; iii. 61 and following. Compare Xenephon, *Cyrop.*, VIII. 1. 23. The legend of Zoroaster with all its developments did not exist at the time of Cyrus. Herodotus, who writes so much about the magi, would have certainly alluded to him too. On the other hand, after Plato and Aristotle, the Greek writers frequently mention him. The definitive arrangement of the Avesta, such as we now have it, does not appear to be anterior to the epoch of the Sassenides. It is parallel to the Talmud, not to the Bible, save for the antique touches found in it.

† The *Cyropedia* is a romance; still, this proves that the old Persian laws had become an ideal in the fifth century. The opinion of the ancients upon the two periods of the life of Cyrus — the one sober and virtuous, the other corrupted by the influence of Babylon — responds to the same general fact.

‡ Pinches and H. Rawlinson, places previously quoted, p. 458. Maspero, pp. 582-584.

clamation to the people, in which he announced that he assumed the royalty by the consent of the national gods. Merodach, irritated by the desertion of Nabonadius, had avenged himself by appealing to Cyrus and inciting him to march against Babylon. He had led the Persian army himself; Cyrus was his friend, his favourite. It is not at all impossible that sacerdotal adulation was carried to this excess. According to Turkish accounts, the French in 1830 seized Algeria by the Sultan's orders to punish the rebellion of the dey. But, in the eyes of the Israelites, Cyrus was none the less the destroyer of the idols of Babylon. He thus appeared to the prophets as a sort of Iahveist, a *mesih*, an anointed one, a man sent by Iahveh; God himself proclaims that he is "the man of his counsel.*" Starting from the Christian idea of the life beyond the tomb, this rôle filled by a pagan is difficult to understand. God would have considered it due to himself to convert to the true faith a man so highly honoured in the execution of His designs. With heaven and hell there can be only the elect and the reprobate. But according to the ancient Jewish ideas, the whole destiny of the individual was accomplished during his earthly life. God had much more liberty of action. The Christian Church has been obliged to make saints or at least Christians of Constantine, and up to a

* איש עצתו. Isaiah, ch. xlvi. v. ii. Compare ch. xli. v. 25; ch. xliii. v. 1; ch. xliv. v. 28; ch. xlv. v. 1; ch. xlviii. v. 14.

certain point of Charlemagne. Cyrus according to the Jews was able to write, "Iahveh, God of heaven, has given unto me all the kingdoms of the earth,"* without entertaining any idea of becoming a Jew on that account.

Certainly the Jewish theory of Providence was subject to one grave objection, which would have ended it if rationalism had been at all exacting at that time. Why did Iahveh always use indirect methods for protecting his people? If he be all-powerful and intend Israel to be the centre of the world, what was the use of these intrigues, to obtain through Cyrus and Nebuchadnezzar the result which it would have been so easy for Him to obtain directly, by giving universal sovereignty to his people without any circumlocutions? It is not consistent. Iahveh rewards pious Israelites by causing them to obtain good situations as stewards, chamberlains, and favourite servants to great personages; surely it would have been more logical to make His protégé himself a great personage. But the plans of Iahveh as a God are very profound. He prefers holding the hearts of kings in His hand to reigning himself. Israel shall be in the good graces of the powerful,† who shall owe their

* Ezra, ch. v. 2.

† This produced one defect amongst the Jews at certain epochs, that vanity shown by subalterns and provincials who are proud to be noticed by the great, the fashion of maintaining that the kings had thought of them and spoken of them with consideration (false

authority to the degree of benevolence they show him. Ostensibly to govern the world is an arduous task. It is better to profit, at the time of their accession to power, by the favour of those who inherit this formidable labour.

The Jewish prophets, pursuing their sole idea that the revolutions of empires have but one aim, the accomplishment of the will of Iahveh towards Israel, are in a very real sense the founders of the philosophy of history, that is to say, of the attempt to subdue all events to a providential design. It is not one of the least singular traits of the Jewish people that they have imposed the chimeras of their own patriotism upon the whole world. Instead of relating Israel predicts, that is, systemizes.* This is why it has no historians, it has prophets. The invasion of the Scythians, for instance, is not anywhere mentioned. The episode of Gog in Ezekiel is a picture of it, transformed into a symbol for the future.† In this curious state of mind everything

---

edicts, false titles, false letters in Esdras, Nehemiah, Esther, Maccabæus, Alexandrines, and Josephus). This is what they call the "glory of Israel," which has often caused the Israelites to render evil service to the States by begging for the favour of the strong. Having no political life of their own they have occasionally troubled the political life of others.

* The impossibility of clearly distinguishing by the tense of the verb, the present, the past, and the future, has greatly contributed to this peculiarity of the Hebrew genius.

† It is thus that all the Old Testament will some day become the figure of that which is realised by the New.

becomes a type and a general formula. The event that happened counts for almost nothing.

In three centuries and a half, the book of Daniel will give a complete statement of the Jewish system, a system which must not provoke too many smiles, since the philosophy of Bossuet's history, which so many persons still take seriously, is only a reproduction of it. The visions of the prophets since the most ancient times are, in their way, humanitarian and highly expressive myths. The whole book of Ezekiel is an historical enigma, a darkness full of bright flashes. The disciple of Jeremiah who interpolated his master's work * also looked far ahead when he proclaimed that the nations weary themselves for vanity and construct all sorts of beautiful things for the fire. Above nationalities, there is, in fact, an eternal ideal. Socialism, according to the Israelite and Christian dream, will probably one day kill the patriots, and make a reality of the words read in the service for the dead: *Judicare seculum per ignem.*

If the prospect of the capture of Babylon so highly excited the imagination of Israel, the effect produced was far worse when the event was accomplished, and the accession of Cyrus to universal rule had opened the way for the boldest hopes. Convinced that the world moved for his benefit only, the Israelite regarded these great upheavals as some of Iahveh's manœuvres to attain His ends.

* Jeremiah, ch. l. and li. See above p. 374, and following.

The rod which he had used for the chastisement of Israel was broken. Cyrus succeeded Nebuchadnezzar as the executioner of the divine will. It is pretended that he confessed and gave thanks to Iahveh for his power. This led to the idea that Cyrus wished to rebuild the temple of the God to whom he owed everything, and we shall soon see this style of imagination developing itself.* It was accepted that Cyrus at least sometimes invoked the name of the true God.† Report never made him a convert to Iahveism; but it credited him with a full acknowledgment of the superiority of Iahveh and a clear consciousness of the mission that he was accomplishing.

In fact, the dynasty of the Achæmenidæ was the rule which the Jews found most favourable to their nation throughout their long history. Inclined as they were to complain, they never murmured against the Persian empire. Under such a rule everything fostered the work of the Jewish pietists. They were free in their own way. On condition of complying with some forms of outward respect, which badly concealed a great deal of contempt, they found themselves protected against their neighbours, always ill-disposed towards them, and sheltered from the great revolutions of the world, upon which they could, as usual, speculate indefinitively.

* See below p. 518.
† Isaiah, ch. xli. v. 25, attenuated by Isaiah, ch. xlv. v. 4, 5.

The Achæmenidian empire certainly realised during its early years a fairly perfect political condition. It was in some respects analogous to the Germanic empire of the middle ages, quickly Latinised and transformed by the Court of Rome or rather to the Ottoman empire in the time of Mahomet II. Corruption followed afterwards, when Babylon conquered her conqueror, and imposed upon the Achæmenidian empire, as later on she imposed upon the Sassenides and the Kaliphs, her civilization, her low morality, profound corruption, and effeminacy. A strong central organization left room for local variations, either under the form of small kingdoms, as in the cities of Phœnicia, or under the form of independent religions. This was exactly fulfilling Ezekiel's dream for his Israel, restored in pure theocracy. This theocracy, which would have killed any kingdom or republic, was perfectly satisfied with a situation which relieved it from all political anxiety and left it free to realise its Utopia. The *nasi* could attend to presiding in state at the festivals surrounded by an army of rich priests. It is thus, in our days, that the Greek community of Smyrna, freed by the Turkish suzerainty from all the political agitation which consumes independent Greece, is more at liberty to follow out its course of internal development than the kingdom of the Hellenes. Under the Achæmenidian protectorate Israel no longer created (the measure of its creative genius was exhausted), but it developed with admirable freedom. Esdras and Nehemiah would have been impossible with a king of Jerusalem. No one can dispose of a society to rearrange it as a religious ideal in the way they did, when this society contains a living principle of national organization, and above all a dynasty.

CHAPTER IX.

THE GREAT ANONYMOUS PROPHET.

Assuredly the Jewish conscience never saw more loftily nor more clearly than at this solemn hour. The finest accents of the prophetic genius are dated from this decisive year, 536. One of the inspired, whose voice we have perhaps already heard in the prophetic manifestoes which marked each phase of the siege,* burst forth at this moment, and in a series of chapters, written all at once, probably during the days which succeeded the capture of Babylon, soared to the highest level to which the mind of Israel ever attained.†

The usual defect of the theology of Israel was particularism. Iahveh shocks us because He is the national god of the sons of Jacob. The book of Job is the most beautiful Hebrew book, because the God of Job is really the absolute God. The

---

* See above p. 370.

† Isaiah, ch. xl.-lxvi. This writer is often called the second Isaiah.

THE GREAT ANONYMOUS PROPHET. 391

great anonymous writer of whom we speak, whose style often recalls the book of Job and who had certainly read it,* also rests upon the heights of the most purified Monotheism.† The junction is accomplished. Iahveh has completely returned to the Elohim of the patriarchs ‡ with the addition of a few fine metaphysical formulas.§

The superiority of the great anonymous writer is also seen in his manner of embracing the whole human race. It is true that in his eyes the mission of Israel is unique, exceptional. But this mission is beneficial to the world. Israel is the leaven that will leaven the whole world. The establishment of the true religion will be the work of Israel. As this formula is precisely the same as that reached by critical science, we cannot rank the unknown man who wrote these pages too highly; they are unquestionably the most beautiful that had yet been traced by the hand of man at that remote date.

We believe that the author of these pages intentionally placed them at the end of the volume of Isaiah, and that he wished them to be attributed to that prophet.‖ Any way they were very promptly

---

* See particularly Isaiah, ch. xl.

† Rare exceptions; ch. lxiii. 1-6. He attributes to Iahveh the thirst for vengeance which he himself feels.

‡ Isaiah, xli. 4.

§ Isaiah, xliv. 6; xlviii. 2 and following.

‖ Isaiah, xli. 21-29; xlii. 8-9; xliii. 9 and following; xliv. 7; xlv. 21; xlvi. 9 and following; xlviii. 3 and following; these passages in which the author wishes that his prophecies should one day be a accepted as his.* We have seen the same thing happen with regard to Jeremiah.† There is a deutero-Jeremiah just as there is a deutero-Isaiah. Predictions thus issued acquired an authority which no private individual could then attain. No man could be a prophet at will, extraordinary assurance was required for the rôle. Since Jeremiah and Ezekiel no one had dared to take up the terrible mantle which denoted a public claim to inspiration and a docility in the crowd which daily became rarer. Our anonymous writer was not therefore a qualified prophet; he was probably as unknown to his contemporaries as he is to us. It was the anonymous conscience of the nation which revived its old inspired writers and made them utter the words that the consolation of the times required. On the whole, prophecy was ending. Men no longer dared to plunge into deep waters; they amplified the ancient books until they arrived at purely apocryphal compositions such as pseudo-Daniel, pseudo-Baruch, pseudo-Enoch, pseudo-Esdras.

---

proof of Iahveh's veracity have no sense except in the mouth of a celebrated prophet. The solemn exordium, lxi. 1 and following, inspires the same reflection. Lastly such passages as xl. 2; li. 16, seem intended to be connected with Isaiah's time.

* It is remarkable that less than twenty years after, Zechariah, vii. 5, 7, 12, quotes a passage of deutero-Isaiah (lviii. 5) as anterior to the captivity. There is no doubt that Zechariah read the book of Isaiah in its complexity just as we have it now.

† See above, p. 374, and following.

THE GREAT ANONYMOUS PROPHET.

Isaiah, for the moment, benefited by this overflow of the heart of Israel. Great in his lifetime, Isaiah became colossal after his death. The rank of the first Hebrew writer, the title of eagle of the prophets, have accrued to him through the pages he did not write. This was only justice. He had written such beautiful things that it seemed that all great and noble thoughts, full of the feverish dreams of the future, ought to be attributed to him.*

The voice of the unknown writer accepted for that of Isaiah was, in fact, so profound that it might easily have been taken for the voice of Iahveh issuing from the depth of his sanctuary to notify the new watchword to His elect.

In fact Iahveh will place himself at the head of the homeward bound caravan. The journey across the desert would be rough (the sceptical asked what would become of the women and children); but Iahveh would himself be the shepherd of His people; He would cause rivers to flow in the desert; † and would carry the sucking lambs in his bosom. Nature should rejoice; the mountains and hills should break forth into singing; the trees of the field should clap their hands.‡

---

* This retrospectively proves the authenticity of the passages by Isaiah that are stamped by Messianism, an authenticity which might have been questioned. See vol. ii. pp. 419 and following.

saiah, xliii. 19 and following.

‡ Isaiah, lv. Compare lvii. 14; lxii. 10-12.

The victory of Cyrus was the work of Iahveh.* Leagues were being formed against Cyrus for the restoration of the Chaldean empire. These efforts would be as much in vain as those of the metal workers to repair a broken idol.† Iahveh's preference for the race of Abraham, his friend, whom He has chosen to be "His servant" requires the ruin of the Chaldean empire. This "worm of Jacob" regulates the fate of the world. His victory will be the victory of the poor and unhappy.

One expression frequently used by our author first appears at this time; it is that of "Servant of Iahveh," taken in a collective sense to designate Israel, not profane Israel, a mixture of good and evil, in which the word of God often finds many obstacles,‡ but pietist Israel, which alone counts, the poor, the *ebionim*, the *anavim*, the depositaries of the religious future. This congregation of the holy may be subjected to criticisms, to reproaches; § but God has no consideration but for it. It conquered the world by an apostleship full of mansuetude.

A new canticle, the canticle of deliverance, will now be heard.‖ Iahveh will gather the scattered

---

* Isaiah, xli.

† Isaiah, xli. 6 and following. The psalm *Quare fremuerunt gentes*, may refer to these plots against Cyrus, Iahveh's Anointed One.

‡ Isaiah, xlix. 1 and following.

§ Isaiah, xlii. 18 and following.

‖ Isaiah, xlii. 10 and following; xliii. 1 and following.

THE GREAT ANONYMOUS PROPHET. 395

members of his elect from all corners of the earth. The Persians, in exchange for the good that they have done to Israel, shall possess Egypt and Ethiopia. The pagan gods have been unable to foresee anything, Israel alone can boast of prophecies fulfilled.

These vague announcements were not enough for the author. He even names the man who has been chosen to carry out the designs of Iahveh.*

In consequence of the reparative acts of Cyrus, happiness will fall from heaven like dew upon the earth.†

The whole world will become tributary to Jerusalem; the people of Egypt and Ethiopia, the tall Sabeans will go to Jerusalem, saying, "Surely God is in thee; and there is none else, there is no God."

God loves life and He wishes the earth to be peopled.‡ Even idolaters may be saved from the impending catastrophes if they will join themselves to Israel and will acknowledge that the prophecies of Israel only have been fulfilled. The whole world is invited to recognise the divinity of

---

* Isaiah, xliv. 28; xlv. 1, and following. This is quite opposed to the usual custom of the prophets, and one questions whether it is not produced by some illusion of the copyist or some marginal note introduced into the text. This is quite possible for the passage xlv. 1; but in the passage xliv. 28 he appears to have really the text as the author wrote it. Compare Isaiah, xlv. 3, 4.

† Isaiah, xlv. 8 and following.

‡ Isaiah, xlv. 20 and following.

Iahveh. Bel and Nebo* are already fallen, their images are carried away in pieces, upon beasts of burden. Zion chants a hymn of deliverance.†

There were doubters and questioners ‡ who did not believe the word of Iahveh, and who said of every prophecy, "We know it already." They insisted upon the impossibility of crossing the desert, and said with feigned politeness and rather keen irony, "Let Iahveh be glorified, that we may see your joy." § A few even dared to say that their false gods had revealed equally fine things. The new Isaiah energetically maintains that Iahveh alone emits genuine oracles. The prophecies uttered in the past, and now fulfilled, were a guarantee that those of the present would also be accomplished. God, who in ancient times had led Israel across the wilderness, would know how to guide the people through it once more, without allowing them to suffer from thirst. The "Servant of God" is hated now.‖ He endures the most unworthy treatment with patience, offering his cheek to receive blows and insults and to be spat upon; but he will be avenged. Jerusalem will gather in her bosom a new generation, born in exile, which she does not know. Every nation will

* Isaiah, xlvi.
† Isaiah, lii. 1 and following.
‡ Isaiah, xlviii. Compare xlv. 9 and following.
§ Isaiah, lxvi. 5.
‖ Isaiah, ch. xlix. and l.

THE GREAT ANONYMOUS PROPHET. 397

bring back these last scions of Israel in its arms, upon its shoulders. Kings shall guard them and princesses shall nurse them. Potentates shall lick the dust from off their feet.

Exciting himself more and more the author then combines, in touches borrowed from the type of Jeremiah, colours which might be said to portray Jesus in advance.* The servant of God will create a law for all nations. He will found a righteousness, a salvation, which will last longer than heaven or earth. Now he is in prison, but he will not die in his dungeon.

In one of the strangest pages that have ever been written,† the Seer then shows us the servant of Iahveh under the form of a victim. Jeremiah had been dead for forty years, and his figure, daily becoming grander, was blended with these hallucinations, and aided to complete the ideal of the Man of Sorrows.

Iahveh adheres to the apotheosis of his great servant, who has become the personification of the people.

* Isaiah, ch. li.
† Isaiah, ch. liii.

CHAPTER X.

THE NEW JERUSALEM.

A SPLENDID future for Jerusalem, and through Jerusalem for the whole world, is the indispensable crown of the prophetic dreams at this time. Israel has been a bride whom a jealous husband has justly abandoned;* she has lost her children; but a reconciliation takes place, thanks to the goodness of the husband; a new family is granted to her, so numerous that the old house is no longer large enough to contain them.

The new Jerusalem will be a city of rejoicing;† a city of saints and prophets taught by Iahveh himself.‡ Nothing in it will recall war nor the implements of force. Henceforth Iahveh will be the sole manufacturer of weapons,§ there will be no more wars without His permission. Thus peaceful

---

* Isaiah, ch. liv.
† Isaiah, ch. lxv. v. 18.
‡ Isaiah, ch. liv. v. 13. Compare Jeremiah.
§ Isaiah, ch. liv. v. 16.

Israel will be master of the world. He will no longer perform material work.

Our great utopist shows but moderate anxiety about the Thora.* He alludes to it only in a general way.† Since the prohibition of sacrifices, the Israelitish law consists in doing righteousness, in observing the Sabbath, and in avoiding pork and unclean food.‡ Adoption into the family of Israel is also rendered as easy as possible, far more so than in Deuteronomy.§ The Gentile, once admitted into Israel, is completely naturalised. Eunuchs, excluded by the law of Deuteronomy,‖ will have a place in the community. After death, instead of children, a cippe (an *iad*, a *sem*) will make his name live. Those Babylonians who wish to join the emigration may do so.¶ Strangers will be admitted to offer sacrifices to Iahveh upon the condition of keeping the Sabbath and of being faithful to the covenant. "For mine house shall be called an house of prayer for all peoples."** It is remark-

* Isaiah, ch. lvi.
† Isaiah, ch. li. v. 4 and 7.
‡ Isaiah, ch. lviii. v. 13-14 ; ch. lxv. and lxvi.
§ Deuteronomy, ch. xxiii.
‖ Deuteronomy, ch. xxiii. 2.

¶ Notice Isaiah, ch. lvi. v. 8, a solemn oracle. Compare Ezra, ch. ii. v. 59-60.

** Isaiah, ch. lvi. v. 6-8. It can be no question here of the *nethinim* only. The poet's imagination once directed towards the heathen becoming servants of Iahveh, returns to the Gibeonites, and depicts the proselytised foreigners as servants in a low position. Compare the servile mark of the name written upon

able that amongst the conditions of admission into Israel there is no allusion to circumcision.

The fast in memory of the ruin of the temple was already established.* The prophet does not wish too much importance attached to it.†

Bravo, Israel! We other revolutionists have also said that and have been crushed for our faults. The servant of Iahveh may be humiliated; but finally he will prevail.

The great consolation of man, in the presence of the incurable evils of society, is to imagine an ideal city, from which he excludes every sorrow and which he endows with every perfection. Jerusalem rebuilt inspires the Seer of Babylon in a marvellous description, which, adopted by the Seer of Patmos and idealised by Christianity, has been the golden dream of poor humanity in its trials, worse, alas! than those of Israel.

This nation of righteous men will be marvellously fertile.‡ The least of its seeds will yield a thousand. The future Israel is a nation of new-born children whom Iahveh will carry in his arms and caress upon his knees. On the other hand, the wicked, those who have opposed the work of Iahveh, will be

the hand, Isaiah, ch xliv. v. 5. The approximations of the prophetic style is an element which must always be taken into account. Compare Leviticus, ch. xvii. 8; xxii. 18; Numbers, ch. xv. v. 14.

* See above p. 364.

† Ch. lviii.

‡ Isaiah, ch. lx. v. 21-22; ch. lxvi, v. 7 and following, v. 12 and following.

exterminated. Their bodies shall lie outside the city in the valley of Hinnom, a place defamed by the burning of children and the execution of criminals. There shall the corpses of the rebellious and unbelievers be seen; they shall never be consumed, but always remain like fresh corpses which worms eat and flames devour. The converted heathen who go up to Jerusalem, will go outside the city to look at them and will be filled with horror.* The new order of things that will accompany the reign of God in a renewed Zion will be perfection for humanity. Israel will feel that he is the cause of the happiness of the world. He will chase away evil, and with evil suffering will disappear. Universal well-being will be complete; longevity will be the portion of all.

All humanitarian dreams are contradictory, for the imagination turns in a narrow circle, and the plans which it traces have, like the lozenge-shaped figures of Oriental mosaics, infinite variety in their many crossings. The programme of the Revolution was liberty, paternity; it carried the Empire in its womb.

The great idealist Germanism of the Herders and Goethes was to end in an iron realism, which declared that it recognised only action and force.

* Isaiah, ch. lxvi. v. 15-18, 24. Compare lxv. 13 and following, and Isaiah, ch. xxx. v. 33. This is the first origin of hell. *Cf.* Sirach, ch. vii. v. 17 ; Marc, ch. ix. v. 43 and following ; Judith, ch. xvi. v. 17.

What can be said of modern socialism and of the change of face which it would make if it ever attained executive power. The great anonymous writer of the time of the captivity is certainly one of the heroes of human history. He is fascinated by justice. His picture of the servant of Iahveh displays abnegation carried to martyrdom; and with that the utmost happiness he can conceive is an agricultural life and longevity. His city of gold and precious stones reigns over the whole earth and exploits it for its own advantage. To enjoy the house one has built, the fruit of the tree one has planted, is the goal reached by this humanitarian. The Aryan, who first of all admits that the gods are not always just, has none of this desire for worldly success. He does not take material enjoyment quite so seriously. Preoccupied with his chimera of the life beyond the tomb (a chimera with which alone great things are accomplished), the Aryan builds his house for eternity; the Semite wishes that it should last as long as he does. A house which defies the centuries, like our feudal constructions or our hotels of the seventeenth century, appears to him an insult towards God. His thirst for justice involves egoism. He does not wish to wait; to him a glory or a benefit which is not felt does not exist. The Semite believes too much in God. The Aryan believes too much in the eternity of man. Both conceptions have been necessary for the foundation of civilization. The Semite has given God; the Aryan has given the immortality of the individual. Mankind has not yet succeeded in dispensing with these two postulates.

This ideal of material comfort without military nobility and of middle-class vainglory not founded upon the heroism of the masses, appears very small to our sentimental romantic races, brought up like Saint Bernard in the confidence of the woods and rocks. Whatever we may do we are the adepts of a wild chivalry, pursuing dreams and fundamentally reposing upon the belief in immortality. But the genius of great races always reasserts itself. Let the so-called materialist, the seeming egoist, say what he likes. His own life will be one of perpetual self-devotion. He has a gift which belongs to himself only, that of hope. The Aryan is resigned, he hopes very little. The servant of Iahveh practises the fine Italian device *Ma spero*. Nothing discourages him. Here is a thinker, two thousand five hundred years ago, sufficiently reflective to write in a very cultivated idiom, sufficiently reasonable to put aside all the aberrations of polytheism, of divination, of the worship of the dead, of the life beyond the tomb,* and who is sufficiently blind to all realities, to believe that justice can govern the world and that the ideal of a perfect state will soon be realised. In this

* Isaiah, ch. lxv. v. 3-4.

respect the second Isaiah much resembles our socialists, whose illusions cannot be destroyed. After each abortive experiment they recommence their work; the solution is not yet found, but it will be. The idea that no solution exists never occurs to them, and in this lies their strength. To have recognised that human affairs are an ever-foiled attempt, without clear purpose or definite result, is a great advance in philosophy, but it is an abdication of every active career. The future lies in the hands of those who are not undeceived. Woe to those of whom Saint Paul speaks, " who have no hope!"

It is through this that Isaiah has been more truly the founder of Christianity than any other religious hero of ancient Israel. Isaiah had the good luck to meet with an anonymous successor who continued his work in a manner worthy of him, who placed him in some measure upon a level with the times, and put into his mouth the words that he might have uttered one hundred and fifty years after his death. The aspirations of these two great souls, so closely associated,* were revived by the sibyllists of Alexandria, by Jesus, by the evangelists, by the author of the Apocalypse of Patmos, by Joachim of Flora, and the votaries of the eternal Gospel. They have been the smoke of the incense with which humanity has intoxi-

* Compare Isaiah, ch. xi. authentic, with ch. lxv. apocryphal.

cated itself during many centuries. Powerful narcotics, consoling mankind by imaginary paradises for the sorrows of reality, will never cease to be necessary until humanity attains the state of material comfort which renders the dream useless. Now, if humanity should ever reach such a state of dull beatitude, it would be so quickly corrupted, so many abuses would be produced, that it would require to rise out of this putrid stagnation a new sacrifice of heroes, victims, expiations, of servants of Iahveh. This is the eternal circle of all life. Let us hope that the final result will be shown in some progress. In the department of science this is secured. In the department of human morality it is more doubtful.

CHAPTER XI.

IAHVEH, THE UNIVERSAL GOD.

THE ancient prophets had announced that after the indemnifications accorded to Israel by its national God, this national Deity would become the universal God of the whole human race. In the second Isaiah this thought is clear, developed, consistent with itself. We must not, in alluding to this remote epoch, attach to the word conversion the dogmatic sense with which it has since been invested. It was not unusual to change the protecting God when a more powerful one could be found.

The conversion of the *goyim* would be the result of the fall of Babylon. Those who escape from the catastrophe would become missionaries for Iahveh.[*] They would travel in all directions, to Tarshish, to Put and Lud, to Tubal and Javan, to the isles afar off that have not heard the name of Iahveh; there they should proclaim the glory of Iahveh, and bring

---

[*] Isaiah, ch. lxvi. v. 18 and following.

back the exiled Israelites, upon horseback, in chariots, in litters, and upon mules and dromedaries, to the holy mountain, Jerusalem. Henceforth Iahveh will be adored by the whole world. The heathen, who witness the favours granted by Iahveh to his people, will wish to become worshippers of a God who bestows such great blessings upon those belonging to Him.*

The whole world will thus try to affiliate itself to Israel, will refer to Israel and flatter it. Israelitish *Kounia* will be freely adopted,† just as the Israelites in Babylon often assumed Chaldean names.‡ The servant of God shall be a light to the Gentiles,§ who will bring offerings to Jerusalem in pure vases. Iahveh will choose priests and Levites from amongst them. A perpetual festival will be held in the temple, lasting from Sabbath to Sabbath, from new moon to new moon; there will be processions of believers always coming to fall down and worship. God, that is to say Iahveh, loves Israel; but He also loves humanity, and one day humanity will not be distinguishable from Israel. Israel will comprise the whole universe. Prayer will replace sacrifice. Keeping the Sabbath will be almost the

---

* Isaiah, ch. lv. v. 5; ch. lx. v. 9.

† Isaiah, ch. xliv. v. 5. The Semitic *Kounia* is the name preferred by the person designated, for instance, Abou Ali, Abou Ibrahim, implying the name of the favourite son.

‡ See above, p. 315. § Isaiah, ch. xlix. v. 6.

sole outward observance of the religion of the future.

The first evangelist of universalism, the *mebasser* of the religion of humanity, is really the anonymous prophet of 536. He is the messenger of good tidings, whose feet appear upon the mountains, like the early dawn. Through him the world first heard the grand words, "The heaven is my throne, the earth is my footstool, but to this man will I look, even to him that is poor and of a contrite spirit."*

All nations shall worship the same God; the universe is His temple; a righteous life is the only offering He will accept. All the prophets since Amos had laboured to purify Iahveh of His naturalistic dross and of His national partialities. Isaiah particularly uses his loftiest accents in favour of universalism.† It is not therefore surprising that it is under cover of his name that we find the proclamation of Iahveh as the supreme God of the universe and of humanity enunciated with the greatest clearness in the sixth century.‡ The anonymous writer of 536 is the last culminating point of three centuries of the greatest religious effort (Christianity excepted) of which history has retained the visible trace. With him we have

---

* Isaiah, ch. lxvi. v. 1-2.
† See vol. ii. pp. 406-407, 419-420, 440 and following.
‡ Isaiah, ch. xliv. v. 6 ; ch lxvi. v. 1 and following.

reached the top of the mountain from whence we perceive Jesus on the summit of another mountain, and between the two lies a very deep valley.

By the loftiness of his sentiments, the boldness of his expressions, the classical eurythmy of his images, the numerous fine impulses that he has suggested to Christian mysticism, the prophet of 536 occupies a special position in Hebrew literature. The unction and gentleness of his words* render him almost a Christian already. The luminous atmosphere of his book is the same as that found in the Gospel. His Iahveh begins to tire of the curiously harsh rôle assigned to him by the ancient prophets; he no longer thinks only of destruction, but would be sorry to exterminate humanity by too much severity.

Man has almost reached the conception of God the Father. The description of the Man of Sorrows has been received for eighteen centuries as the picture of Jesus. The second Isaiah is the book which has provided Christianity with more materials than any other in the Bible. It has passed almost unchanged into the preaching and liturgy of the Church.

With the false ideas of literary criticism so generally diffused, one might be surprised that an unknown writer should have produced such a masterpiece. But the author of the book of Job is

* Isaiah, ch. xliv. xlvi.

also unknown; and so is the compiler of the so-called Iahveist version of the Hectateuch. The finest works of sincere epochs in which men were not tormented by the literary evil are all anonymous. The question of personal vainglory and even of personal merit was non-existent at those epochs. The Gospels are anonymous. No one would ever think of saying that Saint Matthew was a man of talent. Does any one know who wrote Homer, or the *Imitation of Jesus Christ?* Francis de Sales justly described these books when he said, "Their real author is the Holy Spirit."

The unnamed prophet of 536 is therefore the greatest of the prophets, simply because he is unnamed. He is the first humanitarian thinker. All of us whose religion consists in hoping for a future in which humanity will be at last consoled for its sufferings hail him as our master. Greece, that created so many beautiful things, art, science, philosophy, liberty, did not create humanitarianism. She disdained the barbarians too much for that. The Jews certainly despised the *goyim* too, but the Jewish disdain did not produce such disastrous consequences as Grecian contempt. It did not prevent Christianity; whilst the Greek contumely prevented Constantinople from assimilating the barbarians of the Slav race and from thoroughly conquering the Balkan peninsula and the East, a conquest which would have enabled her to stifle Islam in the bud.

The only thing that offends us in the second Isaiah is the name of Iahveh. There is no place for the name of a particular God in a book so entirely universalist. Consistency requires the suppression of this curious word from this time forth. A God who bears a proper name is a false God. He is but one God amongst several others, and even when convincing proof is given that he only is God and that the others are nothing, the fact remains that there has been some rivalry, that he has been in competition with others. But to renounce *Iahveh* would have been impossible at that date. It would have been the destruction of the nation; Iahveh had done so much for it! It would have been philosophy; now it is only in our days that philosophy has had any direct influence over human things. The work of the Israelitish spirit, singularly rationalistic in the main, consists in identifying Iahveh with the supreme God, El, Adonaï, Saddaï, Elohim, to bring Iahveh back to Elohim, to unreservedly pronounce the aphorism, "Iahveh, he is Elohim," to thus return after centuries of wanderings to the divine unity, which the old patriarchs of the desert had caught sight of in their long hours of idleness.*

Yet it seems as though henceforth the name Iahveh became an incumbrance; it was speedily replaced by the vague word *Adonaï*, "the Lord." The utterance

* See vol. i. pp. 71-72, 149 and following, 220 and following; vol. ii. 172, 173, 220 and following.

of the name was avoided (which is one way of suppressing it), and its vowels were consequently lost. Iahveh really disappeared in His victory. Hence this singularity that the name of the God who has conquered the world and has become the only God, is unknown to all but professed Hebrews, and even the latter do not know how to pronounce it. It was right that the individual should be absorbed in the victory of the absolute, and that Israel should forget even the name of the national God who had been the source of all its errors.

Henotheist nations, having one particular God, but having only one, attain Monotheism with great facility; whilst innately Polytheistic races, such as the Aryan, reach it slowly and by many adoptions. Iahveh triumphed over Chemos, Melcom, Salm, and Baal; whilst neither Jupiter nor Brahma ever quite suppressed their rivals. The phenomena of the Duke of France becoming King of France by election amongst his peers, first rendering them subordinate, then stifling them one after the other, did not occur in theology. Neither has the Carlovingian of the middle ages, without any real territory, reigning everywhere, yet reigning nowhere, any analogous place in religious history. Gengiskan, taking twenty years to master a small country of ten or twelve leagues, then invading the world like a cyclone, is far nearer the analogy of Iahveh's victory. Monotheism in humanity originated in the protecting God of one small tribe. The worship of this protecting deity led to wheedlings, to friendly relations, filial on the one side, paternal on the other, which cannot be inspired by an Absolute always identical with himself and impersonal. The abstraction is not propagandist. The fashion in which a pious Christian addresses God would not assume such tender accents if behind the God, in three persons, there were not a more tangible God who has carried his tribe in his bosom like a nurse, has caressed it, and spoken to it as though to a child.*

* Isaiah, ch. xliv. v. 1 and following.

CHAPTER XII.

DOUBTS AND HESITATIONS.

WE have seen that the *anavim* formed but a small proportion of the transported. Misfortune may have produced piety in many persons who formerly had none. Moreover, the pious families must have found their number greatly increased in the second generation. In spite of all this, the lukewarm were still by far the most numerous portion of the community. A great many Jews had shamelessly abandoned themselves to the idolatrous creed of the land [*] and had nearly forgotten Iahveh. The prophet draws many gloomy pictures [†] of their conduct, no doubt exaggerated, as the diatribes of the preachers usually are. The worst practices of Semitic idolatry, the impure rites celebrated under the shadow of the trees, the sacrifices of infants in the ravines, the most inept fetichisms

---

[*] Isaiah, ch. lxv. lxvi.
[†] Isaiah, ch. lvi. lvii. lix. lxii.

DOUBTS AND HESITATIONS. 415

appear to have found great favour amongst the exiles. The upper classes, especially, are treated with great severity by the second Isaiah. Israel has bad dogs, careless in their guard over the flock;* bad shepherds, greedy, sleepy, drunken. For one moment the prophet despairs, and proclaims the greater happiness of those who die; they enter into peace and see no more evil.† Then he fortifies himself in his vocation, which is to announce the good news to the *anavim*, to proclaim the year of deliverance, to bind up the wounded hearts.‡

But the greatest obstacle to the wishes of the enthusiasts is the fact that many of the Israelites had resigned themselves to their exile and found themselves very comfortable in Babylonia. Thanks to their practical dexterity, they were able to find a thousand ways of amassing a fortune in a city devoted to luxury and pleasure. Feeling little sentiment about the religious souvenirs of Zion, they were not at all tempted to leave a country which would retain all its importance for a long time to follow, in order to return to a narrow strip of land, condemned, as it is, to remain eternally poor, through its confined position between the sea and the desert. It even seems that at one time a curious idea sprang up amongst them of building

* Isaiah, ch. lvi. v. 9 and following.
† Isaiah, ch. lvii. v. 1-2.
‡ Isaiah, ch. lxi. 1 and following.

a temple to Iahveh in Babylon. The indignation of the zealots could no longer be restrained. It was decided that in such a temple, if it were built, the sacrifice of the purest animal would be no better than the sacrifice of a pig, and that acts of legitimate worship offered there would be as infamous as an act of idolatry or a human sacrifice.* It is often the fanatics, and not always the delicate spirits, that are found grasping the right thread of the solutions required by the future.

Perhaps there was more judgment and reason in the party opposed to the return than in the opinion of the pietists. The chief argument of the partisans of the return, to wit, that since the cessation of miracles the accomplishment of the prophecies was the great *sign*,† left much to be desired. The prophets were frequently insupportable from their assurance, and through the subtilities which they used, in order that events should never belie their predictions.

Many enlightened spirits were in reaction against the narrow-mindedness of Jeremiah and the acrimonious prophets who had only predicted calamities, of which several had not, however, taken place. The Iahveh of the old school

* Isaiah, ch. lxvi. 1-3. According to other interpreters, this refers to an idea already familiar to the prophets, that the sacrifices, the temple itself, are of little value.

† Isaiah, ch. xli. v. 21 and following, v. 26 ; ch. xliii. v. 9 and following ; ch. xliv. v. 7 and following ; ch. xlv. v. 21 ; ch. xlvi. v. 10 and following ; ch. xlviii. v. 3 and following.

appeared hard, fatalistic, obstinate. A general desire existed for a new Iahveh, who would reconsider His predictions through respect for the liberty of man. The embarrassment which these splenetic prophets would feel on the day when men would decide to be converted, or it would please God to forgive them, was represented in rather a ludicrous aspect. A few jesters bet that on that day the prophets of evil would be grieved and would reproach Iahveh for not carrying out His threats.* This is the fundamental idea of the book of Jonah, the only book of the Hebraic literature upon which one may be led to joke a little.

The author wished to inculcate the idea that there is only one God in the world, Iahveh, God the father of all His creatures, who regrets the severity of His resolutions, always forgives upon repentance, and withdraws His threats when they have attained their object, the sinner's conversion. He relates that the ancient prophet of Israel, Jonah the son of Amittai,† has received a command from Iahveh to go and preach to Nineveh. Nineveh is therefore capable of being converted, a fact in itself singular in the eyes of an ancient Israelite, but which an adept of the universalist school would admit unquestioningly. Jonah, convinced of its impossibility, and caring little about saving

---

* Jonah, ch. iv.
† See vol. ii. p. 351 and following.

the heathen, starts for Tarshish. Iahveh makes him realise his error, then saves him by the burlesque miracle which every one knows, and in which there is surely a grain of irony. In any case, Iahveh is so absolutely the God of all the world, that the sailors, convinced of His power, pray to Him, thank Him, and make vows to Him.

Jonah, rendered more docile, then proceeds to Nineveh, accomplishes his mission, and announces to the Ninevites that their city will be destroyed in forty days. The inhabitants, the king at their head, humiliate themselves before Iahveh. Even the cattle invoke Iahveh, and share the general humiliation by fasting and wearing sackcloth. Iahveh relents, seeing that His threats, which were only intended to create alarm, have produced their due effect. "God repented of the evil, which He said He would do unto them, and He did it not."* The situation then becomes one of the most ludicrous that can be imagined. Jonah gets angry. He reproaches Iahveh, who has thus compromised him to win for himself a name for goodness. Iahveh by naïve and grandiose arguments makes Jonah understand that his personal rôle is to be merciful to all creatures.

This was an answer to the objections of many pious Israelites, who were astonished at not seeing any fulfilment of the ancient prophecies against

* Jonah, ch. iii. v. 10.

the heathen, particularly against Babylon, and who were beginning to doubt the veracity of these prophecies. The destruction of Babylon was not as complete as the fanatics had hoped it would be. We shall soon see the pietists complaining of the indifference of Iahveh and thinking that it would be more profitable not to serve a God who is so meek towards his enemies.* The author of Jonah thinks that an unbeliever, however obstinate he may have been, will obtain pardon. Jonah weeps for the death of a small plant which had given him a little shade. "Thou hast had pity on the gourd, for the which thou hast not laboured, neither madest it grow; which came up in a night, and perished in a night; and should not I have pity upon Nineveh, that great city, wherein are more than six score thousand persons that cannot discern between their right hand and their left hand; and also much cattle?" †

There is no doubt that, amongst the survivors of ancient prophetism, there was more than one Jonah who grieved because Iahveh had employed him to threaten and had then forgiven the culprits. The prophet is always a little out of temper when his oracles are not fulfilled. One of the ridiculous points in Jonah is that he is immediately anxious to

* Malachi, ch. ii. v. 17; ch. iii. v. 13 and following; Zechariah, ch. i. v. 12; ch. ii. v. 1-4.

† It would be hard to allow the unconscious (children and animals) to perish with the guilty.

die about any trifle. If Jeremiah could have seen the pardon of Babylon he would probably have also asked to die. The people began to feel annoyed by the Jeremiads which only predicted death, misfortune, anathema, and after which the condemned cities flourished quite as well as before.

From a literary point of view, the book of Jonah is quite unique in the Bible.* It is a caricature, although its predominant thought is very serious, the details are too much exaggerated. It is a visible imitation of the ancient legends relating to Elijah and Elisha. In modern literature it at times recalls *La belle Hélène,* at times the parables of Krummacher or certain imitations of the ancient agadas, in the style of Heine and Kalisch. Suitably enough in a rough sketch, the narrative is little developed. Probably many readers, even in antiquity, have smiled at the misadventures of the prophet, at his discomfiture and vexation. In doing so, they were not far from the intentions of the author. The canticle, commenced in the belly of the fish, composed of scraps of psalms which have no reference to the circumstances, the preaching to the Ninevites, almost comical in its brevity, the repentance of Iahveh, taken from the oldest Iahveist narratives, the good unknown king who is converted so easily, the beasts that share the fast, Jonah's despair about a gourd, are all touches

---

* It was certainly written in Babylonia, not in Palestine.

which could not have been taken seriously, except at those periods when the interpretation of the texts was accomplished with colossal naiveté.*

These slightly discordant notes do not prevent the current of national opinion from being strongly displayed in it. The servant of Iahveh gently advises the incredulous to attach themselves to the group of saints, who hope and who already possess happiness.† The idea became established that Iahveh would make a choice, that only the good would regain their native land, the others would either be exterminated or miserable. It is probable that several psalms owe their existence to this troubled state of the Israelitish conscience. Some of the chapters which charm us most in the collection of the *tehillim* were perhaps the work of the same unknown writer who had the honour of defining the best, most ingenious, and most durable thoughts of Israel.‡ The possession of the earth is represented as the supreme good; the promises of Iahveh are attached to the land; those who return to their country will be the only ones benefited by them.

* How was it that such a book was preserved? In the same way that Ecclesiastes, the Song of Songs, ch. xii. v. 1-6, Zechariah, ch. ix. v. 13-18, Proverbs, and so many other passages which are at variance with the general design of the sacred book, have come down to us. The collection of the ancient writings was made with some breadth, and suppressions were very seldom made in them.

† Isaiah, ch. l. v. 10.

‡ For instance, Psalms lxix. xcvi. xcvii. xcviii.

The Levites appear to have urged the return very strongly. Their ranks were increased by a rather large number of foreigners, who, admitted into the Israelitish family as " servants of Iahveh," were soon regarded as sacred slaves.* They were called *nethinim* or oblats;† many of the poor became affiliated to this congregation of humble personages in order to obtain a livelihood. This again added to the mass of the pious and poor, from amongst whom *anavism* was recruited. The prospect of an idle existence, provided for by the altar, pleased them better than a laborious life of work in Babylonia. A religious foundation is not solid until it secures idleness to a whole class of men. Islamism is principally defended by the wakoufs, and the foundations which support the idleness of the softas. Save at Utrecht, Jansenism has now ceased to exist because there only a prebend is given for being a Jansenist.

* See above, p. 399. In Isaiah, ch. lvi. 3, 6, notice הנלוים; in Isaiah, ch. xliv. v. 5, notice the servile mark upon the hands.

† This word, of Chaldean form, is not anterior to the end of the captivity. Ezra, ch. viii. p. 20, expressly comprises the *nethinim* with the Gibeonite hierodules.

CHAPTER XIII.

THE RETURN.

ALL the discussions, the hesitations even, which we have witnessed, imply that the Jews felt at liberty to leave their land of exile and to regain their native land. In fact they were free. It was afterwards supposed that on the morrow of his victory, Cyrus, wishing to do homage to the God who had aided him to win it, solemnly published an edict, granting liberty to Israel and permission to rebuild the temple,* and also commanding the restoration to Israel of the sacred vases which Nebuchadnezzar had removed to Babylon. This is the first example of the apocryphal edicts, of which the Jewish historiographers of later times have shown themselves so prodigal. It was thought that the nation gained some importance by showing the potentates of the day occupying themselves with

---

* Ezra, ch. i. v. 1 and following; ch. v. v. 13 and following; ch. vi. 3 and following (a very weak portion). The edict is copied from Deutero-Isaiah, ch. xliv. 28.

the protection of Israel as their first care. It is probable that Cyrus never thought of the Jews, and scarcely ever heard of them. But it is certain that the new order of things which Cyrus inaugurated restored Israel to liberty. The prohibition upon their return did not require a special edict for its removal. In fact the victory of the Medes and Persians restored to all the captives their personal freedom; they could go where they pleased. Doubtless they, at first, formed themselves into isolated bands. The journey through Circesium and Riblah would take at least three months.*
The dangers of travelling must have been very great considering the state of the East at that time. The necessity for large caravans was soon understood. Two principal expeditions were prepared under the direction of princes belonging to the family of David Sheshbazzar a son of Jehoiachin,† was chief of the first band, it appears

* Ezra required four months for the journey. Ezra, ch. vii. v. 9.

† Ezra, ch. i. and v. M. Imbert (*Muséon*, January, 1889, p. 64, note) clearly saw that the ששבצר of the book of Ezra may be the שנאצר, the son of Jehoachim, in 1. Chronicles, ch. iii. 18. Paleography fully confirms this supposition: the same sigle giving either נא or שב, in the writings of the last centuries before our era (see the tables of M. Euting). The Αβασσχρος, of Josephus is certainly the same personage; his name is clearly distinguished in the form ששבצר, which is probably the correct one. Compare 3 Esdra, ch. ii. pp. 12, 15, variations of the Cod. Alex. The identification of Zerubbabel and of Sheshbazzar is quite impossible. In the document, where there is a reference to Sheshbazzar, there is also a reference to Zerubbabel as though he were a different personage (Ezra, ch. v. 2).

to have reached Jerusalem * first, and, according to one tradition, Sheshbazzar received all the credit of the restoration of the city and temple.†

Still the caravan, which decidedly founded the new order of things was that of Zerubbabel, the son of Salathiel,‡ and grandson of Jehoiachin, aided by Joshua, the son of Jozadak, the chief of the Aaronites or Zadokites, the grandson of the priest Seraiah,§ whom Nebuchadnezzar had put to death. Zerubbabel was recognised by the Persian authorities. He bore the Persian titles of *peha*|| or *tirshatha*.¶ Joshua, the son of Jozadak, was far the most capable of the two. From that time it was easy to foresee that the priest would finally supplant the survivor of a lost dynasty, who would have required exceptional ability to enable him to derive any advantage from a terribly weakened position.

* It is difficult not to see in the two contradictory versions, preserved by the last editor of the book of Ezra, a trace of rivalry between the two traditions of the priority of the work of restoration.

† The six first chapters of Ezra are composed of two documents, the one serious, extending from ch. ii. p. 1, to ch. iv. p. 5, then from ch. vi. 13 to ch. vi. 22, the other, almost valueless, and full of apocryphal correspondences, including ch. i., and afterwards all that extends from ch. iv. p. 6 to ch. vi. p. 12. These questions will be resumed in our vol. iv.

‡ 1 Chronicles, ch. iii. v. 17-19, is surely confused.

§ 2 Kings, ch. xxv. 18-21.

|| Haggai, ch. i. v. 1, 14; ch. ii. 2, 21. Perhaps this title was only given to him later on.

¶ Ezra, ch. ii. v. 63; Nehemiah, ch. vii. 65, 70.

The departure of Zerubbabel probably took place in the year 535. The number of the returning Jews could not have been very large.* Fifty-three years had elapsed since the great transportation had been effected. A few of Nebuchadnezzar's exiles still lived, and they started with the caravan.†

A list was made and preserved of those who returned, but it contained many errors and variations.‡ The priests and the numerous classes of the Levites or sacerdotal serf (*nethinim*) formed the greater portion of it. It was almost a troop of priests and Levites. In it were represented all the Chaldean villages § in the neighbourhood of Babylon, of which the populations, in obedience to the invitation of the prophets,‖ had joined themselves to the Israelites.

"They could not," the census-taker stated, "prove their genealogy, nor establish their Israelitish origin."¶ Several families also wished to pass as belonging to the sacerdoce, but they

* The information contained in the book of Ezra (for instance, ch. 2, v. 64) is full of exaggerations or disfigured by errors of the copyists.

† Ezra, ch. iii. v. 12.

‡ This list was recopied into Nehemiah's memoirs (ch. vii.). It is again found with variations in another document, Nehemiah, ch. xii. The total (Ezra, ch. ii. v. 64) and the partial numbers do not agree.

§ See above p. 312, 422.

‖ See above p. 399.

¶ Ezra, ch. ii. v. 59-60.

were unable to produce their title. The *Tirshatha**
forbade their participation in the sacred things,
until a priest should come, " with *Urim* and with
Thummim." † This would seem to be a jesting
equivalent for "never," since this ancient rite had
been abolished for a long time. The train of slaves,
horses, mules, asses, and camels was considerable.
Two hundred male and female singers, mentioned
in addition to the Levites ‡ and consequently
distinct from the sacred singers, seem to have
accompanied the march. There were neither sheep
nor horned beasts, which proves that the agricultural population counted for very little in the
return.

This time the elimination of the indifferent was
complete. All who were not ardent pietists absolutely convinced of Iahveh's fidelity to his promise remained in Babylonia. The troop which
travelled by the banks of the Euphrates and the
deserts of Syria was intrinsically a troop of the pure.
Amongst the *refaim* Jeremiah and Ezekiel must
have been satisfied. They had succeeded. Piety
had increased tenfold in Israel. Through a
thousand trials, a thousand purifications, numerous
exiles and infinite selections, the flock required for
the divine work was set apart. The elimation of
the dross was complete. Henceforth no political

---

* Probably after the reorganization of the ritual.
† See vol. i. p. 228, and following.
‡ Ezra, ch. ii. v. 64.

cares will distract Judah from its vocation. Here on its way is the band of saints, who will realise the ideal dreamed of by two centuries of puritans. It was the greatest triumph of faith and the best proof of what, since Josiah, had been most powerfully constituted in Judaism. Great love alone can work these miracles. If the hill of Zion had not been passionately loved for one hundred years, it could not not have exercised such a strong attraction. Fanatics would not have been seen starting with entire crowds to lead them across the desert, with the certainty of a thousand privations on the road, and the prospect of gloomy misery on their arrival.

Cantate Domino canticum novum.* This was the inaugural song of the era about to open.

Poor humanity needs to tell itself that it chants a new canticle, when frequently it merely repeats the ancient airs. No people ever lived by hope so completely as the Jewish nation has done. Judaism and Christianity are religions of obstinate hope, persistent in spite of all appearances. The return from Babylon was hope carried to folly, and yet, once more, hope was found to be a good counsellor, at least, from the point of view of the general interests of the world. We may say that in the history of Judaism, this is the

---

* Isaiah, ch. xlii. v. 10. The Joachimists, the sects of the eternal gospel, lived upon the internal *susurrus* of this verse, which is used to open several of the psalms composed after the return.

critical hour, the hour which determined life or death. If the return had not taken place, Judah would have shared the fate of Israel; it would have blended with the East. Christianity would not have existed. The Hebrew Scriptures would have been lost. Nothing would be known of these strange histories, which charm us so greatly, and have so often proved our consolation. The small troop which crossed the desert therefore carried the future with it, and definitely founded the religion of humanity.

www.ingramcontent.com/pod-product-compliance
Lightning Source LLC
Chambersburg PA
CBHW022007300426
44117CB00005B/63